Luminos is the open access monograph publishing program from UC Press. Luminos provides a framework for preserving and reinvigorating monograph publishing for the future and increases the reach and visibility of important scholarly work. Titles published in the UC Press Luminos model are published with the same high standards for selection, peer review, production, and marketing as those in our traditional program. www.luminosoa.org

The Dream Is Over

THE CLARK KERR LECTURES ON THE ROLE OF HIGHER EDUCATION IN SOCIETY

The Dream Is Over

*The Crisis of Clark Kerr's California Idea of
Higher Education*

―――

Simon Marginson

UNIVERSITY OF CALIFORNIA PRESS

The Center for Studies in Higher Education at the University of California, Berkeley, is a multidisciplinary research and policy center on higher education oriented to California, the nation, and comparative international issues. CSHE promotes discussion among university leaders, government officials, and academics; assists policy making by providing a neutral forum for airing contentious issues; and keeps the higher education world informed of new initiatives and proposals. The Center's research aims to inform current debate about higher education policy and practice.

University of California Press, one of the most distinguished university presses in the United States, enriches lives around the world by advancing scholarship in the humanities, social sciences, and natural sciences. Its activities are supported by the UC Press Foundation and by philanthropic contributions from individuals and institutions. For more information, visit www.ucpress.edu.

University of California Press
Oakland, California

Suggested citation: Marginson, Simon. *The Dream is Over: The Crisis of Clark Kerr's California Idea of Higher Education*. Oakland: University of California Press, 2016. doi: http://doi.org/10.1525/luminos.17

Cataloging-in-Publication Data is on file at the Library of Congress.

ISBN 978–0–520–29284–0 (pbk. : alk. paper) |
ISBN 978–0–520–96620–8 (ebook)

25 24 23 22 21 20 19 18 17 16
10 9 8 7 6 5 4 3 2 1

To my daughter, Ana Rosa,
who is much loved

CONTENTS

FIGURES AND TABLES

FIGURES

TABLES

The Dream Is Over: The Crisis of Clark Kerr's California Idea of Higher Education is a longer version of the three Clark Kerr Lectures on Higher Education delivered on September 30, October 2, and October 7, 2014, at the University of California Berkeley. I hope that the book is a more considered and evidenced version of the argument made in the fifty-minute lecture format. *The Dream Is Over,* which is first of all about the sixty-year trajectory of higher education in California and the United States, was written from another country but within an early-twenty-first-century global higher education order shaped in a number of ways by public higher education in California. California is where American higher education reaches its high point, and the United States has dominated worldwide higher education since World War II: only now is the rest of the world just starting to catch up. Most of the world's top twenty universities are American, and a number are located in California. All of us who work in higher education in some sense live in California, identifying with its goals and drawing from its fecund freedoms, its vision of growth and opportunity. In examining higher education in California, we reflect on our own deeper beliefs and ideals.

The development of the California Idea of higher education was long in coming. It had its roots in the larger "California Idea," the recurring movements of California Progressives and their agenda for democratic prosperity, as outlined by John Douglass in his account of the century leading up to the 1960 Master Plan. Douglass's clear historical account,[1] which is recommended to all readers, has been one of the foundations of this book. When it came to the systematic implementation of the "California Idea" in higher education, the process was led by University of California president Clark Kerr, the main architect of the 1960 Master Plan for Higher Education, the most important American university president since World War II, and a thinker and writer on higher education whose work is still widely read. *The Dream Is Over* considers where Clark Kerr's notions about the public research university (the "multiversity") and his commitment to a socially inclusive higher education system, dedicated to equality of opportunity and excellence at the same time, continue to be relevant—and where these notions might have become tarnished or rendered obsolete by time. It will argue that while the California Idea of higher education, like all policy-oriented forms, has flaws and limitations, it also contains virtues that have been allowed to deteriorate.

The Dream Is Over argues in part 3 that public higher education in California has become trapped within a high individualist politics that ignores and negates the social conditions in which individual freedoms are nurtured and expressed. These conditions include the role of government, which ought to be (and often is) a positive and not a negative influence in society. But in today's California and United States, as elsewhere in the English-speaking world, many regard taxation as a form of theft, markets are used to value the public good in the social sectors, and wealth and educational power are rapidly concentrating at the top, without regard to those in the middle and at the bottom. The imagined society of the early 1960s, that of a higher education–led meritocracy grounded in equality of opportunity, serving enterprise and justice in equal measure, is over. Hence the bracing title. To find a way forward, we must first acknowledge the situation as it is. The book considers future developments in the circumstances, both rich with possibilities (especially at global level) and troubled in values, in which Californian and American public higher education now find themselves located.

The book has been organized in three parts, each an expansion of one of the Kerr lectures. Part 1 reviews Clark Kerr and the 1960 Master Plan in their time; discusses scholarly works by Clark Kerr, Martin Trow, and Bob Clark that are part of the Californian contribution to worldwide higher education; and opens discussion of the trajectory of the California Idea of higher education within California. Part 2 explores the passage of the California Idea across the world, in the spread of educational capacity and research science in the last two decades, and the rise of new university powers, especially in China and other parts of East Asia. Though the university has many national variations, all local and national institutions are part of a global research system and common patterns of higher education. The imprint of Clark Kerr's multiversity is visible everywhere. The more plural higher education world also poses challenges and opportunities for American institutions. Part 3 brings the discussion back to California and the United States (while remembering that what happens in the United States has global implications). Remarkably, the California Idea of higher education has had a great effect across the world but is losing traction at home. Part 3 reviews the rise of the antistate and antitax politics in California, Proposition 13 and the consequences for the Master Plan, the growth of social and economic inequality in the United States, the "steeper" vertical stratification of higher education, the weakening of equality of opportunity, problems in the relationship between higher education and the labor markets, and the limits on social mobility in American (and English-speaking) society. The epilogue more briefly considers the future: briefly, because we do not know the future, and social science engages in prediction at its peril. Yet this openness, and the scope it gives us for agency, is always our best hope.

The Clark Kerr lecture series is a settling challenge to those of us asked to participate. It invites us to consider our words with more than the usual care and to summon whatever it is, if anything, that might be distinctive in what we say. My concern was always to be worthy of the invitation—and its name. It was an honor and a pleasure to spend time at the University of California, and I now understand a little better the lifelong hold that it exerts on some of my friends. I have benefited from the generous hosting, counseling, and continued collaboration of a group of people in and around the Center for Studies in Higher Education (CSHE) at Berkeley. The weeks at Berkeley were full of good talk and fine stone buildings. Above all I sincerely thank Jud King, who has been a fine adviser and a productive colleague, Sheldon Rothblatt, for his generous engagement with the draft materials, and also Carol Christ, John Douglass, Patricia Pelfrey, and Neil Smelser, Richard Atkinson at San Diego, and Wyatt R. "Rory" Hume. Most of those named read one or more parts of the text. So did Mike Shattock in the United Kingdom. I am very grateful for all comments, while carrying sole responsibility for the narrative and interpretations herein. I also thank Diana Baltodano, Meg Griffith, and Christine Herd, who kindly helped with the visit in 2014. It was good to spend time at CSHE.

The Dream Is Over was developed in several disciplines and draws on many theories and experiences, bodies of commentary, reflective scholarship, and empirical research, as indicated in the bibliography. The book is a synthesis. It is sustained by its own assumptions, organization, and judgment, while working also with the writings of many others: sometimes integrating their insights into the synthetic picture and sometimes bouncing off them in disagreement (the book continues a lifelong preoccupation with the critique of public choice theory). I deeply appreciate the opportunity to engage with this range of scholarship. Again, none of the many scholars cited or quoted in this book are responsible for what is stated here. At least some will disagree with my interpretation of their words and findings, though I trust the text is accurate in matters requiring the "impartial spectator," to use Adam Smith's phrase. Much of the recent research on the political economy of inequality and on social stratification in the United States and China—we need to bring studies of China into the core of social science, given the long-term global importance of that country—was new to me when I began preparing the Kerr Lectures. Research on social stratification, combining sociology and political economy and using both quantitative and qualitative techniques, constitutes a useful direction for higher education studies.

Preparation of *The Dream Is Over* was also informed by conversation with Glyn Davis, a Berkeley alumnus, who is vice-chancellor at the University of Melbourne in Australia, where I worked until 2013, and by the ongoing discussion with my father, Ray Marginson. As vice-principal at Melbourne from 1966 to 1988, Ray Marginson was another of the builders of public higher education, in Australian higher education in the 1960s and 1970s when the world was wide, public investment increased at a rate never seen before or since, and the first system of mass higher education, with broad-based research capacity, was established. The world is still wide but the main arc of creation in higher education has swung to China, South Korea, and Singapore—and maybe to Latin America, Central and Eastern Europe, India, and the Middle East (though new things can happen anywhere). In these zones, not coincidentally, states are in the forefront. When Anglo-American societies rediscover their states as constructive instruments, rather than seeing their public officials as people working behind the back of the common good for solely selfish ends (as public choice theory sees it), those societies will again move forward. The modern Anglo-American higher education systems were mostly formed in 1955–1980, when democratic society charged government, not markets, with the erection of public infrastructure and better systems of institutional provision. The systems, especially, broke new ground. Both the infrastructure and the systems will last much longer than the 1960s dreams that inspired them. If the task had been left to markets, we would be still waiting. We work within the halls built by the postwar generation, first in their heads and then in the world. Clark Kerr was the foremost of the builders. There were many others.

Writing the book had its golden moments. It is a pleasure to work with the rhythm of words in this way, assembling a lattice of thought, testing it against observation and reading and memory and inner synthesis, while one's sense of the world inches slowly forward. Mostly the outcome on the page falls short of the thing we glimpse at the edge of imagination. Sometimes it all springs into view. The weeks on the last third of the draft were good, as months of preparation began to bear fruit. However, it has been difficult to create a book-length study of higher education at the desired level of originality, amid other demands, and at a time of transition and loss. I thank colleagues at the University College London Institute of Education for their forbearance, particularly during the main writing in mid 2014. I am deeply grateful to my wife, Anna Smolentseva, and family. At the time of the Clark Kerr lectures, Ana Rosa began a fulfilling humanities degree at Goldsmiths College in London. I dedicate *The Dream Is Over* to her with love and respect and wish her more great university years.

PART ONE

A City upon a Hill

Clark Kerr and the California Idea of Higher Education

Today the eyes of all people are truly upon us—and our governments, in every branch, at every level, national, state and local, must be as a city upon a hill—constructed and inhabited by men aware of their great trust and their great responsibilities.

—JOHN F. KENNEDY, JANUARY 9, 1961, ADDRESS TO THE GENERAL COURT OF MASSACHUSETTS, JUST BEFORE FORMALLY ASSUMING THE PRESIDENCY

1

An Extraordinary Time

The later 1950s and the 1960s were an extraordinary time, especially in the United States. The period climaxed in the explosion of ideas, identities, popular culture, and political rebellion in the second half of the 1960s. That great outpouring of civil energy in America, brilliant and sustained, has tended to block from view the decade before, which was marked by rising expectations and all-round creativity in many spheres, including universities, research, ideas, and government itself. State action did not carry the stigma it later acquired. The memory of World War II was still green, helping to maintain the potential for ambitious collective solutions. American society was on a highway somewhere between, on one hand, the war years with their sleeves-up common commitments, improvised plans, and governmental management of resources and population and, on the other hand, the emerging social movements, higher aspirations, and larger personalities breaking out in many quarters. It was the time of the civil rights movement and the time of Lyndon Johnson's Great Society. Both government and critics wanted to make a better world. Both believed that this was possible. In higher education there was the 1960 Master Plan in California. Something of the same optimism and faith in common and constructed solutions was evident in Europe and Britain—for example, in the 1963 Robbins Report, which called for a major expansion in British higher education.[1] As Sheldon Rothblatt puts it, "the period was one in which the very idea of planning in itself was held in high esteem."[2]

In his historical account of economic and social inequality, *Capital in the Twenty-First Century* (2014), Thomas Piketty shows that special circumstances after 1945 opened the way to greater social mobility and a larger role for social allocation in higher education in the industrialized countries in the United States,

United Kingdom, Western Europe, and Japan. Before World War I, inherited wealth and capital incomes had retarded the potential for upward social mobility through work and education, especially in Europe and the United Kingdom but also in the United States. However, the world wars and the 1930s depression evacuated many of the great fortunes, and this partial emptying out of the upper echelon of society provided more space for social mobility after 1945. Progressive income tax, capital taxes, and inheritance taxes, which had been used to mobilize resources for the war effort, continued into the postwar era, reducing intergenerational transfer and creating more room for the expansion of the middle class.[3] The top tax rate was high and managers' salaries were restrained. Until the 1970s, savings from labor were the main source of wealth, rather than capital incomes, which facilitated the spread of home ownership by what Piketty calls the "patrimonial middle class." There was more room at the top and (partly because of that) more room in the middle of society, while the long thirty years of economic growth between 1945 and 1975 further enlarged the scope for merit. This brought higher education into a more central place in American society. It was the pristine source of science and technology. It was the way of the future for families, the economy, and the nation. It was the great engine room of the growing middle class.

Nowhere in the world was higher education practiced on a larger scale and with more original thought and far-reaching innovation than in the fast growing state of California, which had moved to the front rank of American development. The central figure in the fashioning of higher education in California was Clark Kerr, chancellor of the University of California at Berkeley from 1952 to 1957 and president of the multicampus University of California from 1958 to 1967. Kerr was the principal architect of the 1960 Master Plan, the best known of all blueprints for system organization, one that helped to shape higher education across the country and across the world, and the author of perhaps the most influential book on modern research universities, *The Uses of the University* (2001/1963). Stories of individuals can tell us much about history when those stories are at the heart of the time. Kerr's life and work help to open up the motives and methods of the generation of postwar leaders that used public programs for the common good, establishing institutions of lasting value—institutions that were enabling and ennobling of a modern democratic community: the "city upon a hill," as John F. Kennedy called it prior to his inauguration in 1961, when reflecting on the high potentials of public service.[4]

It is with the emblematic figure of Clark Kerr, whose work peaked in building the California Idea of higher education in the world, that *The Dream Is Over* begins.

2

Clark Kerr

Who was Clark Kerr (1911–2003), what did he accomplish, and what was in his mind that still survives? Kerr's physical memorial is visible from Berkeley to San Diego, and his memory remains green. He was fortunate in his friends and colleagues. They consider themselves to be especially fortunate in him. Those who worked directly with Kerr repeatedly said, and continue to say, fine things about his personal and intellectual qualities. According to Sheldon Rothblatt, citing Matthew Arnold, Clark Kerr saw life clearly and saw it whole. He "read widely, was learned and had a wonderful capacity" to ask good questions and find the right answers.[1] "His observations were compelling, and he spoke with clarity and direction in sentences often pithy."[2] For Christina Gonzalez, Kerr was "intensely interested in ideas."[3] Neil Smelser emphasizes his "ability always to grasp the big picture." At the same time he was down-to-earth, his visions embedded "in the realities of social, political and economic life."[4] Kerr himself said that he was an "American pragmatist."[5]

As a university president and then the head of the leading think tank on higher education, Clark Kerr never stopped being a social scientist. For Patricia Pelfrey, he had "a singular ability to look at mountains of information and discern patterns and trends where others saw only a jumble of unrelated facts and statistics"; and "he was a particularly acute observer of higher education."[6] He grasped the detail, but he was not a specialist. He saw the world whole and in its many parts at the same time. Kerr was a masterly synthesizer. Rothblatt remarks that although he "possessed the social scientist's inclination to anticipate the future"[7] and his solutions tended towards the structural—he eschewed talk about the inspirational dimension of leadership—he was a humanist rather than a calculator, and he never lost sight of human freedom. Thus like many social scientists that seek to understand change in modern societies, Kerr was acutely aware of the structure/agency dilemma. While he could readily imagine the long trends and the forces of history, he found a place for agency within them.[8] Prophetically, and rightly, Kerr forecast that within industrial societies, the scope for individualism and personal liberty would increase. As a leader he valued talented people and wanted them to be free to do whatever they could do.[9] His own life showed that one person could achieve much when the conditions were right and the will was there.

In Clark Kerr's time the dominant intellectual force in the practical social sciences was John Maynard Keynes, whose *General Theory of Employment Interest and Money* (1936) argued that the state should induce economic growth by stimulating aggregate demand, pointing the way out of the 1930s Depression. Kerr's mode of thought recalls Keynes's account of his method: "profound economic intuition and an unusual combination of keeping an open mind to the shifting picture of experience and of constantly applying to its interpretation the principles of formal thought."[10] In common with his teacher Alfred Marshall (who also influenced Kerr), Keynes used not just abstract reasoning but "trained common sense" to interrogate complex material, and he varied his interpretations to fit the context.[11] Like Keynes, Kerr was big on common sense and contextual sensitivity, though in his case the intuition was that of a sociologically minded political scientist, not an economist. His method of achieving understanding was to apply his wide-ranging perception to the scene he was observing, to apply the principles of formal thought by posing contrasting poles of interpretation of those observations, and then find his way to a summary judgment that was mostly in the middle ground. The method was akin to the dialectical.

Rothblatt makes the telling comment that Kerr saw the world in terms of in-betweens rather than absolutes.[12] One example is his comment that the multiversity was both public and private and something more.[13] By moving beyond the dualism, without discarding it as an analytical tool, he could see things that the dualism alone would not have permitted him to see. He was an intellectual pluralist as well as a political pluralist. He wanted to encompass the complexity of the world rather than reduce it. Thus in his concept of the multiversity, multiplicity enables an inclusive, many-sided idea of the university. Likewise, while Kerr had beliefs and moral concerns, the simplifications of the ideologue were outside his frame of reference.

Kerr's mode of leadership paralleled his in-between intellectual method. As University of California president and later as head of the Carnegie Commission, he led inclusively, by consensus. Drawing from his research in industrial relations and his own experience as a mediator in labor disputes,[14] in the Godkin Lectures Kerr argued that mediation was the supreme function of leaders (note that the text reflects the male domination of both the lexicon and the university presidency in 1963).[15]

The president in the multiversity is leader, educator, creator, initiator, wielder of power, pump; he is also office-holder, caretaker, inheritor, consensus-seeker, persuader, bottleneck. But he is mostly a mediator.[16]

Crucially, however, the role of the mediator was not to find the midpoint between the contending parties or reaffirm the status quo. Rather it was to find a higher level of synthetic agreement, a solution that contained everyone's ideas or concerns and that all could endorse. This might be called *transformative mediation*. For Kerr, moving a plural group or institution to a higher level of agreement, and in doing so bringing the common enterprise forward, was a lifelong skill.[17] Arthur Levine, who worked with him at the Carnegie Commission, states that many times he saw Kerr perform "an almost magic trick":

He would preside over a meeting in which there was a heated discussion with participants, saying black, white, red, blue and on through the rainbow. At some point, the conversation would wind down, and Clark would turn to the group and respond, "I think I heard you saying magenta." The usual response was nodding of heads around the table.[18]

There was more to this than the capacity to see several moves ahead. Kerr knew that it was important that all parties not only own the solution but also share the common interest that it was designed to address. Everyone had a contribution to make, to something larger than themselves. He had been an active Quaker in his youth and took from that the belief that "there is that of good in every person" (though he noted that this adage came under strain when he was a university leader).[19]

These ways of thinking and operating translated into an individual political style, based in keen and continuous observation, that was inclusive, responsive, and practical. One of Kerr's methodological assets was a capacity to step back and analyze dispassionately events in which he himself was involved. Smelser calls this ability to secure distance, the attribute of the social scientist, Kerr's "power of objectification."[20] It rendered him a reliable witness when describing tumultuous events. Likewise, Kerr mistrusted slogans and symbolic political actions and instinctively rejected extremes. He supported the advance of liberty in the movements for racial and sexual equality and decolonization, and he saw higher education as "a great force in the liberation of the human spirit."[21] But he did not like the "aggressive politicization" of academic life. It disturbed both the tranquility of scholarship and "the public acceptance of academic institutions."[22] He believed, rather to his cost amid the student unrest of 1964, that any political problem, especially one in his immediate setting, could be addressed by negotiation and persuasion. However, as Neil Smelser points out, "these were years of ideological confrontation, not pursuit of practical interests." Not everyone wanted to make peace.[23]

CLARK KERR AND POLITICS

At the levels of society and nation, Kerr's political perspective was nuanced and moderate. Like almost everyone in his environment, he was a nationalist rather than a globalist, and he was a moderately spoken American exceptionalist. He shared the growing optimism of the 1950s and 1960s, the hopes that something special could be made in the United States and that its civilizing influence in the world was (or at least could be) benign. He was a patriot but not jingoistic. He was conscious of the dangers to freedom that lay in jingoism, as he famously showed in his liberal and conciliatory stance in the loyalty oath controversy. This helped bring him the Berkeley chancellorship[24] and earned him the long-term suspicion and surveillance of the FBI. Kerr signed the loyalty oath and supported the University of California (UC) regents' 1949 ban on the employment of Communist Party members. "I was totally opposed to communism—to its emphasis on total monopoly by one party over all political and economic life, and its reliance on force to assert its will." At the same time he did not think that communism was a serious internal threat. As Berkeley chancellor and later as UC president, he "refused to act against alleged communists without full proof."[25]

An in-between in politics and an in-between in his social vision, Kerr was an unabashed modernist. He saw industrialization as both transformative and inevitable, and technology as largely beneficial. He also placed markets at the center of the economy. Nevertheless, he had little faith in neoclassical theories about pure markets, as Rothblatt notes.[26] He was a critical supporter of capitalism, which he saw in terms of in-between, as an amalgam of pluses and minuses. As a young man in the early 1930s Kerr railed against social injustice. He enrolled in a master's degree program at Stanford to work for "a better social and economic and political order."[27] His 1939 doctoral dissertation focused on workers' cooperatives for the unemployed in California during the Depression.[28] In its subject matter, the work had something in common with John Steinbeck's Pulitzer Prize–winning novel *The Grapes of Wrath*, about migrant workers in California, which was published in the same year. Kerr believed the world could be made a fairer and a kinder place, somewhere "in between free markets and a command economy." For Kerr, government was a necessary part of the mix.[29] He did not share the idea from public choice theory, published in 1962, the year before Kerr's *The Uses of the University,* that politics necessarily turns on self-interest and that there is no such thing as the general welfare or social altruism distinct from private interests.[30] Kerr was more high-minded. He saw the public good as more than the aggregation of private goods. "The university ought to remain a neutral agency devoted to the public welfare, not private welfare," he stated in 2001, meaning that the university was a common resource in which the private interest of one person or corporation should not be privileged over others.[31] Likewise, he believed that much could be expected of government, though little could be assumed. The experience of the Depression made him a Roosevelt New Dealer in politics and a Keynesian in economics. He respected Nordic social democracy. He advocated public planning though he knew that legislatures were not always reliable and governments could be overbearing, especially in relation to higher education. Universities had to hold to their missions, despite the tendency of government to know best and the seductions offered by market interests.[32] Kerr's position will seem contrary for those for whom politics turns on an absolute polarity between market and state or for whom the state is absolutely subordinated to the freedom to trade in the market, but it was a classical liberal position, one shared by many in higher education today.

Transported into the present, it is likely that Kerr, the 1940s–1960s New Dealer, would be uneasy with today's neoliberal eclipse of a broad-based notion of the public good, especially in economic policy and universal regulation on the basis of financial values. He would probably blanch at today's level of economic inequality. One of his aphorisms was that while money was not the root of all evil, it was the root of some.[33] He might also criticize military engagement in such theatres as Iraq and Afghanistan. Kerr had attended student peace conferences as a young man in the 1930s.[34] Later he opposed the American intervention in Vietnam: "a bad war for Americans to be in." He became national chair of the Committee for a Political Settlement in Vietnam, which he described as "an antiwar but pro-American group."[35] Yet at one stage Lyndon Johnson had Kerr under consideration for the posts of American ambassador to South Vietnam and director of the CIA, so compelling were his credentials.[36] There were also firm offers of cabinet posts. When President Kennedy took office in 1960 he asked Clark Kerr to serve as secretary for labor. "I was then involved in working out the Master Plan for Higher Education in California and starting three new campuses, and so I declined," stated Kerr.[37] In early December 1964, during a meeting of the president's Labor-Management Advisory Committee, Johnson asked Kerr to take the position of secretary for health, education and welfare. "You'll have more money to work with than anyone else has had in American history," said the president. To Johnson's surprise and annoyance, Kerr, in the throes of the Free Speech Movement at Berkeley, said he would have to think about it. Again, the time was not right to walk away. Meanwhile, reports Seth Rosenfeld in his 2012 book, *Subversives*, the president asked FBI head J. Edgar Hoover to conduct a routine background check of Kerr's character, associates, and loyalty. Hoover, who had long been gunning for Kerr, produced a misleading report, recycling old charges against the University of California president, allegations the FBI itself had dismissed. Kerr decided to stay in California. Simultaneously, Johnson withdrew the offer.[38] Kerr was never again offered a cabinet post in a Democratic administration. There was no prospect of such an offer under the subsequent Republican administrations of Richard Nixon and Gerald Ford.

Kerr was too in-between for Hoover. He was also too in-between for Ronald Reagan, who took office as governor of California at the beginning of 1967 and

unlike Kerr advocated the forcible repression of student activism.[39] Reagan coop-
erated closely with Hoover. On 19 January 1967 the newly elected Governor Reagan instigated Clark Kerr's dismissal as university president by the UC regents.
Within hours Kerr moved his constructive energies to the Carnegie Commission
on Higher Education, followed by the Carnegie Council on Policy Studies in Higher Education, as chair and director (1967–1980). At Carnegie the influence of the
author of *The Uses of the University* and the leader of the California Master Plan
was amplified on the national stage. Kerr moved seamlessly from speaking on behalf of a campus, a multicampus system, and higher education in a state to speaking "to the enterprise as a whole."[40] Research at Carnegie underpinned the start of
the Pell Grant scheme for needy students in 1972, the main federal contribution
to equality of opportunity.[41] In its annual roundup of American leaders in selected
fields of endeavor, *U.S. News and World Report* chose Kerr as the most influential
leader in education in 1974, 1975, and 1976. The American Council on Education
named him as the first recipient of its Annual Award for Outstanding Lifetime
Contributions to American Higher Education in 1980.[42]

3

Clark Kerr and the California Idea

Arthur Levine states that Kerr's achievement was fourfold. He modernized the public research university, managing the transition from the modest-sized university typical of the pre–Second World War period to a much larger institution that sustained its commitment to high quality and maintained its social status. He cloned that public university successfully within the University of California. He grounded its social rationale and organizational form in the concept of the "multiversity." And he located this within a larger system of higher education,[1] based on the principles of social equality of opportunity and a managed division of labor, through the 1960 California Master Plan for Higher Education. This comes close to it. Kerr led the building of the high science-research university, the building of a networked system of such universities, and the building of a larger higher education system in a state that was one of the world's ten largest economies. He did this both discursively and in bricks and mortar at a key phase in the evolution of higher education, and at the highest level, and the structures and activities that were established and clearly explained by Kerr became known everywhere that higher education is practiced.

This double achievement, in the world of ideas and the practical world, is what the social sciences have been designed to do. The tools of social science, its critical imagination, were fashioned in the later nineteenth century as an adjunct of government programs for the purposes of modernization and improvement. The subject matter of the social sciences is human society, but joined to power the social sciences also help to form human society. At the same time higher education and research are among the makers of society in more ways than this: through sciences, medicine, and culture, through engineering and technology, through business studies, and through teaching of government. Few social scientists have enjoyed Kerr's opportunity. He worked at a time when there was a broad consensus about public planning, an unusual excitement about the expansion of educational opportunity, an optimism about institution building in higher education, and a willingness to fund it. It must also be said that Kerr and his contemporaries used to great effect the window of opportunity that they had.

The American research university first emerged in the forty years prior to World War I and came to dominate higher education and knowledge in the second half of the twentieth century and into the twenty-first. The 1960s, when the institutional forms of the American research university were reset on a larger scale and at a higher level of social, economic, and cultural potency, were the "golden age" of the American institution. These were the Kerr years.[2] According to Jonathan Cole in *The Great American University* (2009), Kerr "made the most significant advance in the idea of the American university"[3] in his long lifetime. Like Wilhelm von Humboldt, who conceived the research university in terms of the freedoms to teach and to know, Kerr built institutions as well as ideas. Like J. H. Newman's notion of teaching dedicated to knowledge rather than individual or social utility, Kerr's idea of the institution has proven especially compelling.[4] Though Kerr's multiversity is less high-minded than Newman's "idea of a university," the multiversity is more realistically grounded and has become much more widely achieved.

Yet Kerr's historical importance is more than just a catalogue of his individual effects on the environment. To render his achievements solely as an outgrowth of his biography, let alone his personality, would be to understate and decontextualize his contribution. The Clark Kerr story is part of a larger story with a long history. The Kerr legacy is the emblematic figure in what can be called the "Californian Idea of higher education." This has older roots and embodies a particular approach to public system and public institution. The California Idea combines excellence with access and equality of opportunity in the service of state, society, and economy through the device of a managed division of labor between institutions, with missions both comprehensive within their own frames and distinct from each other. Here the "public" character of the California Idea seemed natural to Kerr and his contemporaries, even to many working in private universities, though "public" is more problematic to some today. In the multiversity and the Master Plan, it was taken for granted that higher education served private interests. That in itself was not in conflict with the public idea of higher education and with the neutrality of the public multiversity. Private goods were contained inside the idea as it was manifest, on the basis that, to the extent possible, each person would pursue those goods without prejudice to the interests of others. Market forces operated, but "within carefully designed legal parameters."[5] It was also the task of the public higher education institutions, and the system managers, to ensure that as many citizens as possible would benefit, directly and indirectly, within the common weal.

The California Idea of higher education took its mature form in Kerr's time as a set of norms, structures, and practices within an enabling public order. It was also expressed in and supported by a clear-minded scholarship of higher education to which Kerr was a leading contributor. All of these elements—norms, policies, institutional forms and behaviors, and scholarship of higher education—supported each other and made manifest the wider effects of the California Idea of higher education within and beyond the United States. Since World War II the California Idea of higher education has been much more influential than any other. Mature national systems are still drawing closer to the practical forms and animating spirit of the California Idea, especially the California forms of research organization, its research freedoms, and the enterprising California university executive. Emerging higher education systems tend to bear the stamp of the California Idea, and the similarities are reinforced by university rankings. Though the multiversity is more than fifty years old, Kerr's description still rings true in most respects, particularly for university presidents when they contemplate their tasks.

At the same time, the California Idea has now been articulated through a wide range of other policy cultures and educational traditions. While it has promoted a convergence in higher education and in science across the world, the outcome has not been universal homogeneity. Notions of "public," "excellence," and "equality of opportunity" are open to interpretation. System designs vary, even more than institutions. The flow of time has also lapped at the base of the California Idea. Its position in California has been eroded, as will be discussed. Its norms are now partly in question. It seems too difficult to provide access and excellence on a common public basis. The system falters. The public multiversity in California is travelling less well than it did. The Tier 1 private multiversities are doing better and threaten to overhang public excellence at the top. At the bottom of the system that manifests the California Idea, the promise of inclusion and social mobility has frayed. Yet the imagined alternative idea of higher education, that of the universal higher education market, ticks fewer boxes. Nothing as large and compelling has replaced the California Idea of higher education as a way of combining elite and mass higher education, while meeting multiple social and economic goals in a transparent manner.

THE 1960 MASTER PLAN

Clark Kerr's in-betweenism and his instincts for inclusion and for transformative consensus were all at play in the preparation of the 1960 California Master Plan for Higher Education. While many people had their hands on the Master Plan, Kerr is generally seen as its principal architect. Patrick Callan observed, "He was the instigator, framer, principal negotiator and advocate, and public face of the Master Plan." The successful bill for the preparation of a Master Plan was proposed in 1959 by Assemblywoman Dorothy Donahoe at Kerr's suggestion.[6] The conditions for a plan were clear enough: there was a growth crisis in California; there was unregulated sprawl and competition between sectors of education, with no clear division of labor; and the state had money. The question was, whose plan? As John Douglass puts it in *The California Idea and American Higher Education,* from the beginning Kerr "realized that the University needed to take the lead in building a consensus, particularly if the University wanted to maintain its unique role in the tripartite system."[7] The eight months of discussions over the California Master Plan were intense and difficult. The Plan was not so much a system blueprint as a hard-negotiated bargain between contending parties, on two fronts. But it was not a quick fix. It was designed to set a system in place for at least two decades, and it lasted longer.

First, the Master Plan was a bargain between the University of California and the well-organized state colleges, which wanted to become a second fully fledged university system (and later became the California State University). One of the origins of the plan lay in Kerr's judgment that the political pork-barreling of new college campuses and the potential for academic drift, with the colleges demanding growing funding for research, posed clear long-term dangers to the UC position.

> The strategy of the University was clear. Our three new campuses . . . along with the expansion of programs at Davis, Santa Barbara, and Riverside, were adequate to fill an anticipated void in facilities for training PhDs and conducting research and in the political map of fast-growing population areas without a UC campus. We did not want to share resources with sixteen additional "university" campuses (the twelve established state colleges and four more then being developed) who would then claim lower teaching loads for their faculties and higher research subsidies at greater cost. And we did not want to watch the state colleges abandon their highly important skill training functions for teachers in the hot pursuit of the holy grail of elite research status. The state did not need a higher education system where every component was intent on being another Harvard or Berkeley or Stanford. An upward drift was desirable in quality but in the direction of several models. What we needed were three improved models—the open-access model, the polytechnic model, and the research university model. If the state colleges "went university," some new colleges would have to be founded to serve the polytechnic role.[8]

In the outcome, though the colleges gained coherence and autonomy as a sector, they were unable to secure the research role and doctoral degrees that they wanted. California already had 9 percent of the nation's population but 15 percent of its elite research universities, argued Kerr.[9] It did not need more research universities. Kerr worked hard to ensure the University of California would protect its near monopoly of research, holding his nerve as the matter went down to the wire.

Second, the Master Plan was a bargain between higher education on one side and the legislature and governor on the other that reduced the state's role in decision making about postsecondary provision. It ended "the open market approach of lawmakers and local communities towards creating new campuses," as John Douglass puts it.[10] The state allowed its budget to be tied down for the long term, with its management left in the hands of the University regents and their state college counterparts. Why did the state of California agree to close off its fiscal and political options? The larger answer lies in the Californian and national political cultures.

The Master Plan was in continuity with the older tradition of what Douglass calls "the California Idea." The California Idea derived from the California Progressives, a middle-class political reform movement that aimed to reshape California at the end of the previous century. The Progressives believed that education would usher in "a modern and scientifically advanced society" and that all high school graduates should have the opportunity for postsecondary training. They argued that the state should progressively expand the number of public higher education institutions, especially in emerging population centers. Progressive thinking was in the van in the first two decades of the twentieth century, coinciding with the evolution of the University of California under President Benjamin Wheeler. Wheeler secured a major increase in public funding and positioned the University, in Douglass's words, "as a great engine of equality and prosperity for the state."[11] He was much assisted by the structure created in the state constitution of 1879, which gave legal status to the University and the board of regents, removing both from direct political interference. By 1920 the University of California consisted of two campuses—UC Los Angeles was managed by a provost who reported to the president at Berkeley—and two research stations. There was also a large system of public junior colleges and the teachers' colleges. The Progressive educational spirit in California dipped in the Depression years but began to gather a new and stronger momentum in the decade after World War II.

THE MERITOCRATIC 1960S

In the period from the 1950s to 1970s the United States came closer to becoming a meritocratic nation than at any other time before or since. Merit was generally understood to mean talent plus hard work. Thomas Piketty states that: "During the decades that followed World War II, inherited wealth lost much of its importance, and for the first time in history, perhaps, work and study became the surest routes to the top."[12] It was widely, though not universally, agreed that the fairest and best means of sorting the continuing competition for social position and success were higher education and the nexus between education and professional occupations. Though the idea of society organized as an educational meritocracy was utopian, because there were widespread opportunities at this time, especially in California, the notion of meritocracy seemed credible and it stimulated new thinking. Merit became the springboard for the two narratives that still in one form or another shape expectations of higher education all over the world: education as human capital, as economic progress, and education as equality of opportunity, as social justice. Human capital theory and equal opportunity: these are the foundational myths of modern higher education systems. There are tensions between investment in human capital theory, which presupposes a selective system grounded in value to employers, and universal opportunity. Yet each myth is essential to the meritocratic ideal.

Piketty notes that Gary Becker's (1964) influential mathematization of human capital theory is permeated by the belief that capital, other than human capital, has lost its determining importance.[13] Human capital theory imagined that when students acquired the right educated attributes, the embodied productivity required by graduate employers, salary and success would automatically follow. The implication was that providing graduates were "employable," there was no end to the social wealth that education could generate by this mechanism, until saturation educational participation was reached. This notion of an open supply-driven potential for economic growth and enrichment, personal and social, rendered economically rational each additional student place. Thus each foundational myth, human capital and equality of opportunity, was needed by the other, and each also positioned higher education, especially the university, at the very center of human affairs. Each told the public that higher education had a great role in making a just and efficient society in which merit conquers all. Human capital theory made education responsible not just for personal development but for universal career success and collective economic growth. Equal opportunity had solved the problem of democracy, it seemed. Yet in reality higher education, in California or anywhere, was far from being this powerful. It did not determine future society. It had little control over the economic and social settings that constituted its possibilities and limits.

The meritocratic vision of equity and economy advancing together was irresistible to educational leaders. It promised them legitimacy, though at the price of future burdens. It was equally saleable in government and the public space. The two meritocratic paradigms quickly colonized the policy world. The social science research programs that were mobilized to support educational reform focused on widening equal opportunity and the barriers (particularly the financial barriers) to equality, on the private and social returns to higher education, and on smoothing the passage between the heterogeneous zones of education and work. Nor was the meritocratic vision threatening to the already rich and successful. For them human capital acquired on the basis of equal opportunity, floating free of other forms of capital, implied that those with social advantages succeeded not because of their birth and connections but because of their abilities and powers of application.[14]

In this curious backhand way, human capital theory modernized ("meritified") privilege and made progressive educational leaders complicit in the maintenance of privilege and its barriers to equality, though their own normative commitment was to equality of opportunity.

GROWTH AND ACCESS

Meanwhile, however, the rising tide was lifting all boats. Tensions between privilege and opportunity could be safely postponed. Nor was there much debate about the need for a public presence in higher education. Increasingly, state and federal intervention and investment were not just legitimate, but they were expected, and the national importance of education and research was magnified when they were drawn into the center of Cold War strategy. The 1957 Soviet Sputnik, the first satellite launched into space, followed by the first cosmonaut, Yuri Gagarin, in 1962, stimulated American competitiveness and pushed science and universities up the policy agenda.

Hanna Holborn Gray argues that for Clark Kerr the sixties were a time of "great possibility" in which several factors came together—"generous federal funding, expanded access to higher education, and general prosperity"—creating conditions that favored change, innovation, and experimentation.[15] More urgently, growth in higher education was a problem to be solved.[16] Participation was moving from mass access towards universal access for high school graduates. In California demographic growth was driving additional demand for higher education on an unprecedented scale, with 300,000 immigrants entering the state each year. In these circumstances a well-documented plan for higher education, promising shared opportunities in the national interest, had strong appeal. State politicians had much to gain by aligning themselves to the Master Plan and nothing to gain by opposing it. Kerr notes that California governor Pat Brown took little active part in the early evolution of the Plan but "later became an ardent supporter." Perhaps his main contribution was to tell the negotiating parties, at a crucial moment, that if they could not agree on a plan, the state would make one for them. This intervention achieved its objective, catalyzing movement to a solution. Eventually, Brown claimed responsibility for the Master Plan. He came to consider it as "one of the greatest accomplishments of his term as governor."[17]

In 1960, 45 percent of California's college-age population matriculated to a higher education institution. At that time the national average was about 25 percent. The Master Plan promised to keep California ahead of the country. The Plan endorsed the continued growth of participation in response to economic need and popular demand, which were conflated. It proposed a tripling of the enrollment by 1975. More grandly, it held out the heady prospect of the equalization of opportunity and removal of access barriers. The Plan promised a place in college for every high school graduate and all other persons qualified to attend. The promise of access to all those qualified to enter is now a policy commonplace in many countries. Its significance in 1960 should not be lost. The Master Plan in California was the great exemplar that pioneered it for everywhere else. Kerr and his colleagues were trusted by the state and public because, as Patrick Callan states,

> they advanced institutional aspirations in the context of a common policy goal: the commitment that every Californian high school graduate who was able to benefit from college could attend a college or university. California became the first state or, indeed, governmental entity to establish this principle of universal access as public policy.[18]

The Master Plan constituted a major innovation in social as well as educational policy. It also had long-term economic implications for California. However, while universal access was normatively compelling, in fiscal terms it was not as lavish as it might appear at first sight. For the first fifteen years the Master Plan promised to save money by shifting part of the expected growth from four-year to two-year institutions.[19] Community colleges were to be established within commuting distance of almost every resident in the state, but this was less expensive than new research universities. In the outcome, the maintenance of a firm division of labor between research universities, the state colleges, and two-year community colleges was to be as definitive of the California Master Plan as was the expansion of social access overall.

The elite, research-intensive University of California recruited from the top 12.5 percent of the school graduate cohort. Thus the UC secured its role as "excellent" by guaranteeing the quality of its incoming students and concentrating the public investment in research. The UC was separated from the volume-building community colleges by the Master Plan's middle sector, the state colleges, that recruited from the top 33.3 percent of school graduates. The colleges were located more on the mass than the elite side of the system because their potential for research and doctoral training was truncated. This firm downward segmentation of opportunity—with highly selective doctoral universities and the firm barriers to academic drift in both the two-year and the other four-year institutions—was to be leavened by guaranteed upward transfers between the sectors. Given that most enrollments were to be located in the bottom tier, if the Master Plan was to sustain and expand equality of opportunity, much depended on the transfer function and on the capacity of the school system to adequately prepare students from all districts and all social and ethnic backgrounds.

THE PUBLIC MISSION

The Master Plan for Higher Education in California was quintessentially public in its commitment to universal access and in its systemic character, in the organizing of three subsectors on the basis of a division of labor. It embodied the idea of higher education as more than a collection of individual institutions; rather, these were interdependent institutions operating within the framework of common public structures and with a commitment to a single set of ideas. Institutions, and within them individual schools and research groups, competed with each other but within structured limits. The constrained missions and the formal cooperation between sectors were a major departure from the idea of university as stand-alone firm that was influential then in the private sector and is more dominant in all thinking about higher education today. The Plan also sustained the long-term autonomy of higher education in a highly politicized state. It meant that, provided all sectors kept to the rules, higher education could more or less regulate itself. The constituent campuses of the University of California were protected by the Office of the President from the direct interference that plagued public universities in other states. Legally, the UC campuses were not owned by the state government or the people of California, but by the regents. It was a formal independence highly unusual in the university world, though the funding relationship with the state underpinned continuing ties.[20] The state colleges, later the California State University, were likewise sustained by a new board of trustees, which also ensured that they no longer engaged in unrestrained competition with each other. Instead of an overarching governing board, there was a low-key coordinating council to ensure cooperation between the sectors. Their autonomy did not necessarily contradict the public character of the Master Plan. Higher education in California was positioned as a kind of public civil society, universal but separate from government. The public connectivity of the institutions was sustained through both their relations with their boards and their direct dealings with the world, but they could choose the ways in which they would be socially responsive. This was a different kind of "public" to that of state government administration: democratic in purpose, access, and transparency and in the sheer range of its social engagements, while closed to electoral contest or political capture.

At the same time, institutions could not retreat too far from the public sphere. The trust inherent in the Master Plan rested on their capacity to effectively identify and meet emerging public needs on a voluntary basis, to listen to vocal groups, and to continually persuade them that higher education for all was a high priority of the state. In this gift economy, what the higher education institutions offered to the public, jointly and severally, was the gifts of mass education, meritocracy, and discovery. The two-year colleges provided an open door to all comers, undertaking to provide for the common literacy of California as well as its social opportunities. The elite UC campuses were committed to providing scientific infrastructure, general disciplinary education, and professional training at the highest possible level—vast missions. In public production there is no natural limit to the volume and quality of outputs. There are merely opportunity costs when, within a bundle of finite resources, one course of action is chosen over another. There are also limits to the imagination, but this is less of a constraint in research universities in which there is scope for bright people to take decentralized initiatives. In return the UC campuses gained the freedom to accumulate resources and local, national, and global power on a secure basis, providing the public subsidies continued to flow. In charge of their own destiny, they could become institutionally distinctive and creative. This structure freed the multiversity to do public good and to be itself while holding it at the pinnacle of the system.

Though the Master Plan now has its problems, as will shortly be discussed, its stability has been impressive. In a state in which both demographics and the political economy have transformed fundamentally since 1960, perhaps it has been too stable. There have been few structural changes. In 1967 a state board of governors for community colleges was created, completing the set of sectoral boards. In 1973 the modest common coordinating board became the California Postsecondary Education Commission. This was abandoned under fiscal pressure in 2011. The State University gained sole authority to offer doctoral degrees in education in 2005. Meanwhile the fame of the Master Plan spread across the world. In 1963 the Organization for Economic Cooperation and Development (OECD) urged member nations to adopt "development plans of the California type." Two and a half decades later, in 1989, the OECD said the Master Plan was "recognized throughout the OECD world as a blueprint for preserving universal postsecondary education opportunity, while preserving the separate "missions" of the three types of public institutions."[21] After more than half a century, it is still the formal frame for public higher education in California, though its resource base and its promise of universal access look very different than they did in 1960.

4

The Uses of the University

Three years after the Master Plan, Clark Kerr put the seal on his understanding of the multiversity, in the Godkin Lectures at Harvard on 23–25 April 1963. The three lectures were published by Harvard University Press as *The Uses of the University* later the same year. Kerr added more chapters in successive editions of the book, until the fifth and final version in 2001,[1] issued two years before his death. He retained the original three lectures. Kerr spoke and wrote much during the course of his career, but it is to these three lectures above all that he owes his influence and reputation as a scholar of higher education. They are unparalleled in clarity of exposition and insight into modern higher education, especially the comprehensive American research university. Kerr was wholly familiar with the 1950s transition to large megauniversities, when quantitative growth transformed into a Hegelian change in quality, because it happened in front of his eyes during his own career, and he became responsible for its ordering. The multiversity described by Kerr still stands, the most visible and lasting component of the California Idea of higher education.

Kerr's prose is not as transcendent as J. H. Newman's in *The Idea of a University*.[2] Newman's writing is quite extraordinary. Among the major authors on the university, Newman brings the reader closest to the subtle, almost indefinable processes of teaching and learning, and his polemic is deeply persuasive, drawing us to an archaic and unrealistic ideal. Newman refuses the role of research in universities, determinedly turns his back on Francis Bacon's practical knowledge, and dismisses the whole idea of learning for vocation. It is another world from this, but it is a world as beautiful as truth and the reader is carried with it. Kerr reaches into our minds in another way. He uses spare and simple prose, a panoramic vision across the sector, and a pellucid clarity and realism in analy-sis. Not a philosopher like Newman, he is a humanistic social scientist: at home with numbers but not ruled by them, lifting us to a medium height with language without losing his anchor in the material world. The observations are immediate, plausible, and witty. They make one's own experience more clear to oneself. The lectures also create a larger reflexivity. They open higher education to a more ef-fective public scrutiny and trigger discussion about institutional form, feeding the evolution of all institutions.

"A CITY OF INFINITE VARIETY"

Though it is often assumed that Kerr was describing the Berkeley campus, he had Harvard at least as much in mind.[3] The lectures are nevertheless general to the large American research universities. The first Godkin Lecture provides a history of ideas of the university and reflects on the evolution of the American institution with its twin nineteenth-century foundations: the land grant movement and the research and graduate university that began at Johns Hopkins. It traces the passage of the university from the pristine world of J. H. Newman to the comprehensive research institution devoted to mass higher education:

> The "Idea of a University" was a village with its priests. The "Idea of a Modern Uni-versity" was a town—a one-industry town—with its intellectual oligarchy. "The Idea of a Multiversity" is a city of infinite variety. Some get lost in the city; some rise to the top within it; most fashion their lives within one of its many subcultures. There is less of a sense of community than in the village but also less of a sense of confine-ment. There is less sense of purpose than within the town but there are more ways to excel. There are also more retreats of anonymity—both for the creative person and the drifter. As against the village and the town, the "city" is more like the totality of civilization as it has evolved and more an integral part of it; and movement to and from the surrounding society has been greatly accelerated. As in a city, there are many separate endeavors under a single rule of law.
>
> The students in the "city" are older, more likely to be married, more vocationally oriented, more drawn from all classes and races than the students in the village; and they find themselves in a most intensely competitive atmosphere. They identify less with the total community and more with its subgroups.[4]

"A city of infinite variety." In the easy rhythm of this beautiful passage, much of Clark Kerr's sensibility is contained. We feel the power of a plain poetry, nestled within prose as simple as a Mozart sonata, that holds our loyalty to practical vi-sions and ends. We see the deftness and directness and the common sense fluency of his thought. Here Kerr's historical phases and sociological categories have given way to a more human story, in which his empathy of feeling is punctuated by moments of sharp-eyed realism. Actors from everywhere throng the multiversity, moving through its glow, striving and retreating by turns. Kerr's deep emotional engagement with the university is apparent. For the whole of his life, this institution sparked his curiosity and energy. It was the place where he found his full voice, and it was the object of his service, and of his love, for like others before and since, he found in the university a space of freedom. There is also a hint of that utopianism that Gray sees as an essential component of Kerr.[5] Perhaps utopianism was always part of the 1960s, looking up at the shining city on a hill.[6] It was certainly part of the Master Plan.

It may be that Kerr's rich picture renders the multiversity more attractive than he intends, but the burdens of executive coordination, strategy, and identity are also apparent. As Smelser puts it, the multiversity is not only larger but has many more "moving parts."[7] The multiversity acquires ever more "accretions," the product of new opportunities and new problems, yet when conditions change it cannot rid itself of those accretions.[8] In the multiversity there is an irreducible plurality of communities, functions, disciplines, internal interests, external constituencies, agendas, and beliefs. The plurality, always threatening to pull in every direction, is somehow contained within an unspoken consensus about the common good of the multiversity. This consensus, this residual harmony, never explicitly stated but sensed instinctively by all, is almost the defining feature of Kerr's institution. Certainly it is essential. It was to be interrupted by the radical student movement, beginning with the Free Speech Movement at Berkeley in 1964. Kerr never really understood this. But the multiversity outlasted the student movement.

The lecture also reflects on the changing character of faculty life, with the growth of administrative functions and external consultancy; on problems of governance (Kerr's thoughts about faculty and governance develop further in the third lecture); and on the different styles of presidential leadership in universities, culminating in the president as mediator. The lecture is notable for the frank and self-deprecating humor with which the multiple roles of multiversity president are introduced:

> It is sometimes said that the American multiversity president is a two-faced character. That is not so. If he were, he could not survive. He is a many-faced character, in the sense that he must face in many directions at once while contriving to turn his back on no important group. . . .
>
> The university president in the United States is expected to be a friend of the students, a colleague of the faculty, a good fellow with the alumni, a sound administrator with the trustees, a good speaker with the public, an astute bargainer with the foundations and the federal agencies, a politician with the state legislature, a friend of industry, labor, and agriculture, a persuasive diplomat with donors, a champion of education generally, a supporter of the professions (particularly of law and medicine), a spokesman to the press, a scholar in his own right, a public servant at the state and national levels, a devotee of opera and football equally, a decent human being, a good husband and father, an active member of a church. Above all he must

enjoy travelling in airplanes, eating his meals in public, and attending public ceremonies. No one can be all of these things. Some succeed at being none.

He should be firm, yet gentle; sensitive to others, insensitive to himself; look to the past and future, yet be firmly planted in the present; both visionary and sound; affable, yet reflective; know the value of a dollar and realize ideas cannot be bought; inspiring in his vision yet cautious in what he does; a man of principle yet able to make a deal; a man with a broad perspective who will follow the details conscientiously; a good American but ready to criticize the status quo fearlessly; a seeker of truth where the truth may not hurt too much; a source of public policy pronouncements when they do not reflect on his own institution. He should sound like a mouse at home and look like a lion abroad. . . . He is a marginal man but at the very center of the total process.[9]

Lecture 2 situates the multiversity in the American federal policy setting. The larger issue, with resonance in other national systems, is the impact of funded science on the plural institution. Research funding has created the "federal grant university," though the research role is more concentrated than the land grant role. Direct relations between granting agencies and disciplines skew the balance between fields, resources are increasingly unequal, and disembedded faculty stars and research centers achieve an operational distance from the institution that is often frustrating for university presidents. Research functions and income have compromised the commitment to undergraduate teaching. These have become familiar issues.

Lecture 3 brings together the two sets of themes. The great shifts in higher education have been the adoption of the principle of universal access and realization of the idea of progress through science. Expectations of the multiversity are rising. It is seen as the driver of economic growth and all-round solver of problems. It now includes all students, regardless of their social and economic background. The faculty are conservative and tend to resist, but the external factors driving change are irresistible: the growth of participation, the spread of credentialing to all professions and occupations, the university's multiplying involvements in society. Above all there is the increasing centrality of knowledge in human affairs. At the same time that "the knowledge industry" had become central to business and government, universities have become more like an industry themselves. Resources are becoming more concentrated in those units that produce useful knowledge, stratifying the sector. Competition between universities has become intense. (Clark Kerr did not name it "academic capitalism," as Sheila Slaughter and Larry Leslie were to do in 1997,[10] but he described some of the signs.) There were three challenges ahead: to improve undergraduate instruction; to create a more unified intellectual world, with a relative strengthening of the humanities and social sciences; and to "relate the administration more directly to faculty and students in the massive institution."[11] Those challenges still lie ahead.

A THEORY OF THE UNIVERSITY

Clark Kerr's grasp of what Smelser calls "the realities of social, political, and economic life" is such that for the most part *The Uses of the University* still stands as a valid description of the research university, half a century after the lectures were delivered. A reflection on the present and never intended as a theory of the university, it became one. Given the pace of change in higher education, this requires explanation.

In part Kerr's argument has remained relevant because in California in 1963, most of the crucial features of today's university were already in place, ahead of most of the rest of the world—such as mass higher education, large institutions, professional administration, the accretion of occupational degrees, corporate linkages, and the national government structuring of funded research. In part it has remained relevant because Kerr could see where things were going. In part it is because of Kerr's method. He was strong at the level of generic concepts and syntheses, and he separated fact and value in the manner of Weber. He wrote as a social scientist, not as an actor within the politics of higher education with axes to grind, points to prove, and programs to protect. Again, he drew on that capacity to achieve critical distance from the things that mattered to him. Though the fact/value separation is a fine methodological tool, it is never absolute. Explanation can be used to inform a range of normative projects, and Kerr's observations, like those of all persons, were shaped by his values. One the strengths of critical distance, though, is the capacity to treat both facts and values as partly open systems. Kerr routinely took in new evidence and listened to new ideas, and he saw even some values as susceptible to evidence and change over time. One of the strengths of *The Uses of the University* is its air of curiosity and its openness to new explanations.

In the 1963 preface Kerr stated that his task was to uncover how the multiversity worked and how it related to the environment in which it sat, not to preach one or another normative position on what the university should be. He saw the multiversity not as an ideal model but as a complex living institution with pluses and minuses. To his cost, amid a highly charged debate about the character of the university, given that he was a university president under attack from students on his own campus, others saw his notion of the multiversity as a defense of the status quo or an ideal institution to be achieved, as Newman's *Idea of a University* had been. "Unfortunately many listeners or later readers thought that I had invented— or was uncritically endorsing—the "multiversity" instead of merely describing the tremendous changes I had observed."[12] Kerr later said that with hindsight he would have been less frank, less the social scientist, more guarded in his commentary in the Godkin Lectures. "I paid a heavy price for being an honest and realistic commentator."[13] We are fortunate that he did not have that hindsight, though we can sympathize with his predicament.

None of us can control the way our words are used. Despite Kerr's intention, the multiversity is read not only as an explanation or a commentary but as an ideal type, as the research university that emerging systems want to create. Arguably, it is better that such normative propositions should be grounded in the empirical. Nevertheless, Kerr's multiversity was also specific to his time and place, to the American research university in 1963, and it is impossible to translocate every sinew of that beast into other national systems. What is surprising is the extent to which Kerr's conception of the multiversity *does* translocate. This is one sign of the Americanization of the sector that has occurred—not least because of Kerr's masterly synthesis. It is, to say the least, ironic that Kerr's realism, grounded in a conscious renunciation of the normative, fashioned a project that functions like that of Newman. Clark Kerr's multiversity has become the principal imagined form of the research university across the world.

With hindsight, it is apparent that the Godkin Lectures were not perfect. They did not predict Silicon Valley, the Internet, and post-1990 communicative globalization, the spectacular advance of China in the economy and higher education, the offshoring of American manufacturing industry, or the collapse of Keynesian regulatory frameworks and the rise of neoliberal policy. However, Clark Kerr was not alone: no one else predicted these developments either. Perhaps the only element that might have been better handled was Kerr's account of the coherence of the multiversity.

Clark Kerr had an unquestionable grasp of what Smelser calls the "systemness" of the university—the manner in which it combined the disciplines and combined first degrees with extension and with graduate studies and research; the interrelationships between its many parts and its openness and connections to its environment—just as he understood a multicampus network as a system and higher education as a system of different types of institutions. "By 'system'," says Smelser, "I mean an entity with identifiable but interrelated parts, such that changes in one part influence the other parts and the entity as a whole."[14] What then sustains the whole, beyond a myriad of bonds between one part and another? In the first Godkin lecture Kerr remarks tellingly that "universities have a unique capacity for riding off in all directions and still staying in the same place." He knew about the need for decentralized authority and successfully reformed the University of California so as to facilitate it,[15] yet all within a "single rule of law."[16] In the 2001 edition of *The Uses of the University,* he notes that the integration of the multiversity into the outside world tends to trigger its disintegration within. Yet as noted, his argument also presupposes an unspoken consensus, the shared assumption that all within it want the multiversity to continue and flourish. All of this poses the questions, "what holds the multiversity together," what is its institutional personality, given its several "animating principles"[17] and many missions, interests, pressures, and inconsistencies? Kerr has various answers, mostly implicit. One answer, implied by the absence of an explicit argument, is the postmodern answer: "nothing."

Nothing holds the multiversity together. This would be consistent with Kerr's trope of multiplicity, which again anticipates the postmodern sensibility. Another implied answer is "the university president," the unspoken centripetal counter to the centrifugal tendency that almost defines the multiversity. An institution too varied to be held together by normative synergies at the least needs good management.[18] But Kerr makes no overriding claim for presidential coordination. There is even a hint the multiversity could function without it. A third answer is more explicit, the university's "name":

> This means a great deal more than it sounds as though it might. The name of the institution stands for a certain standard of performance, a certain degree of respect, a certain historical legacy, a characteristic quality of spirit. This is of the utmost importance to faculty, and to students, to the government agencies, and the industries with which the institution deals. Protection and enhancement of the prestige of the name are central to the multiversity. How good is its reputation . . . its "institutional character"?[19]

This is closer to the mark and begins to supplement the California Idea of higher education. Arguably, the multiversity is held together by its prestige and the desire to sustain it, which is more than the desire for revenues, for money is merely a means to a greater end. What matters is the social power of the multiversity and its visible manifestation as status. The mechanisms for reproducing institutional status are twofold and time-honored. They are selective student entry and research performance. These two mechanisms are heterogeneous but linked. Revenues from student tuition underpin stellar research performance. Research reputation helps to sustain the value of the university "name" that attracts high-scoring students. (This symbiosis suggests another kind of "teaching-research nexus", differing from that imagined by Wilhelm von Humboldt). All parties in the multiversity have an interest in the growth of institutional status through these two mechanisms. Students want to gain access to selective institutions, and as graduates they stand to benefit from the multiversity's name. Faculty want to work in high-status universities. Industry wants to follow the research strength as well as brand power. Donors want to back a winner. University presidents guard the institutional reputation closely. Increasingly, since Kerr's time, presidents focus on improving the university's ranking, now the most visible sign of its prestige. In the third Godkin Lecture Kerr does note that "interuniversity rivalry" had become very intense, but this suggestive theme is not further explored.[20] More than a lopsided competition for federal research grants, dominated by a few universities,[21] was driving that rivalry. The motors of status competition were larger than Kerr saw, and they affected not just the research universities but the whole higher education sector and all its students. The dynamics of status competition, interacting with and reproducing social inequality, help to explain the failure of the Master Plan to achieve the promise of equality of opportunity, as will be discussed in part 3.

5

Martin Trow

Higher Education and Its Growth

The Uses of the University is one of three pathbreaking contributions to the common understanding of higher education by scholars working at the University of California in Clark Kerr's time and the next generation. The second is an essay prepared for the Organisation for Economic Cooperation and Development (OECD) by Martin Trow, *Problems in the Transition from Elite to Mass Higher Education* (1973). Trow was a sociologist who was founding director of the Center for Studies in Higher Education (CSHE) at Berkeley, a post he held from 1976 to 1988. In the expansion of participation, California was ahead of the curve, and like Kerr, Trow anticipates issues that arose later in many places. The argument is insightful and explanatory. It has influenced thinking in many countries. It is scarcely possible to overstate its impact.

Martin Trow focused on the growth of higher education. He argued that there was a "broad pattern of development of higher education" in "every advanced society," manifest in three phases: elite higher education; mass higher education, where participation reached 15 percent or so of the age group; and universal systems, where participation exceeded 50 percent. In the transition between the three phases, higher education changed its character "in fundamental ways."[1] Access to higher education shifted from being a privilege in the elite phase to a right in the mass phase and then to an "obligation" in universal phase, when higher qualifications became mandatory for full and effective social engagement, and "failure to go on to higher education from secondary school is increasingly a mark of some defect of mind or character that has to be explained or justified or apologized for."[2] Along the continuum, the main purpose of higher education shifted from "shaping the mind and character of the ruling class" in the elite phase to preparing a larger group in professional and technical skills in the mass phase, to preparing the whole population in "adaptability" to social and technological change in the universal phase.[3] Trow's three phases were Weberian ideal types.[4] He used the categories elite, mass, and universal in two distinct ways. On one hand, he imagined them as separate historical stages in the evolution of higher education. On the other hand, he saw them as differing constellations of practice that existed alongside each other in the present.

The three-part historical sequence recalls Clark Kerr's passage from Newman's university village to modern university town, to the multiversity as the city of infinite variety. However, whereas Kerr explained the research university alone, Trow considered the higher education system as a whole. Kerr's multiversity was affected by growth and massification, but Trow's system was defined by them. Using the three sequential phases, Trow develops prescient narratives about change in the sector. Student selection proceeds from the primary use of the criterion of academic merit in the elite phase to programs designed to create social equality of opportunity in the mass phase and then to open access in the universal phase, because "social inequalities show everywhere a stubbornly persistent effect on educational achievement."[5] In the elite phase, the student enters directly after school. In the mass phase, some students delay entry "until after a period of work or travel." In the universal phase, "there is much postponement of entry" and periods of broken attendance, and vocational training and mixed work-study modes become a larger proportion of higher education. "The emphasis on 'lifelong learning' is compatible with a softening of the boundaries between formal education and other forms of life experience."[6] The curriculum moves from a "highly structured" program based on mandatory intellectual or professional requirements in the elite phase to a more flexible modular structure that facilitates choice in the mass phase, to the collapse of sequencing, structure, and assessment requirements in the universal phase, "where no single conception of higher education obtains."[7] The pedagogical relationship between student and teacher moves from personal mentoring designed to shape individual development in the elite phase (for example, in an Oxford college) to formal instruction in large classrooms in the mass phase, with emphasis on the transmission of skills and knowledge, to subordination of the student-teacher relationship in the universal phase as the student is exposed to "new or more sophisticated perspectives" such as correspondence programs, "video cassettes and TV's," the "computer and other technological aids."[8] No doubt if Trow had been writing today he would have added Massive Open Online Coursework (MOOCs) to that list, but the forecast made more than forty years ago has not dated.

In the transition from elite to mass to universal higher education, institutions change. Elite systems "tend to be highly homogeneous." The institutions are small and resemble each other, and they share strong notions of membership, clear boundaries between institution and society, and ("at least in their meritocratic phase") high standards. Mass systems are comprehensive and diverse in functions and standards, with institutions of up to 40,000 students in size and more fuzzy and permeable external boundaries. In the still more diverse systems of universal access, when the boundary between higher education and society is vanishing, "the very notion of standards is itself challenged and problematical." Fragmented student populations of unlimited size have merely nominal connections. Students "do not in any sense comprise a community" united by frequent association, values or identity.[9] Governance also changes. Elite institutions are run by small homogenous groups inside and outside the university. Part-time amateur academic leaders are served by a handful of administrative staff. In the mass phase, institutions maintain an elite leadership but are increasingly affected by interest groups and democratic process inside and outside the sector. Academic administrators are full-time, and beneath them the university bureaucracy mushrooms. In the universal phase, financial managers and specialist services flourish, the diversity of functions and units drives standardization, and higher education becomes the property of the public media. Academic values and processes appear archaic and are habitually questioned.[10]

Having framed higher education in this linear narrative, Trow then desimplifies it. Movement from elite to mass to universal higher education "does not necessarily mean that the forms and patterns of the prior phase or phases disappear or are transformed." Each phase survives in some institutions and parts of others, even as the system broadens its enrollment and functions. "In a mass system elite institutions may not only survive, but flourish; and elite functions continue to be performed within mass institutions."[11] A Master Plan–style division of labor, in which expansion was centered on nonelite institutions, allowed the pristine environment of the elite public universities to be protected. They "defend their unique characteristics in the face of the growth and transformation of the system around them." Nevertheless, Trow was concerned that elite universities were "not always successful" in doing so.[12] Public agencies find it difficult to nuance regulation for diverse structures and values and impose standard treatments in the name of equity. Anxiety about elite research-intensive universities in a mass-to-universal era is a repeated theme in Trow.[13] He may have worried too much. Arguably, elite public universities like UC Berkeley came to face greater challenges from private competition and public defunding than they did from public intervention and from contamination by mass educational styles within. In the end, it was the mass and universal public institutions, especially the community colleges, whose social role came into greater question.

Martin Trow's account of elite, mass, and universal, supported by its undertone of historical inevitability, offers a plausible framework for sorting higher education systems and their trajectories. Though the real world does not always fit with

Trow's three-phase schema—for example, elite universities often lead in modernization reforms—the examples that he uses to illustrate elite, mass, and universal are pungent, locking into the common perception. Over the course of his career, Trow was ambivalent about the question of the universality of his account. In the 1973 essay, he firmly predicts that the American patterns will play out across Europe, the United Kingdom, and the "advanced industrialized" world,[14] while providing little support for the claim. In a later essay, in 2000,[15] he emphasizes the differences between American and European higher education and provides an exceptionalist reading of the American sector. But his argument has resonated as much outside the United States as within.

THE DRIVERS OF GROWTH

Nonetheless, the larger intellectual achievement of Trow's 1973 essay lies not in his narrative of transition from elite to mass to universal, but in his explanation of the social dynamics of the growth of participation in higher education. This explanation says much about the nature of modern society. Arguably, Trow's sociological imagination better explains long-term patterns of educational participation and the social character of higher education than the alternate explanations of growth.

In Trow's time, the main explanation of the relationship between higher education and the economy was that provided by human capital theory, which was formulated by Jacob Mincer, Theodore Schultz, Gary Becker, and others in the decade prior to the 1973 essay. Human capital theory remains the dominant intellectual framework in this domain. It is entrenched as the policy orthodoxy. It has sustained many thousands of empirical studies since the early 1960s.[16] According to the orthodox narrative, the expansion of higher education is shaped by government and/or market forces in response to the economic need for educated human capital. Higher education expands more or less in step with growing demands for graduate knowledge, skills, and certified professional competences. Economic demand for human capital is signaled in the labor markets by the wage returns to skill. Prospective students focus on graduate wages and employability, calculating the likely financial benefits. People, or governments on their behalf, invest in education in terms of time, income forgone, and the cost of tuition to the point where the lifetime returns to degree holders equal the costs of investment. Economists note that higher education can lag behind economic need, overprovide graduates, oversupply places, and hype up qualification levels ("credentialism"). However, in the long run, believes the orthodox economist, higher education tends to equilibrium with economic demand. If there are too many graduates, the price of their labor falls and the expansion of higher education slows or reverses. If this does not happen, then the market is not clearing. There must be a blockage of some kind in higher education or in government policy that prevents market signals from being followed.

Trow could have adopted the human capital orthodoxy, and at the time he might have been expected to do so. He did not. His picture of higher education is closer to the action, more documentary and less abstract. He notes that the service sector of the economy is expanding, triggering greater demand for graduates.[17] But this "economy pull" factor is not the main driver of educational growth. Social demand for education does not fluctuate in proportion to changes in employment or earnings. It is unquestionable that most families see higher education first in terms of future careers and that students want their degrees to facilitate pathways to work. The question at issue is whether education and the economy are connected by a human capital logic. For Trow the motor that drives the rising demand for participation is not economic rates of return but family aspirations to maintain and improve social position. Families and students invest time and money in higher education to augment their position, as human capital theory suggests, but for the most part they do not know what the outcome will be. They know only that whatever the state of the labor market at the point of graduation, it is better to be a graduate than not.

This leads Trow to three insights. First, because there is no intrinsic limit to positional aspirations,[18] there can be no limit to desires for social betterment through higher education and hence *no ultimate limit to participation growth*. It is not subject to economic scarcity. There will be "continued popular demand for an increase in the number of places in colleges and universities," he states. "It seems to me very unlikely that any advanced industrial society can or will be able to stabilize the numbers."[19]

> Despite much loose talk about graduate unemployment or an oversupply of educated men, it is still clear that people who have gone on to higher education thereby increase their chances for having more secure, more interesting, and better paid work throughout their lives. . . .
>
> Growth and the movement from elite to mass higher education itself creates a set of social and psychological forces that tend to sustain it. As more and more people go to college or university, and as an even larger number become aware of it as a possible and reasonable aspiration for themselves and their children, higher education enters into the standard of living of growing sectors of the population. Sending one's sons or daughters to college or university increasingly becomes one of the decencies of life rather than an extraordinary privilege reserved for people of high status or extraordinary ability. . . . But in addition, sending one's sons and daughters to college or university is already, and will increasingly be, a symbol of rising social status. Not only does it give evidence of status mobility in the adult generation—in this respect resembling the purchase of a home in the country or an automobile—but it also lays the necessary foundation for the social mobility of a family across the generations.[20]

Trow says that in the longer term graduate unemployment is not a problem because, as well as the expansion of services jobs, there is the "educational inflation of occupations."[21] Labor markets respond to changes in higher education, as well as vice versa. A growing number of occupations require degrees at the point of entry, and graduate jobs move down the occupational scale as the number of graduates expands, for employers take the best-qualified applicants on offer. Graduates tend to displace those without college, often using their educated capabilities to enrich the jobs. "What mass higher education does is to break the old rigid connection between education and the occupational structure" that otherwise would prevent graduates from taking what were nongraduate jobs, states Trow. People with higher education can now "seek employment without loss of dignity wherever the jobs may exist."[22] This explains why since Martin Trow's time, in nearly all countries, participation has kept expanding despite the fact that graduates are no longer guaranteed professional employment and some face unemployment in the medium term. Participation growth falters only when the equation of costs and rewards—which include not just additional earnings but social status and personal pride—becomes so unfavorable as to erode the graduate premium, which is the advantage that graduates hold over nongraduates. This happens only for lower tier graduates in highly stratified higher education systems (though as will be discussed, it has now happened in California).

Though Trow and the economists are on separate tracks, his fellow sociologists and sociologically minded political scientists—who take into account elements such as the drive for status (as distinct from earnings), the impact of stratification in the labor market and higher education, and the fragmented structure of the labor market—are more likely to agree with him. For example, Trow's understanding of the loose fit between jobs and higher education is shared by other scholars familiar with both sides of the divide. Clark Kerr remarks that "there is . . . no precise way to relate rising job content to higher educational requirements," and "the correlation between a higher education degree and a good job" has weakened.[23] In an overview of four decades of research, *Higher Education and the World of Work,* published in 2009, leading European scholar of higher education Ulrich Teichler emphasizes that "a match between the number of graduates and the corresponding positions, or between the competences acquired during study and job requirements, cannot be expected."[24] There is perennial concern about "overeducation." However, research shows that "most persons seemingly overqualified do not face major hardships on the labor market but acquire mostly a position only slightly less than that they strive for."[25] Educational sociologist David Baker confirms Trow's point that education shapes work, as well as vice versa: "The usual version of the human capital model considers the effects of education too literally and narrowly, thus missing the reciprocal transforming relationship between highly educated populations and the nature of work."[26]

Trow's second insight, implied rather than stated, is that in the long run government policy must follow the growth of social demand for higher education. Governments will be under pressure, especially from middle-class families, to facilitate growth until saturation is reached, using expanded supply and if necessary financial aid to support participation. This was plausible in 1970s California with its active electorate and sensitive polity. The prediction that participation would expand without limit around the world was bolder, given that participation was mostly much lower than in California; early 1970s governments were still enamored of manpower planning, as it was then called, using rates of return and employment data to plot a rational fit between education and the labor markets, or so they hoped; and few polities were as open to popular pressure as that of California. Yet in the long run Trow has been proven right. Whether in multiparty or single-party polities, it seems that almost all governments now support continually expanding aspirations for higher education, though these are often financed by shifting part of the cost to families. In many countries the resort to mass private education as one medium of mass expansion has facilitated the deregulation of supply in demand-driven systems. Old ideas about restricted ability distributions or restricted labor market take-up of graduates have gone.

The third insight is especially pertinent in relation to California. Trow notes that high and growing participation in higher education does not necessarily trigger upward social mobility on a broad scale when social stratification is aligned to the vertical institutional segmentation of higher education:

> It is hard to imagine a successful move to end the expansion of higher education, although that is certainly talked about in conservative circles in all Western countries. But the establishment of different sectors of higher education, reflecting the status hierarchies in the larger society, is a more effective way of using higher education to buttress rather than undermine the class structure.[27]

A three-tier system of the California type limits the extent to which the framework of equality of opportunity can be realized as upward social mobility. Trow's 1973 realpolitik showed California's conservatives they had little to fear from the Master Plan. However, he highlights a tension within it, for the promise of educational and social opportunity was always basic to popular consent to the Plan. As Trow put the matter in his later essay comparing Europe and America,

> in most countries, higher education trained and educated the ruling strata, selected and recruited to government service and the learned professions. It conferred status on those who earned degrees and qualified them in various ways for the society's most challenging (and prestigious) jobs and occupations. In recent decades it has expanded those functions to provide education and training in a wide range of new and semi-professions. In the United States, colleges and universities perform those functions, but also, and most importantly, they give substance to the idea that anything is possible to those with talent, energy and motivation. This sense of society

with limitless possibilities for all, largely (though not exclusively) through higher education, is what is usually meant by "the American dream." The end of the American dream is continually proclaimed, usually by intellectuals who never believed in it to begin with, and wished no one else would. But this faith, fundamental to the American political system, survives hostility and cynicism, and underpins America's peculiar mixture of conservatism and radical populism. Through its role in fostering social mobility and the belief in a society open to talents, American higher education legitimates the social and political system, and thus is a central element in the society as it is nowhere else.[28]

In the longer term, the California Idea of higher education could retain its legitimizing functions—and sustain its own legitimacy—only if enough of the faith in it was fulfilled. If participation in the community colleges failed to generate sufficient value; if the routes to upward mobility were too attenuated, or were blocked; if economy, society, and education became more unequal, then the shiny exceptionalist ideals would become tarnished.

6

Bob Clark

The Academic Heartland

The third University of California scholar who has made a front-rank contribution to the global understanding of higher education is Burton R. (Bob) Clark. Clark worked at Stanford, Harvard, Berkeley, and Yale, where he served as chair of sociology, and then became the Allan M. Cartter Professor of Higher Education at the University of California, Los Angeles, in 1980. Of Clark's major books and papers,[1] *The Higher Education System* (1983) is the most important. As with the works of Clark Kerr and Martin Trow, the mark of the book is its close grasp of the realities of higher education and its relational dynamics. Each social scientist has a somewhat different vantage point on the problem, however. Rather than examining higher education at the level of society (Trow) or from the university president's office (Kerr), Bob Clark sets out to "detail systematically how higher education is organized and governed"[2] from the bottom up. Higher education is organized in "two basic crisscrossing modes: by discipline and by institution."[3] In discussing systems and institutions, Clark develops the perspective of the academic department. He identifies knowledge as the principal organizing and differentiating element in higher education. The generative effects of knowledge are largely missing in Trow's study of growth, and they are discussed in general rather than specific terms by Kerr. Yet research repeatedly shows that faculty identify with their field. As Clark states, "the discipline rather than the institution tends to become the dominant force in the working lives of academics."[4] Higher education is continually diversified by the evolution of new fields and subfields of knowledge, which creates a problem of systemic and institutional coordination.

This allows Clark to define what is distinctive about the higher education sector when compared to other social sites. Higher education has become a relatively independent sector with its own "action patterns."[5] To understand its complexity requires us to "retreat somewhat from general theorizing across the major sectors of society and concentrate on analysis of particular realms."[6]

> It does not make much sense to evaluate business firms according to how much they act like universities, nor economic systems according to their resemblances to higher education systems. Nor does it make any sense to do the reverse; yet it is built into current commonsense and management theory that we do so.[7]

The knowledge-centered nature of the tasks of higher education fosters diversity of outlook, the endemic autonomy of persons and groups, the peculiarly flat structures often found in academic communities, and also the uncertainty and ambiguity that is endemic to the sector. Reciprocally, the way higher education is organized shapes the way knowledge is bundled.[8] "Knowledge materials . . . are at the core of any higher education system's purposes and essences."[9] The centrality of knowledge, Clark concludes, is "the root cause of the many odd ways of the higher education system."[10]

The Higher Education System investigates academic work, beliefs, power and authority, system integration, and the handling of change. Like Martin Trow, Clark was a comparativist and the book is grounded in a succession of empirical studies that he conducted in the United States, the United Kingdom, France, Italy, Germany, Japan, and the Soviet bloc. "To define what is basic requires that we move among nations and confront their common and varied structures and procedures," he said. This is a corrective to "the unconscious assumptions that possess our vision when we study only a single country, generally our own," which Clark calls "the hometown view."[11] Clark explains the role of symbolic factors, the integrating role of shared beliefs, the different permutations of system structure, kinds of hierarchy and status, forms of academic career, and modes of institutional and system coordination. If the book were to be prepared today, it would say more about competition, rankings, university brands as symbolic and integrating factors, and managed faculty behaviors, issues that Clark explored more fully in *Creating Entrepreneurial Universities* (1998), fifteen years later.

The Higher Education System is best known for its triangle of coordination. Clark locates three Weberian ideal types at the points of the triangle: systems driven by states, systems driven by market forces, and systems driven by academic oligarchies. He positions each national higher education system within the triangle, with the United States closest to market coordination, Soviet Russia closest to state control, Italy closest to academic oligarchy, and so on. Japan is the most difficult to place as it has strong elements of all three.[12] Modes of coordination make a difference. For example, Clark observes that while state control tends to aggregate, markets tend to fragment. "The state system thereby encourages a student class consciousness: the market system restrains it."[13] Clark's triangle is still widely used by doctoral students for analytical purposes. It is not without ambiguity. Clark wrote the book before the full evolution of neoliberal systems in which government deploys quasi markets as means of allocation, control, legitimation, and performance management. Two points of the triangle, state and market, can overlap, as Clark himself suggests.[14] Another problem is where to place the university executive: with the academic oligarchy, with the state, or at a point of its own? Should the triangle be a square? Despite these problems, Bob Clark's triangle has yet to be superseded.

THE MULTIVERSITY AS CORPORATION

Creating Entrepreneurial Universities: Organizational Pathways of Transformation (1998) has been cited more often than the *Higher Education System*. It appeared at a moment when universities in many countries were moving towards enterprising missions, corporate forms of autonomy facilitated by government, more active relations with stakeholders and local communities, and an emphasis on raising funds; these had long been features of the American university but were novel in institutions that had long been administered and funded by the state, as in Europe. Clark's research was conducted in 1994–1997 in five universities that were early adapters of the entrepreneurial turn: Warwick and Strathclyde in the United Kingdom, Twente in the Netherlands, Chalmers in Sweden, and Joensuu in Finland. All had been successful, particularly Warwick. Clark focuses on the individual institution without regard to system dynamics—in the book he argues that a university-specific strategy has become crucial, so that the multiversity in effect becomes a firm competing with other firms. However, what lifts *Creating Entrepreneurial Universities* above the how-to-succeed-in-business textbook is Clark's focus on the knowledge-related dimension. He argues not for the holus-bolus importation of business and public sector management into higher education but for the hybridization of executive-led organization with academic culture and faculty agency.

Clark identifies five elements crucial to institutional transformation: "a strengthened managerial core; an enhanced developmental periphery; a diversified funding base; a stimulated academic heartland; and an entrepreneurial culture."[15] All five universities had developed "a greater systematic capacity to steer themselves," using varied local combinations of "centralized decentralization."[16] They had strengthened lines of authority from president/rector to dean to department head. Individuals and units were newly accountable, while at the same time the executive took an enhanced responsibility for the financial health of the institution as a whole. "Most important, the administrative backbone fused new managerial values with traditional academic ones."[17] In part this was ensured by drawing on the faculty when composing the leadership. For the new generation of professional managers and strategically focused executive leaders, the model was Clark Kerr's multiversity president.[18] In the "enhanced developmental periphery," alongside the traditional departments were new, temporary, and flexible units that handled commercial consultancy, outreach teaching, or cross-disciplinary research projects. This provided an enhanced responsive capacity in the face of the growing demands on universities. At the same time and most importantly, "impressive in the universities studied was the extent to which the heartland departments had been brought into entrepreneurial change."[19] Even the humanities and humanistic social sciences found ways to explore policy analysis and multimedia production, providing that they were selective and retained core academic identities—always provided that they could be subsidized by the units with higher income-earning potentials, such as the business school.

When *Creating Entrepreneurial Universities* was published, the case for the diversified funding base was becoming obvious in many countries. For Clark, funding from a range of sources created opportunities and protected autonomy, while allowing university presidents to protect less enterprise-focused disciplines—but in any case it was inevitable. The problems of public funding were a function of mass education:

> The state mantra becomes: do more with less. It has become a virtual iron law internationally that national and regional government will not support mass higher education at the same unit-cost level as they did for prior elite arrangements.[20]

At the end of the 1990s, it was becoming an iron law in California also.

Whither the California Idea of Higher Education?

So this is the California legacy. The California Idea of public higher education is an ideal to be realized ("the city upon a hill"), as well as a vast workshop of practical activity in which people are prepared for work and society, opportunity is allocated, and new ideas are formed and disseminated. It embodies a society-wide commitment to universal access to higher education, with tuition free of charge or low enough to constitute only a minor barrier to entry and financial aid for the needy as required. It is a self-regulating system of higher education that expands continually to meet social demand, affordable in both private and public terms, while providing for the vocational needs of the state on behalf of the state. It includes a front-rank research establishment in the University of California, which together with the private sector does much to drive the economy. It is an interdependent higher education system, comprising an ordered and hierarchical division of labor between three kinds of institutions with defined missions, sustaining access while augmenting the quality of the elite sector of autonomous research universities. The barriers in this institutional hierarchy are moderated by rates of transfer from community colleges to the California State University campuses and the University of California, and between the CSU and the UC, which enable educational and social mobility on a scale that is consistent with the promise of equality of opportunity. Or at least that is how it is meant to happen. That is the ideal.

In this manner the California Idea, realized in a practical way in the world, is meant to ensure the simultaneous advance of the public good and the many private goods via higher education. The Idea is informed by nation-leading and world-leading wisdom in system design and guidance, institutional organization and management, academic leadership, and in ideas about higher education. It is also normatively powerful. It plants higher education at the center of society. If the vision takes the form of American exceptionalism, that sense of a special people chosen for a promised land, the California Idea of higher education emphasizes those ideas that render modern America (especially California) attractive to the rest of the world: openness, optimism, the buzz of continuous change, forward vision, and larger opportunity amid the common enterprise on a new and fertile frontier. Above all, there is that open, California sense of freedom. The California Idea is compelling.

The separate components of the California Idea were not especially original, especially in the American context. The central positioning of public education in the future of the state was not California's invention. Other states developed a tripartite division of labor, student transfer between sectors, and even the notion of universal access. The multiversity concept was general to the American research university, not the California research university, and was always at least as much Harvard as Berkeley. What makes the California Idea unique is that all of these features were systematized together in a single Master Plan with long-term life and that, along with the Master Plan, California led intellectual thinking about higher education, as embodied in the scholarship of Clark Kerr, Martin Trow, and Bob Clark. The Master Plan was more a developed and coherent system design than those that evolved in most other American states. It guaranteed not just a division of labor between institutional mission types; it protected the multiversity within that division of labor from competition in the form of upward drift, which most other states did not do, or did not do as well. The California combination of research university excellence and social access is the aspect that is most often cited, even though outside the United States, there are often qualms about the firm hierarchy between the three segments of the system and the narrow entry into the doctoral universities. More generally, the Master Plan legitimated the idea of a planned system itself,[1] stimulating system blueprints in many jurisdictions in the United States and abroad, even though no other nation or region exactly copied California's forms (see part 2).[2]

Peter Scott argues that the Master Plan and the works of California scholars including Kerr, Trow, and Clark constitute the first "general theory" of higher education. Though the theory is "highly coloured by the particular experiences of America" it "still dominates" worldwide imaginings of what is possible in higher education. The California Idea of higher education is underpinned by "a powerful secular faith, a belief, at its most intense in America but general across the developed world, in the inevitability of social progress underpinned by economic growth." Despite economic shocks, this belief remains largely unshaken.[3]

THE EXCELLENCE OBJECTIVE

"Between the idea / and the reality / . . . falls the Shadow," as T. S. Eliot famously said.[4] Imagined social forms never shine as brightly in practice as their ideal version would suggest. Large-scale and far-reaching constructions are more likely to fail than most. All the same, there are no iron laws here. The distance between idea and reality, the extent of the failure of the plan, varies from case to case. Policy constructions falter when the imagining was patchy in its coverage or was internally contradictory, when conditions and resources change, when the will to implement them falters, or when intentions shift from the original design. In the case of the California Idea of higher education, the political, fiscal, and social conditions are now very different to those of 1960/1963, and there is continuing commitment to some aspects of the vision but not others. The multiversity has travelled better than has the overall system design. The goal of excellence has been realized more completely than that of access. Equality of opportunity through public education seems a long way from realization. If Trow's 1973 analysis was right, the goal of equal opportunity was never going to be fulfilled.

Some parts of the California legacy have been effectively realized. First, the division of labor between the three subsectors has proven stable. In some other segmented systems, upward academic drift, with nonresearch campuses moving into research and graduate degrees, has exploded the vertical division of labor. Australia (1988) and the United Kingdom (1992) dissolved their binary systems into unitary systems, though the premerger universities have remained dominant in research.

Second, the University of California has sustained unquestionable research excellence across all campuses, except UC Merced, founded in 2005, which is still in formation. In the Shanghai Academic Ranking of World Universities (ARWU), focused solely on research, seven UC campuses are in the top sixty in 2014. UC Berkeley is fourth, behind Harvard, local rival Stanford, and MIT, and ahead of the University of Cambridge in the United Kingdom, Princeton, and Caltech. UCLA is twelfth and UC San Diego is in fourteenth place; UC San Francisco is eighteenth; UC Santa Barbara, forty-first; UC Irvine, forty-seventh; UC Davis, fifty-fifth; UC Santa Cruz, ninety-third; and UC Riverside, in the top 150[5] (table 7.1). If science is one of the hopes of the world, then much of that hope is invested in California. The UC research capacity, the outcome of the 1960s policy implemented with state and federal support, recalls the vision of the "city upon a hill" that John F. Kennedy proclaimed in 1961 soon after the Master Plan had been signed into law.

The University of Leiden Centre for Science and Technology Studies (CWTS) provides detailed comparisons of university research output. Table 7.1 shows that Berkeley is fourth among the major research universities in the proportion of its published research papers in the top 10 percent in their field by citation rate in 2010–2013 behind only MIT, Harvard, and Stanford. Santa Barbara, San Francisco,

TABLE 7.1. University of California campuses in the Shanghai Academic Ranking of World Universities 2014, and Leiden research ranking for 2010–2013 citations

ARWU ranking 2014	University	Index in 2014 ARWU ranking (max. = 100.0)	Proportion of all research papers in top 10% of field 2010–2013 (Leiden ranking)	Number of high-citation research papers* 2010–2013 (Leiden ranking)
1	Harvard	100.0	22.1%	6,892
2	Stanford	72.1	21.9%	3,083
3	MIT	70.5	24.8%	2,486
4	UC Berkeley	70.1	21.8%	2,573
5	Cambridge (UK)	69.2	17.3%	2,100
6	Princeton	60.7	21.5%	1,110
7	Caltech	60.5	21.4%	1,092
8	Columbia	59.6	17.5%	2,064
eq. 9	Chicago	57.4	17.6%	1,238
eq. 9	Oxford (UK)	57.4	17.8%	2,301
11	Yale	55.2	18.5%	1,913
12	UC Los Angeles	51.9	17.4%	2,438
13	Cornell	50.6	16.6%	1,910
14	UC San Diego	49.3	18.1%	2,124
15	Washington, Seattle	48.1	16.6%	2,276
16	Pennsylvania	47.1	17.2%	2,178
17	Johns Hopkins	47.0	15.8%	2,348
18	UC San Francisco	45.2	19.8%	2,017
19	Federal IT Zurich (Switzerland)	43.9	17.1%	1,403
20	University College London (UK)	43.3	15.8%	1,959
41	UC Santa Barbara	34.3	20.3%	864
47	UC Irvine	31.9	15.2%	949
55	UC Davis	30.4	13.9%	1,477
93	UC Santa Cruz	24.7	18.6%	366
between 101 and 150	UC Riverside	n.a.	15.3%	459

SOURCE: Author, adapted from data in ARWU 2015; Leiden University 2015
NOTE: ARWU = Academic Ranking of World Universities. n.a. = data not available
* Papers in the top 10 percent of their research field in terms of total citations.

Santa Cruz, and San Diego all outperform Cambridge, Columbia, Chicago, and Oxford. The final column in Table 7.1 shows the number of high-citation papers produced in each university. This is a useful measure of a university's scientific "firepower," as indicated by the quantity of high-quality research published in the years 2010–2013. Here Harvard performs remarkably, with more than twice as many papers in the four years as the world number two, Stanford. The University of Toronto, not shown in the table, is third (with 2,738), and the University of Michigan (2,616) is fourth. UC Berkeley is fifth and UCLA is seventh. UC San Diego and UC San Francisco are also in the first fifteen universities. If UC Berkeley and UC San Francisco are combined, their total 4,590 high-citation papers is 50 percent larger than the output of Stanford, and two-thirds that of Harvard. This is a plausible combination—Berkeley and UCSF share the same urban space; San Francisco is solely a medical school, and Berkeley does not have a medical school.

In the Leiden field-specific measures of research performance, UC Davis is first in the world in high-citation papers in Life and Earth Sciences and UC Berkeley is third. Berkeley is second in Physical Sciences and Engineering, after MIT, and fifth in Mathematics and Computer Sciences. UC San Francisco had the third largest number of high-citation papers, after Harvard, in Biomedical and Health Sciences.[6]

The University of California's research preeminence has been achieved with endowment funding much less than that of leading Tier 1 private universities. One reason is that, more than most universities, the UC is unambiguously committed to the merit principle. Fostering and supporting the best people enabled the spectacular rise of the San Diego campus to a leading world position in only three decades. Like Clark Kerr, the successive USD chancellors believed in freeing researchers to act. For example, in her biography of Richard Atkinson, San Diego chancellor (1980–1995) and UC president (1995–2003), Patricia Pelfrey notes that "Atkinson operated on the conviction that nothing is more important to organizations than encouraging talent and that talent is best encouraged by giving it the widest possible scope, without overly specific prescriptions about outcomes." It has been a winning formula.[7]

THE ACCESS OBJECTIVE

When the focus moves from the excellence objective to the access objective, the picture is more mixed. The public character of higher education, and especially its contribution to equality of opportunity, is shaped not by whether tuition is charged or by the sticker price but by the combination of price, subsidies, exemptions, student loans, student selection, graduation rates, and the value of qualifications in terms of social status and labor market power. The public value of higher education has different meanings depending on the character of institutional mission and who uses the institutions.

Perhaps the ultimate determinant of the public character of the University of California is who gets in and benefits from the social mobility its valuable degrees enable. Here the UC campuses—including Berkeley, Los Angeles, and San Diego—take in more students from socioeconomically disadvantaged backgrounds than do most leading research universities. In total, 42 percent of all UC students receive federal Pell Grants, allocated to students from families with incomes of $44,000 a year or less, suggesting significant social mobility. A third of all UC tuition dollars are directed to financial aid. This is exclusively needs-based aid. Berkeley has developed a progressive tuition regime whereby 40 percent of students pay no tuition, financed by tuition from higher-income families. Those with family incomes below $140,000 per annum have discounted tuition. Progressive tuition has spread to the other UC campuses.[8] UC campuses also take in a high proportion of students with at least one parent born outside the United States. Rothblatt cites a figure of 60 percent of entrants at Berkeley in 2004 and notes also that 27 percent of students were in the first generation of their family to go to college.[9]

In the outcome, students from poor families and first-generation higher education students are much better represented at UC Berkeley than in the Ivy League private universities. In his study of Yale, *The Power of Privilege* (2007), Joseph Soares reports that in the 1988–2000 period, 64 percent of the students of Tier 1 institutions in the United States and 44 percent of the students from Tier 2 schools were from the richest 10 percent of households in terms of family income. In Soares's study, Tier 1 institutions are the leading private universities, and the major public research universities are in Tier 2. He compares these intakes with the UC system in the period 1991–1996. The most socially exclusive UC campus was Santa Barbara, with 31 percent of its students from the top 10 percent of families. The other campuses had ratios of 28 percent at Berkeley and San Diego, 24 percent at Santa Cruz, 23 percent at Davis and Los Angeles, 18 percent at Irvine, and 15 percent at Riverside.[10] Berkeley's school-leaver intake is as academically accomplished as the Tier 1 intake. At the same time, according to John Douglass, both UC Berkeley and UCLA now *each* have as many low-income students as the *whole* Ivy League; 40 percent of Berkeley undergraduates pay no tuition; 65 percent receive at least some financial aid; and half graduate with no debt. The average debt of $19,000 was just over two-thirds of the national average of $27,000. In addition, UC's undergraduate completion rates are unmatched by any other research-intensive public university.[11] Like the data on research outputs, these are impressive numbers and consistent with the spirit of the Master Plan.

However, the UC takes in a relatively small minority of the age cohort. It cannot on its own sustain a successful equality-of-opportunity regime across California's society. The outcomes from higher education as a whole have been less good.

The Master Plan sought to control costs yet at the same time provide universal access and high social mobility *and* a UC system that could compete with the best private and public universities in the country.[12] Both access and excellence carried a price tag, but more so, universal access in combination with high social mobility. After the Plan was announced, California's population and the social demand for higher education grew more rapidly than predicted. Inevitably, as Martin Trow suggested in 1973, once the principle of universal access was established, social aspirations for higher education grew at pace. Under these conditions, the scope for upward social mobility depended on the capacity of the schools to bring students from all California's communities and social groups to the starting gate for higher education, on the capacity of the community colleges to bring students through to successful completion, on the capacity for upward transfer from the community colleges through to the CSU and the UC, and on a proportional expansion of the UC and CSU in line with the growth in the bottom-tier sector, the community colleges. In turn, each of these positive developments depended on the maintenance of the necessary public resources in schooling and in all three tiers of higher education, as well as continued no or low tuition. A primary difficulty, especially in the longer term, was that the resource needs of the expanding system have been much greater than were envisioned in 1960.

In the outcome, California and its public education have failed to deliver. First, as was planned in the 1960s, growth was concentrated in the community colleges, and the CSU and UC systems were not expanded in proportion, so that opportunities for upward mobility were attenuated. In most other nations that provide research universities, the proportion of young people entering those institutions has expanded markedly in the last forty years—through growth of the institutions or, more often, the opening of new research universities—in line with social demand and economic need. This expansion has helped to broaden the highways for mobility into the professional and managerial occupations. This is not the case in California, where the research-university sector remains confined to the top 12.5 percent of school graduates. From the point of view of equality of opportunity, this was a flaw in the original system design, as it placed too much pressure on the transfer function. Transfer between institutions in a vertical hierarchy is always a second-best form of social access because it requires greater stamina of aspiration.

Second, for reasons that will be further discussed in part 3, over time the state's tax-spend compact has severely deteriorated. For the last twenty-five years, California has been unable to properly support the Master Plan. Funding declined especially sharply in the cutbacks triggered by the recession of 2008 and after. This has affected all three sectors, including the University of California, which has become less competitive vis-à-vis Stanford in competition for top global research talent. UC tuition has been pushed up for the growing number of out-of-state students, helping to keep the in-state price down, but the cost of attending UC graduate professional schools now comes close to equaling that of the major private universities. This has required ever more nimble footwork with tuition discounts and student aid.

Third, there has been a decline in the resourcing, quality, standing, and accessibility of mass public education across the nation, and in California both the public schools and the community colleges are undersupported. Public schools' graduation rates have stagnated, and there is pronounced locational and ethnic inequality.[13] In the community colleges there are again regional and ethnic inequalities in graduation and transfer rates, and the combined graduation and transfer rates in both the community colleges and the state universities are disappointing. In a system in which social opportunity is reduced, fragmented, and punctured at many points, the outcomes of public education in California—as in the country—are increasingly differentiated on the basis of location, socioeconomic background, and its partial correlate, ethnicity. Access, retention, graduation, and transfer rates all sharply favor the white middle class and Asian Americans, with students from African American and Hispanic families, which are disproportionately located in the bottom half of the income distribution, doing noticeably worse. It is far from the 1960 promise of equal opportunity through higher education.

Fourth, and most seriously, public higher education no longer provides for universal access. California's community colleges first began to turn away students in bad state budget years in the 1980s. They currently turn away at least 200,000 potential students each year. Enrollment in the CSU campuses was first reduced by 50,000 in the early 1990s. Following the cutbacks triggered by the 2008–2010 recession, they are once again not accepting all eligible students.[14] This is a major retreat. Across the world, a growing number of national systems provide near universal access to higher education (see part 2). In California universal access has never been a utopian goal. It was and is achievable. California was the first political jurisdiction in the world to achieve it. Apparently it is now the first to lose it. This is the most serious failure of the expectations called up by the Master Plan. It signifies a historic decline in California's public higher education on both the national and global scales—in its provision to its people and as an idea, an exemplar.

In 1960 state participation was double the national average. Fifty years later, in 2010, California was the forty-third state in the proportion of 18- to 24-year-olds with baccalaureate status. In the United States as a whole, the proportion of the population graduating with a degree has fallen in relative terms to be only slightly above the OECD average.[15] California has massively deteriorated relative to the rest of the country, yet in a curious way this is part of the historical pattern in which national trends are led from California. The United States is following California as it goes up and down.

There will be a dramatic demographic surge in the next generation. The state will have 50 million people in 2050, compared to 38 million in 2013.[16] What will happen? Will a new Master Plan appear to lift the sights of the state and secure a renewed social consensus on the need to fund and provide public education that combines excellence with universal access and prospects of mobility? Is the will there for that?

THE FUTURE

Clark Kerr would have been half, but only half, pleased at the outcome of his work. In the long outcome, the Master Plan has functioned very well overall in the research multiversities. There it has provided for excellence limited only by the imagination and for a high level of social access, given the elite academic character of entry. It has partly failed at the system level, especially in relation to the promise of universal access, and the vehicle of planning itself seems to have run into sand. In the end the execution of the Plan has faltered in the way that the original Plan was especially strong: in the big picture, in the economics and the politics. California has fallen short of the public values of the "city upon a hill" that sustained the 1960s' commitment to common social advance through higher education. To anticipate part 3, it must be said the failure of the Plan was not its own work. The dominant political philosophy has undermined its enabling conditions. High individualism in California's culture has valorized private good without regard for the common good.

Are the principles that animated Kerr and his colleagues now obsolete? Is the public research university to be the only strong survivor of the California Idea of higher education? What is its future in the present ideological and economic setting, which favors the Ivy League alternative and in which the public university is now becoming more beleaguered? What are the implications of declining mass education and closing mass access for the opportunity structure and for growing social and economic inequality? Has the prospect of widespread social mobility through higher education been broken? What is the future of public higher education in California—and everywhere? These questions will be explored further in the chapters that follow.

One thing is clear. There will be no return to 1960 or 1963, any more than there is a way back for JFK from Dallas. As Clark Kerr remarked in the 1963 preface to the Godkin Lectures: "Instead of platitudes and nostalgic glances backward to what it once was, the university needs to take a rigorous look at the reality of the world it occupies today."[17] Part 3 will return to the future of the California Idea of higher education. Before that, part 2 examines how the California Idea, with its high participation and institutional diversity and its compelling notion of the research multiversity, crossed the waters, radiating outwards from California to the whole higher education world, the ultimate success of that vision of a city upon a hill.

PART TWO

Crossing the Waters

The California Idea in the World

There is no reason for the West to be pessimistic. The West will not lose power. It will have to share power. . . . The massive new middle classes emerging all around the world have begun to accept many of the aspirations and values of the Western middle classes.

—KISHORE MAHBUBANI, *THE GREAT CONVERGENCE* (2013), PP. 11–12

8

The Idea Spreads

Four decades after the publication of *The Uses of the University* in 1963, its full worldwide effects became clearly apparent. In 2003 the first reputable ranking of the world's top five hundred universities appeared. Fifteen of the top twenty universities were American. The ranking looked credible. It used transparent metrics of research prizes, publications, and citations, from known sources. Outside the United States, media, government, university presidents, and many faculty were fascinated by the new ranking table. For each university it seemed to provide a neat measure of the distance between its research quality and the global standard, which was mostly an American standard.

Unlike most of their counterparts abroad, American universities were used to ranking. The National Research Council had ranked research university departments for most of the postwar period. *U.S. News and World Report* had begun ranking colleges in 1983 and published an annual survey from 1985 onwards. *U.S. News* modeled competition in higher education as a student market in degrees. When the global ranking appeared in 2003, the United States was largely indifferent. Few people grasped that with the new ranking an open global competition in higher education had begun, that it was a competition about research science, not the student market, and that its effects would be transformative.[1] After all, why should a global ranking matter? Only national standing was important. As in baseball, so in universities, the "world series" was a contest inside the United States. Few noticed where the new ranking had been prepared, and fewer realized that this too was a sign of the times. The new ranking had been created in a university on the east coast of China.

Many later observers assumed that the Shanghai Academic Ranking of World Universities (ARWU), as it became known, came from the Chinese government. This was incorrect. The ranking was conceived and prepared by a Shanghai Jiao Tong University engineering professor who also worked in higher education planning: Liu Niancai. Shanghai Jiao Tong was a comprehensive research university, strong in engineering, and beginning to contend with Fudan University for the leading role in the nation's second city. An extended partnership with the University of Michigan was bearing fruit in research. Liu developed the ARWU to lift Shanghai Jiao Tong's position, principally by advancing the university's contribution to China's science and technology. The aim was to measure how far universities like Shanghai Jiao Tong must travel to catch up to the West, meaning the United States.[2] Thus a Chinese university began to rank American universities and to frame the world market, including common aspirations for "world-class university" status, on the terms that it set.

Some responded to the new ranking by hunting for methodological flaws and dubious interpretations. A Chinese ranking could not get it right. But revised and streamlined in the second year in 2004, the ARWU proved robust and soon began to shape strategies of universities and governments. Universities focused on how to lift themselves into the top 500, 100, or 30, depending on where they were placed. Submissions to *Nature* and *Science* rose. High-citation researchers received job offers at more lucrative rates of pay. Governments began to invest in programs to increase their numbers of world-class universities as defined by the ranking. The term *world-class universities* (WCU) was popularized by the Shanghai group, which began to hold biennial WCU conferences, cementing its global leadership role, just as the volume of science papers published by researchers in China's universities was taking off.

The Shanghai ranking did not set American university agendas. Rather, it propagated American agendas. In framing his ranking, Liu adopted the norms of the large, comprehensive American science university (see table 8.1). The better a university's English-language science and the more it published, the more articles it had in *Nature* and *Science,* and the more Nobel Prizes that it won, the higher it would be ranked. This was a ranking of global multiversities. Universities with a disciplinary coverage that was substantially different from Harvard's or Berkeley's did not do well in the ARWU. Those with strong research in all sciences and quantitative social science, especially in medicine and engineering, did very well. The ranking, and the performance incentives it created, not only symbolized but sustained the world domination of the institution that Clark Kerr had described and had patterned in the University of California campuses.

In the decade since the ARWU began, ranking-induced reforms in many countries have pushed world higher education closer to the multiversity idea and quickened investment in R & D. Huang Futao notes in relation to China:

TABLE 8.1. A means of Californization: Indicators used in the Shanghai Academic Ranking of World Universities

Indicator	Weighting
Nobel Prizes* and Fields Medals for Mathematics won by alumni (sliding scale, more recent prizes score highest)	10%
Nobel Prizes* and Fields Medals for Mathematics won by currently employed faculty	20%
Faculty who are high citation researchers according to lists kept by Thomson-Reuters (roughly the top 300 in each research field)	20%
Papers published in the journals *Nature* and *Science* in the previous five years	20%
Papers indexed in the Thomson-Reuters Science citation index and Social Science citation index in previous year	20%
Per capita indicator: Standardized sum of the above indicators divided by the number of full-time equivalent faculty	10%
Total	100%

SOURCE: Author's summary of listings in ARWU 2015
NOTE: This is the 2014 set of ARWU indicators, not the initial set used for the first ranking in 2003. The Shanghai ARWU ranking underwent modest changes in the early years, but most of its elements have been continuous; it has been more stable than the global rankings by the *Times Higher Education* (2015) and QS World Rankings (2015). The main change was the introduction of the 10 percent per capita indicator, designed to compensate for the bias in favor of institutional size in the other indicators. That change assisted smaller high-performing research universities such as Princeton and Caltech.
* Does not include the winners of the Literature Prize and the Peace Prize

"The significance of the emergence of global rankings systems on the formation of China's world-class university, especially the publication of ARWU, . . . cannot be overestimated."[3]

This is not the only way in which the higher education world has followed American practices, practices (not limited to California) that were popularized by the California Idea of higher education. The 1960 Master Plan's approach to access and the growth of higher education—essentially one of open access and demand-led participation—has become the norm in most higher education systems, except in the poorest nations. In this manner the California formula of a higher education system that combines the excellence mission and the access mission through research multiversities (now often called world-class universities) and mass higher education institutions has become very widely used. The patterning of higher education on this basis is not universal. For example, some Western European system structures consisting of single-mission types or binary systems based on the principle of parity between institutions with different missions have continued and are influencing the evolution of dual academic-technical systems in East Asia. In many countries the division of labor is not as firm as that enforced by the Master Plan. Nevertheless, the power of the American and particularly the California Idea is especially apparent in two ways. First, in emerging higher education countries, system forms are mostly closer to California than Western Europe. Second, as noted, in nearly every country the classical Clark Kerr multiversity, the comprehensive research-intensive university with a broad set of functions and many parts and constituencies, has been adopted or has set the template for institutional reform.

At global level, it is more accurate to refer to the part "Americanization" of higher education than its "Californization." Harvard and the rest of the Ivy League exercise a great influence, admired everywhere, and the Midwestern public universities are also widely known. Nevertheless, at system level it is the ideas embodied in the Master Plan and the work of Kerr, Trow and Clark, together with the stellar success of the University of California, that above all have come to stand for the modern virtues of American higher education, just as the ideas of Wilhelm von Humboldt came to signify the essence of the nineteenth-century German university. California public education, centered on the state and a public policy compact, is closer to the political forms of higher education in other countries than is the Ivy League. Replicating Harvard and Yale around the world is no more possible than replicating Oxford and Cambridge. While the achievements of Berkeley and San Diego place them in the same league as those historic foundations—it is no easier to reach the research output of Berkeley than that of Oxford or MIT—the fact that the UC campuses are the product of a visible process of state-driven construction, implemented by modern planners such as Clark Kerr, makes them an example to strive for rather than an impossible fantasy. The California dream is a dream of modernity. As such, it appears to be in reach.

It is therefore ironic that although the California Idea is no longer fully honored in California, and U.S. higher education is widely criticized at home, especially for galloping tuition costs, U.S. and especially California higher education continue to be idealized, admired, praised, envied, and part-emulated abroad.[4] The California Idea is still radiating outwards, still transforming higher education.

Not every feature of the California Idea has become normative. No system beyond the United States and few systems within the country combine California's highly developed public mission with its equally well-defined institutional and sectoral autonomy, in which the institutions are understood as public organizations in civil society, obliged to states and stakeholders but located at arm's length and free to manage their own affairs—though the American idea of academic freedom is widely understood as essential to California/U.S. research creativity. More generally, the California/U.S. multiversity and system forms have not been *adopted* as such anywhere. Rather, they have been *adapted,* often with widely varying results. American forms and behaviors in higher education have been a major but not the only influence in countries with their own histories and cultural practices, state forms, and political economies. Other foreign influences are often also at play, such as the British, German, and French institutions and in emerging systems the more recent examples of the Dutch, Nordic, Singaporean, and Chinese approaches. The California Idea has been mixed and matched. Yet all of these other norms and exemplars are also affected by American higher education, especially the multiversity.

Part 2 explores the global radiation of American approaches to higher education, popularized above all by the California Idea, and the kind of higher education world that has resulted when American practices have been combined with other traditions and other modern forms in circumstances often very different from California's. It also considers what this partly Americanized and increasingly multicentered higher education world, one that Clark Kerr might have glimpsed but never experienced, means for American universities. The account begins with the worldwide growth of participation in higher education.

9

Participation without Limit

In 1973 Martin Trow forecast that there would be "continued popular demand" for higher education on an open-ended basis in all societies. "It seems to me very unlikely that any advanced industrial society can or will be able to stabilize the numbers," he said.[1] In a later essay in 2000, Trow seemed disappointed in the pace at which his prediction was bearing fruit. Europe, where participation was at 30–40 percent, was two or three decades behind the United States on the "continuum" to "universal access."[2] However, fifteen years further on, it is apparent that Trow's 1973 prediction is being realized, and not only in Europe.

The best source of information on rates of participation in higher education is the UNESCO (United Nations Educational, Scientific and Cultural Organization) Institute for Educational Statistics (UIS). The institute compiles a data series for the gross tertiary enrolment ratio (GTER), which measures the total number of students in university and college programs[3] as a proportion of the school-leaver age cohort. The GTER must grapple with the problem of standardizing worldwide offerings, codifying courses and hours, and coping with varied rates of mature-age and foreign student entry.[4] However, despite its limitation, it is the best available statistic for comparing participation between nations and over time because data for most countries are available.

The UNESCO data series begins in 1970, a decade after the Master Plan. In 1972 the United States had the highest rate of participation in the world, with a GTER of 48.0 percent. The only other nation where more than one-third of the population was in higher education was Soviet Russia, which routinely strove to match America in all departments. Russia's GTER was 43.9 percent. Just nineteen national systems had GTERs above Martin Trow's 15 percent threshold for mass

TABLE 9.1. From elite to mass to universal participation, 1972–2012

	1972 (%)	1982 (%)	1992 (%)	2002 (%)	2012 (%)
United States Gross Tertiary Enrolment Ratio (GTER)	48.0	56.9	76.9	78.8	94.3
Worldwide Gross Tertiary Enrolment Ratio (GTER)	10.1	12.7	14.0	21.5	32.0
Number of systems with GTER over 15% (Trow "mass")	19	47	59	96	107
Number of systems with GTER over 50% (Trow "universal")	0	1	4	34	49
Higher education system with highest GTER*	USA 48.0	USA 56.9	Canada 97.1	Korea 85.8	Korea 98.4

SOURCE: Author, based on data in UNESCO Institute of Statistics 2015.
*Data for Canada available only for 1992. For 2012 Greece recorded a GTER of 116.6%, compared to 66.7% in 2002, an implausible rate of increase in school-leaver and/or mature-age participation. The UIS series can be only as consistent as the national agencies collecting participation data.

participation. The United Kingdom was at 15.3 percent, Japan at 19.4 percent. This was far from the high participation and limitless growth in higher education that Trow was imagining. Nevertheless, ten years later, in 1982, the United States had broken through the "universal" barrier to reach 56.9 percent, the only nation to do so—Russia was at 47.1 percent—and there were forty-seven "mass" higher education nations with GTERs of over 15 percent. The overall world GTER moved only from 10.1 to 12.7 percent, however[5] (see table 9.1).

Over the next decade, the 1980s, the worldwide GTER continued inching up slowly, reaching 14.0 percent in 1992, though by then four nations had exceeded 50 percent—Canada, the United States, New Zealand, and Finland—and no less than fifty-nine higher education systems had crossed the 15-percent mass education threshold. In 1992 the worldwide participation ratio was still held down by low GTERs in three of the four largest countries in population: only 2.8 percent in China, 6.0 percent in India, and 9.6 percent in Indonesia. The United States had achieved a high GTER of 76.9 percent. Russia, where the Soviet Union was fragmenting, was stuck at 49.3 percent.[6]

GROWTH TAKES OFF

In the second half of the 1990s, as the full impact of the communications revolution unfolded and air travel cheapened and expanded in volume, the rate of growth of participation in higher education quickened. The enrollment in middle-income and lower-middle-income countries began to increase at the same rate as in wealthier countries. There was a surge of student growth in the post-Soviet countries after the state regulation of enrollments was removed, with an enrollment boom in the market-oriented fields of business studies and law. In Latin America, the post-Soviet bloc, and parts of Asia, much of the growth took place in mass private sector institutions, some of them for-profit institutions, and fee-paying places in the state sector. The worldwide GTER jumped from 14.0 percent in 1992 to 21.0 percent in 2002. The number of systems with a GTER of 15 percent or more reached ninety-six, and those above 50 percent rose from four in 1992 to thirty-four in 2002. New "universal" systems included not only the English-speaking nations and most of Western Europe but the Baltic states, Poland, and Russia, as well as Greece, Argentina, and Libya. South Korea and Finland moved ahead of the United States, with Korea the new world leader at 85.8 percent in 2002.[7]

The pace of change further accelerated in the 2000s. The world GTER increased by a remarkable 1 percent a year to reach almost one third (32.0 percent) in 2012. Forty years before, just prior to Trow's 1973 essay, only two national systems in the UNESCO data had GTERs above 32.0 percent: the United States and Soviet Russia. The world as a whole was catching up to the American level of four decades before. There were forty-nine systems with a GTER of more than 50 percent, and one hundred and seven above the 15-percent mark. New nations with GTERs above 50 percent in 2012 included Albania, Armenia, Barbados, Bulgaria, Iran, Jamaica, Kazakhstan, Kyrgyzstan, Mongolia, Palestine, Saudi Arabia, Serbia, and Thailand. It was apparent that when the GTER exceeded the "universal" level of 50 percent, the rate of participation kept on rising. By 2012 it had reached 90 percent in South Korea, Canada, the United States, Finland, and Belarus. In Argentina, Australia, Cuba, Denmark, Estonia, Greece, Iceland, the Netherlands, New Zealand, Puerto Rico, Russia, Slovenia, Spain, and Ukraine, it had passed 75 percent. South Korea's GTER, sustained by the nearly complete retention of the age group plus mature-age participation, with students enrolled in two parallel systems of academic universities and technical-vocational universities, was 98.4 percent. New "universal" systems included Albania, Croatia, Turkey, Iran (where the GTER had risen from 19.1 to 55.2 percent in the previous ten years), Mongolia, and Thailand. Aggregate progress had been made on gender also. From 1990 to 2010 the female-to-male ratio of total years of education lifted from 82 to 91 percent.[8]

Most significantly, in the large-population countries, China had lifted its GTER to 26.7 percent; participation in India was also growing rapidly, especially in the private colleges, and had climbed from 10.4 to 24.8 percent between 2002 and 2012; and the GTER in Indonesia, with expansion again mostly in the private sector, was at 31.5 percent.[9] It looked likely that China would achieve its official target of 40 percent by 2020. In the Beijing and Shanghai regions, the GTER was at 60 percent by 2010.[10]

In 2012 the overall GTER in North America and Western Europe was 79.0 percent, while participation in Central and Eastern Europe at 70.9 percent was moving closer to the Western European level. The regional GTER was 42.8 percent in Latin America and the Caribbean, exceeding 50 percent in four countries. In all systems in East Asia except China, the GTER exceeded 50 percent. It was still low in South Asia, at 22.8 percent in 2012, but was growing more rapidly in that region than in the world as a whole. Only in Central Asia, where the GTER was 24.5 percent in 2012 had overall participation not grown since 2002. The gap in the worldwide pattern of participation was sub-Saharan Africa where per capita incomes were low, most states lacked the economic resources to begin building mass higher education, and the middle class was relatively small. From 2002 to 2012 the regional GTER rose from 4.9 to 7.8 percent in sub-Saharan Africa. In 2012 the GTER was below the mass level of 15 percent in all systems for which data were available except Mauritius.[11]

The gap in educational participation in Africa has global consequences. Family size and birth rate are correlated to education levels, especially women's education. Educated women tend to control family size and thereby limit national birthrates. When enough women reach higher education, growth of population slows sharply.[12] The world population projections were revised in 2014. During the previous twenty years, it had been expected that global population would peak at 9 billion in 2050. The revised projections stated that population will keep on increasing, reaching 11 billion in 2100, with no peak in sight. The change of expectations centers on sub-Saharan Africa. Fertility rates have come down in most countries but not in sub-Saharan Africa with its low GTERs. Regional population is expected to grow from 1 billion in 2014 to more than 4 billion in 2100. In Nigeria alone, the expected population growth is from 200 to 900 million. Currently, the average Nigerian woman has six children.[13] These population projections assume no change in the GTER. That is, population in Nigeria will grow to 900 million unless high-participation higher education is established. In sub-Saharan Africa, it is a race between higher education and fertility. In the worldwide rollout of the California ideal of universal access, there is much at stake.

At the same time that participation in higher education surged all over the world, it continued to rise also in the United States, reaching 94.3 percent in 2012, second in the world among the countries from which data were available. The nation was not as well placed in its comparative gross graduation rate at first-degree level (three-year programs or more), being the world's twenty-fourth higher education system at 40.1 percent on that measure.[14] This reflected the facts that a relatively high proportion of American students were in two-year colleges, transfer to four-year programs was limited, and degree completion rates were lower than in some countries. In 2012 the leading nation in the proportion of the age cohort with degrees was the Russian Federation, at 61.6 percent, followed by Iceland and

Poland. South Korea was at 50.0 percent and the United Kingdom, with most of its cohort in three-year rather than two-year programs, was at 47.8 percent. Cuba's degree graduation rate of 50.8 percent in 2012 also exceeded that of the United States.[15] These comparisons do not reveal the quality of higher education in different countries—for example, the student children of many of the families in India and Indonesia enter small local private colleges with undertrained teachers and no scientific equipment. Though populations have been successful in demanding educational opportunities from government and market, popular demand alone is not enough to lift the threshold of quality on a universal basis—especially in market-based systems that stratify higher education into high- and low-quality streams. Nevertheless, the rapid spread of higher education and labor market qualifications throughout the world is unmistakable.

ECONOMY AND SOCIETY

What are the dynamics of this now almost universal California-style open-ended growth of participation? Martin Trow's explanation is that growth in participation is driven fundamentally by rising popular demand, which in turn is sustained by rising social aspirations—by the spread of the desire for the positional advancement of the family through higher education (see part 1). A further factor sustaining growth is that while students from affluent backgrounds, well represented in higher education, have means other than higher education of advancing their social position—for example, social and cultural capital at the point of entry into work—this is less true of students from social groups with a lower propensity to participate. At any given time the disadvantaged student is particularly likely to benefit from higher education.[16] This drives successive extensions of aspirations to the whole society (see part 3).

The growth of educational enrollment is mostly accompanied by an expansion of occupations requiring skilled labor. As participation increases, not all graduates enter professional occupations. The point, however, is that those who do not enter higher education experience an increasing disadvantage in the labor market. This maintains the graduate premium, grounded not just in higher earnings but also the social status attached to degrees, that is essential to the continued growth of participation. These factors shape the movement from elite to universal higher education. In developing countries, the dynamic of participation growth begins to take off once the urban middle class reaches sufficient size, as long as state policy facilitates expansion. The infrastructure of higher education is located in urban areas, so that urbanization expands and concentrates popular demand; states respond sooner or later to pressure from urban middle-class families for educational opportunities, and the middle class helps to finance education through taxation and tuition payments.

Since the mid 1990s, when the worldwide growth of participation quickened, four factors have been at work. First, the pace of urbanization has also increased, with more families moving from the rural economy to the cities. Between 1970 and 2010, the proportion of the world's population that was located in urban areas rose from 36.6 to 51.6 percent. The pace of urbanization was uneven by region. It was most rapid in nations in which precapitalist rural economies were being absorbed by modern capitalism. In South America the urban share climbed from 59.8 to 82.8 percent, in China, from 17.4 to 49.2 percent, and in Indonesia, from 17.1 to 49.9 percent, though it grew more slowly in India, from 19.8 to 30.9 percent.[17]

Second, and associated with urbanization, there has been a marked growth in the size of the world's middle classes, persons capable of discretionary and aspirational spending. In a study for Brookings and the OECD, Homi Kharas and Geoffrey Gertz define the middle class as persons living on US$10–$100 per day in purchasing power parity terms. In these terms 1.8 billion persons were middle class in 2009, 28 percent of world population. A further 2 percent were "rich."[18] Thus 30 percent of all persons were middle class or above, similar in proportion to the world GTER of 28 percent in 2009.[19] Third, globalization has increased the opportunities for city-based graduate labor in developing countries, in such fields as international trade, finance, and public administration. Fourth, policy support for the open-ended growth of higher education has become nearly universal. All international agencies now advocate the continuing growth of participation. In the year 2000, with the release of a landmark report on higher education in the developing world,[20] the World Bank moved away from its earlier advocacy of growth in primary rather than higher education. The Bank now advocates simultaneous expansion of educational provision at all levels. With its member countries mostly in the advanced industrial bracket, the OECD has long advocated high participation in higher education, for both economic development and social inclusion. Nearly all individual governments embrace this orthodoxy. Some struggle with the cost of expanding systems, while others transfer an increasing proportion of costs to students and families, especially in the lower-status institutions. Fiscal pressures have driven the pronounced growth in the role of private sectors and of low-cost online and distance delivery in many countries.

In a 2005 data-based review of worldwide growth in participation, national system by national system, Evan Schofer and John Meyer found that the older notion of higher education as constituting a closed society and occupational system has been replaced by an open-system picture of education as constituting useful human resources for unlimited progress and individual growth. This is the California Idea of higher education writ large. Schofer and Meyer also link the worldwide expansion of participation to the global spread of democratization, human rights, and global linkages. That argument is more tendentious. While, all else being equal, higher education fosters personal agency and a critical approach to knowledge, this does not mean that it is necessarily located in a Western liberal political agenda, nor that global imitation and policy borrowing in one arena are necessarily joined to others. The great growth of higher education extends to multiparty states like Norway and South Korea, single-party states like Russia and Singapore, and dynastic regimes like China. Everywhere, states that once restricted participation and worried about "over-education" now accommodate demand. It is easier for states to offer access to higher education than to guarantee employment. Responsibility for outcomes is transferred from state to families. At the same time, as was concluded in a major survey of educational growth in the BRICS countries, "states use the expansion of education, including university education" to promote "political legitimation with the mass of families who want to enhance their children's employability and social mobility."[21]

Governments continue to use human capital rationales to explain the expansion of higher education, recycling expectations about careers, status, and widespread mobility that universal higher education systems cannot fulfill. If the statistical fit between investment in education and economic outcomes were sufficiently close, high-skill work would be growing in proportion to graduate numbers. But the higher education/economy relation is not one of fit. The fact they are still seen in a linear continuum points to the power of the human capital myth. Though the empirical relevance of human capital theory is questionable, it survives.[22] In some fields, such as medicine, there is a close match between training and labor market outcome. From time to time, labor markets "pull" additional educational supply in specific areas—for example, when there is a shortage of accountants or engineers. Yet as Roger Geiger puts it, on the whole "labor markets and education markets are on separate tracks."[23] The two sectors, higher education and work, are heterogeneous. The transition from higher education to work is articulated by structural factors—the stratification of families and institutions; social networks; ethnicity, locality, and gender segmentation; job selection; information flows—that do not embody a human capital logic.

Macro-level research on the relationship between the economy and participation in higher education has reached similar conclusions. In their data-based study of world participation trends, Schofer and Meyer note that "the rapid expansion of higher education in the 1960s does not coincide with especially large historical changes in occupational structures, job skill requirements, or labor market demands that would create a need for massive expansion of higher education." After the 1960s, the relationship between the growth of participation and economic factors became weaker.[24] Similarly, a country-by-country comparison between economic growth rates and rates of growth of tertiary education enrollment in 2000–2012 suggests a weak to moderate association. There is a stronger correlation between rates of urbanization and country-specific GTERs.[25] This does not mean that urbanization "causes" participation growth, or that skilled work has not grown. Rather, the demand for skills, urbanization, and educational growth are all functions of the larger process of capitalist modernization. Compared to rural living, urban settings provides more favorable socioeconomic and cultural conditions both for the expansion of the middle class and the provision of education infrastructures and for the extension of aspirations and participation to poorer families as well. Though other cities across the world mostly look very different from California's cities, they share the California educational dream, nuanced with local characteristics.

GROWTH TO COME

The economic consequence of universalizing higher education is that in many countries, the pool of potentially high-skilled graduate labor will eventually constitute the majority of the workforce—although the extent to which graduates are used effectively is an open question. There is no iron law of either "over-education" or "graduate take-up." It is certain that in an increasingly mobile world, more labor will move offshore in the hunt for career opportunities or simply jobs. Still, remarks Peter Scott, "much more radical may be the social effects of mass participation." Already,

> the fact that so many people now have some experience of higher education has created a new kind of society, with multiple effects. For example, initial education has been prolonged and entry into the labor market delayed. Student lifestyles have morphed into mid-life consumerist lifestyles. The prevalence, and popularity, of "creative" and portfolio careers have been boosted. . . . There has been an explosion in the number of knowledgeable (or, at any rate, knowledge-hungry) citizens transforming the role played by professional expertise in our society. Levels of participation, albeit in virtual as well as physical forms, have been enhanced. Older social demarcations have been eroded (without necessarily leading to greater equality). . . . Educative capacity has leaked out into wider society not only through the future lives of graduates but also, more immediately, through the mass media, transforming culture, politics, social behaviors, consumption habits.[26]

There is much more Martin Trow universalism to come. In their Brookings/OECD research, Kharas and Gertz remark that in the next twenty years "the world evolves from being mostly poor to mostly middle class." In their estimates, the middle classes will increase from 1.85 billion persons in 2009 to 3.25 billion in 2020 and 4.88 billion in 2030. Most of the estimated growth is in Asia Pacific, from 0.53 billion to 3.23 billion, principally in China and India. In Latin America and the Caribbean, the growth is from 181 million to 313 million. Using a more restricted definition of middle class, the World Bank expects the middle class share of global population to more than double by 2030.[27] These families will all want higher education for their children. Across the world, middle classes have similar aspirations.

Education is driving cultural globalization and facilitating economic globalization. It is also part of the evolution of a more plural global power system. Kishore Mahbubani calls this process "the great convergence": "There is no reason for the West to be pessimistic. The West will not lose power. It will have to share power. . . . The massive new middle classes emerging all around the world have begun to accept many of the aspirations and values of the Western middle classes." Mahbubani attributes this to the education of emerging country elites in Western countries, or in Western-style universities at home. "In the past few decades, the world has produced the greatest flock of university-educated brains ever seen in human history. Never before have we nurtured talent at the scale occurring today. The rising tide of new talent is one of the key driving forces producing the great convergence."[28]

A doubling of global participation is in prospect, in a single generation. This heralds a different world. Across the world better-educated populations will deal more effectively with governments, corporations, and each other. It is less clear how higher educational expansion will be paid for, where the jobs will be for graduates, and whether there will be concurrent increases in upward social mobility. In these questions and problems, California is again being replicated everywhere across the world.

10

The Spread of Science

When Clark Kerr wrote *The Uses of the University* in 1963, world scientific capacity was concentrated in North America, Great Britain, Western Europe, and Russia. There was limited exchange between the Western nations and science in Russia. Japan built its government science laboratories and research universities in the 1970s. Though from time to time nationals from other countries contributed important discoveries, they nearly always did so in the laboratories of one of the leading science powers. In some science systems, including those of the English-speaking nations, research capacity was primarily concentrated in large higher education institutions of the multiversity type. In others, including France, Germany, and Russia, separate public research agencies played the primary role in many fields of science, leading doctoral training or sharing it with the universities. In Russia many of the universities were specialist institutions confined to specific disciplines and linked to particular government ministries, though the national flagship Moscow State University was comprehensive in form. Following the Russian example, China also adopted the dual model of scientific research and established more specialist higher education institutions than multiversities. Before the 1990s, research in China was underdeveloped and had a negligible global role.

In sum, the spread of scientific capacity was limited, as was the reach of the multiversity, and they were not always in the same places. Some nations in Europe, Latin America, and Asia had comprehensive universities of the multiversity type in terms of disciplines but were minor players in the science literature. Many nations sent bright students to the United States, Britain, or Western Europe for doctoral training, but only some of those that returned remained active in research.

In the 1990s communicative globalization changed the structure of scientific practice. This was another development led from California: information and communications technologies at Stanford and Berkeley and in Silicon Valley in the 1980s led to the personal computer and then to the World Wide Web. In the early 1990s Internet penetration began to spread. In *The Rise of the Network Society,* first published in 1996, Manuel Castells explains the economic logic of network growth: "The morphology of the network seems to be well adapted to increasing complexity of interaction and to unpredictable patterns of development arising from the creative power of such interaction," states Castells. "Yet this networking logic is needed to structure the unstructured while preserving flexibility, since the unstructured is the driving force of innovation in human activity." Further, he argues, "when networks diffuse, their growth becomes exponential, as the benefits of being in the network grow exponentially, because of the greater number of connections, and the cost grows in a linear pattern. Besides, the penalty for being outside the network increases with the network's growth because of the declining number of opportunities in reaching other elements outside the network."[1]

In a partly networked environment, the opportunity costs of exclusion grow over time. Yet in electronic networks, the unit cost of each new connection is negligible. These two facts together drive explosive growth until universal coverage is reached. So it has been with the Internet. There were 14 million users worldwide in 1993, 121 million in 1997, and 501 million in 2001, 8.1 percent of the world's population.[2] Scientific communities and research universities were often early adopters, ahead of business and government. All research universities became immediately visible to each other as part of a single networked community. Cross-border e-mail ballooned. Potentials for active collaboration were much expanded. The Internet enabled complex data transfer and as bandwidths and technology improved, so did the use of video communications for meetings. In disciplinary conversations in research universities, suddenly everyone was in synchrony with everyone else. With journals and papers published on the Web instantly accessed from everywhere, the Internet soon came to constitute a single world library of scientific knowledge that was continually updated. Because of the dominance of the English-speaking countries (principally the United States) in business, research, and the Internet itself, that single world library and most cross-border research communication were in the English language. The older global roles of French, German, and Russian faded. Spanish, Chinese, and Arabic had global potentials but were yet to establish themselves in more than regional science.

Here the growth and diversification of disciplinary knowledge, with its endless multiplication of specialisms (a process long endemic to higher education, as Bob Clark had pointed out), became joined to the new multiplication of networks, nodes, and participants. Conversation splintered and combined within one communicative grid. In this setting, strategic institutional creativity and intellectual creativity catalyzed each other, though they were not the same process. Bob Clark captures the international dimension emerging in the late 1990s in *Creating Entrepreneurial Universities*:

> Internationally, no one controls the production, reformulation and distribution of knowledge. Fields of knowledge are the ultimate uncontrollable force. . . . Just by itself, the faculty of a university, department by department, expresses an inexhaustible appetite for expansion in funding, personnel, students and space. Rampaging knowledge is a particularly penetrating demand, rooted in the building blocks of the system: it shapes basic-unit orientation, organization and practice. Since it has no stopping place, it never ceases. As one field after another stretches across national boundaries and brings more parts of universities into a truly international world of science and education, growth in the knowledge specialities also becomes the ultimate internationalizing force for the higher education sector of society.[3]

THE GLOBAL SCIENCE SYSTEM

The Internet has mediated the emergence of a single system of global science and technology in English. Charles Vest calls this "an evolving global meta-university."[4] Prior to the Internet, there was a worldwide conversation in most disciplines. What has changed is the fluency and volume of that conversation, so that the visible pool of common knowledge has larger presence and coherence. In turn, this change has reworked the balance between national and global elements. Lex Borghans and Frank Cörvers note: "If the transferability of research findings increases, the costs of international research decrease, or the scale effects increase, researchers participating in the national debate will switch to the international debate when this threshold is reached."[5] The Internet increased transferability and decreased the costs of collaboration, while enhancing the number of researchers that could be brought in. It also rendered communications instantaneous. These effects were all substantial.

The global science system has not consumed national science systems. It has changed and relativized them. In all countries apart from the United States, the vast bulk of innovations, whether in basic research or in commercial applications, are sourced not from national science systems but from the global science system. Even in the United States, global knowledge has become crucial in most disciplines. The majority of high-citation papers are now published by non-Americans, a significant change. According to the National Science Foundation, 26.6 percent of the journal papers published in 2008–2010 had American authors, as did 46.4 percent of the leading papers by citation rate (the 1 percent of world papers most cited) through the year 2012. American science was very strong in 2012 but was not as dominant as it had been ten years before, in 2002, when 57.0 percent of the top 1 percent papers had American authors. In other words, the citation measure indicates that between 2002 and 2012 the role of non-American countries in lead-ing science expanded from 43.0 to 53.6 percent of top 1 percent papers.[6]

Since World War II there has been a continuous expansion in the role of knowl-edge-intensive production, a trend that exercised Clark Kerr in *The Uses of the University*. For all nations, the ability to access the global science and technology system is now essential to scientific effectiveness and industrial competitiveness. To access the global science system, nations need their own trained scientific ca-pability. They need to be able to interpret, understand, and apply global science; to do this, they must actively engage in it. This means that they need their own trained personnel, capable not only of understanding research but also of mak-ing it and collaborating with others who do so. This means that nations also need their own infrastructure, including doctoral training in at least some disciplines. Those that lack indigenous research capacity are locked into continuing depen-dence and locked out of new technologies and knowledge-intensive production. The outcome is that research science is no longer the preserve of North America, the United Kingdom, Western Europe, Russia, and Japan. It has moved from the margins to normal business in both established and emerging states. All nations need science capacity—though not all can pay for it—just as they need clean water, stable governance, and a globally viable finance sector.

In policy, the spread of science is imagined as an arms race in innovation. Yet states lack purchase on innovation. International comparisons in that domain are elusive and few governments direct business activity (China is one exception). Policy makers provide tax breaks and other schemes to encourage industry-relat-ed R & D but more directly focus on science output in universities and state-sector laboratories, where they provide the funds, enjoy policy sway, and have visible indicators. Global research rankings allow states to compare nations and identify their competitive position. It is ironic that the shift in the balance between na-tional science systems and the global science system has fostered national capacity building in many countries, and the growing importance of research and com-mercial applications in industry and national security has strengthened the policy emphasis on building basic science.

Global rankings also point policy towards basic science. Emphasis on science has been central to American federal policy since the Manhattan Project, Hi-roshima, and Vannevar Bush's report *Science: The Endless Frontier* (1945).[7] At a world level, the policy emphasis on science—not just research but education in the STEM disciplines (science, technology, engineering, and mathematics)—has been intensifying for the last fifty years. This tendency in policy is associated with the growth of total scientific output, the spread of science capacity to more nations, the growing impact of global rankings on state policies and institutional manage-ment and on increasing the number of high-prestige science universities, and the global hegemony of a post-Kerr version of the California multiversity—the large,

TABLE 10.1. Annual output of published journal papers in science, 1995–2011

	1995	2000	2005	2010	2011	2011 (1995=1.00)	Average annual growth 1995–2011
World	564,645	630,459	710,294	799,599	827,705	1.47	2.4%
United States	193,337	192,746	205,565	209,542	212,394	1.10	0.6%
European Union	195,897	222,688	235,121	250,031	254,482	1.30	1.6%
Russia	18,604	17,181	14,425	13,500	14,151	0.76	---
China	9061	18,479	41,604	79,991	89,894	9.92	15.4%

SOURCE: Adapted by Author using data from NSF 2014. Original data from Thomson-Reuters Science Citation Index and Social Science Citation Index
NOTE: Includes selected social science but not humanities.

comprehensive science university that is not only multiple but entrepreneurial and increasingly performance managed, to ensure that science output is maximized and brought into dock with industry.

The output of published journal papers in science and social science has grown steadily at world level in the last two decades. Output rose from 564,645 papers in 1995 to 827,705 in 2011, or 46.6 percent growth in sixteen years, at an annual rate of increase of 2.4 percent (table 10.1).[8] Part of the growth reflects an expansion of capacity. Part of the growth reflects pressures to publish in performance-oriented universities, especially in countries keen to accelerate their evidence of scientific progress: an expanding journal list feeds these ambitions. Nevertheless, signs of the new science countries are unmistakable. Most of the growth has been concentrated in emerging science systems in East and Southeast Asia, Southern and Eastern Europe, the Middle East and North Africa, and Latin America. The standout is China. In China between 1995 to 2011 the annual output of science papers rose by 892.0 percent, at the remarkable rate of annual increase of 15.4 percent. In Iran, journal paper numbers increased from just 280 in 1995 to 8,176 in 2011, constituting a growth rate of 23.5 percent a year, the highest in the world among significant research nations. Much of this output was concentrated in the physical sciences. Other nations with rapid growth in journal output included South Korea, Turkey, and Brazil. Table 10.2 has details. In 1995, thirty-seven nations each published at least one thousand research papers per year, a benchmark which indicates an indigenous capacity to generate science in at least some disciplines.[9] By 2011 the number of such nations with their own science system was fifty, now including Chile, Romania, Slovenia, Croatia, Serbia, Tunisia, Iran, Pakistan, Malaysia, and Thailand.

In the established research countries, some of the same performance pressures apply, but the growth of scientific output has been much more modest. Between

TABLE 10.2. Fastest-growing national science systems, by country, 1995–2011

	Published journal papers in:		Average annual growth, 1995–2011
	1995	2011	
Iran	280	8,176	23.5%
China	9,061	89,894	15.4%
Tunisia	143	1,016	13.0%
South Korea	3,803	25,593	12.7%
Thailand	340	2,304	12.7%
Malaysia	366	2,092	11.5%
Turkey	1,715	8,328	10.4%
Portugal	990	4,626	10.1%
Pakistan	313	1,268	9.1%
Singapore	1,141	4,543	9.0%
Brazil	3,436	13,148	8.7%
Taiwan	4,759	14,809	7.4%

SOURCE: Adapted by author, using data from NSF 2014.
CRITERIA: 1,000 papers in 2011, growth rate of more than 7.0% per annum.

1995 and 2011, there was low growth in journal papers in Germany and France and little change in the United Kingdom. U.S. journal-paper output, three-quarters of which was generated in universities, rose 9.9 percent, at an annual rate of 0.6 percent. In Japan, paper volume rose by 21.3 percent between 1995 and 2000 and then fell by 17.5 percent between 2000 and 2011. In Russia output fell dramatically, by 23.9 percent between 1995 and 2011. Research infrastructure built in the Soviet period has not been adequately renewed, and Russian science and technology are not as strongly engaged with global science as those of many other countries. In some sciences the published conversations are largely conducted in the Russian language.[10] However, Japan and Russia are exceptional. Elsewhere global scientific output has been stable or has grown.

At the same time, foreign collaboration has increased at pace within the expanding networks of global science, reflecting the ease of collaboration via the Internet. Between 1997 and 2012, the proportion of papers with international coauthorship rose from 16 percent to 25 percent. In many countries a majority of papers are coauthored across borders: in 2012 there was intensive coauthorship within the Europe Research Area and between Asian countries. People working in large science systems, such as that of the United States, are less likely to coauthor abroad because a high number of domestic partners are available. However, the United States had high-intensity collaboration in Canada, Mexico, Chile, Israel, China, South Korea, and Taiwan relative to the overall pattern of collaborations by each pair of nations.[11]

11

The Global Multiversity

The increased focus on basic science in many countries, consistent with Clark Kerr's 1963 discussion of the growing social role of knowledge and a point he returned to in successive revisions of the Godkin Lectures,[1] is associated also with strengthened support across the world for the kind of research multiversity that he described.

First, while patterns of research provision continue to vary by system, the overall tendency is to center an increasing proportion of science in the comprehensive research universities. Where there is an inherited structure of state academies and laboratories, for the most part it survives, but the role of the academies is contracting overall. In China and, to a lesser extent, Russia, where in both cases the national academy of science continues to conduct a high proportion of funded scientific research,[2] the state has nonetheless encouraged mergers in which specialist universities have become part of comprehensive institutions,[3] while some activities previously sited in research academies are now in universities. This has increased the proportion of all researchers found in higher education. The fact that these countries and others with strong national institutes—such as France, China, South Korea, and Germany—have all focused recently on investments in the global performance of their leading research universities[4] will over time diminish the nonuniversity research organizations. This again strengthens the hegemony of the multiversity form.

Second, in some countries where elite professional preparation was separated from research universities, government has focused on bringing the two strands of higher education together, again moving closer to the multiversity. The classic case is France, where the 2010 IDEX program rewards cooperation between the profession-focused *grandes écoles,* comprehensive research universities, and the private sector.[5]

Third, in all these countries and many others (though not all), governments have implemented funding and performance management policies designed to elevate the globally referenced research outcomes of a designated group of elite institutions ("world-class universities") akin to the University of California. Global referencing is most often applied on the basis of global ranking. Global rankings are mostly lists of individual institutions, so that they, too, normalize the comprehensive multiversity.[6] Large institutions with broad coverage of research do best in rankings, because they maximize the weight of research output and concentrate resources and international prestige. Between them the global rankings variously measure publication and citation volume and quality, reputation via multinational surveys of academic and employer opinion, the proportion of staff and students with international origins, income for research, and faculty as a resource. Rankings will be examined first and then the various national programs to create world-class universities, or WCUs.

GLOBAL UNIVERSITY RANKING

Global higher education is a complex field in which institutions and national systems engage with each other in a lattice of relationships of cooperation and competition. Global rankings have radically oversimplified that field, normalizing it as a market competition between research universities and countries, stratifying it on the basis of the template of the American multiversity, and summarizing the complex activities of multiversities with a handful of ordinal numbers.[7] Yet the work of policy makers and university leaders everywhere is shaped by this global template. Through it, Clark Kerr's multiversity, or rather a highly reified sketch of the multiversity of *The Uses of the University,* has become the idea of a global multiversity. This in turn has encouraged the homogenization of real-life universities along American lines.

The three principal rankings are those of the Shanghai ARWU, the *Times Higher Education,* and the QS, a marketing and consulting company that has built worldwide business services on the back of its global ranking. Though the three rankings use varied methodologies with varied rigor,[8] all valorize the Anglo-American science university. The top-50 lists strongly overlap. There is more diversity at lower levels.

The indicators used by the Shanghai ARWU were outlined in table 8.1. The *Times Higher Education* uses thirteen separated indicators: reputational surveys for research and teaching constitute 34.5 percent; bibliometric indicators, 34.5 percent; income indicators, 10.75 percent; PhD studies, 8.25 percent; internationalization (the proportion of students and staff who are of international origin and international copublication), 7.5 percent; and the student-staff ratio, 4.5 percent. The individual rankings in each of these areas are not closely correlated.[9] Though the *Times Higher* ranking purports to be a measure of all aspects of higher education, there is no direct measure of teaching quality or learning achievement; there is only the survey of reputation for teaching and the student-staff ratio. In total, 73.25 percent of the *Times Higher* ranking is constituted by one or another aspect of research performance: research reputation via survey, citations, research volume, research-related income, international research collaboration, and PhDs. The use of surveys suggest that the *Times Higher* ranking has been designed as a reputational table, not a performance table.[10]

The same comment can be made about the QS ranking, which is 50 percent survey dependent and 20 percent determined by citation indicators, with the remaining indicators related to staff-student ratios and internationalization.[11] The QS ranking is the least research metric dependent of the major rankings and, not coincidentally, is also the least rigorous. However, shifting the balance between academic opinion surveys and research metrics does not greatly change the ranking outcome. This is because the quantity and quality of research play a central role in shaping the global reputation of institutions of higher education, while at the same time, there is a reciprocal movement from prestige to research outcomes. Global reputation is instrumental in drawing talent, ideas and resources from all over the world.

Research by Ellen Hazelkorn and others finds that outside the United States, global rankings shape the choices of many international students and influence the investment decisions and judgments of foundations, donors, and companies, not to mention high-performing faculty and prospective doctoral students. Highly ranked universities are global magnets for talent. Highly ranked universities also attract income from the sources that sustain their position. For many university presidents, improved rankings have become the principal performance indicator. By installing strategies designed to increase measured research inputs and outputs and other indicators that feed into rankings, university leaders normalize resource priorities, developmental strategies, and faculty management according to the content of the global rankings.[12] These effects are magnified when system managers directly focus on higher rankings as an institutional objective. Remarkably, the overprecise and undercertain technologies of global university rankings have also become installed in the funding and decision regimes of many nation-states. For example, in 2007 immigration policy in the Netherlands was revised to include a provision that defined as a valued skilled migrant anyone who graduated from a world top-150 university as measured by one of the principal rankings. The governments of Qatar, Kazakhstan, and Mongolia, among others, allocate scholarships for foreign study to universities ranked in the world top 100, ensuring that about half of their globally mobile doctoral students will go to the United States.[13]

Rankings shape people's lives. And as in France, many other governments have set strategic goals based on increasing the number of national universities in the world's top 500, 200, 100, or 50, just as individual research universities set ranking-related targets for themselves.[14]

WORLD-CLASS UNIVERSITIES

Global ranking feeds into the flourishing "world-class university" industry with its conferences, papers, special journal editions, monographs, reports, consulting companies, and superannuated professors in the market in strategic advice. In this industry, creating a world-class university (WCU) is universally understood to mean achieving a globally ranked institution. WCUs have a number of meanings for national governments: WCUs signify research innovation power and, through that, economic status; WCUs' programs resource local social elites; and WCUs at home might be seen to challenge Anglo-American neoimperial sway in higher education. "Developing prestigious institutions helps to legitimize the state as a national power."[15]

In 2009 the World Bank published *The Challenge of Establishing World-Class Universities* by the coordinator of its tertiary education program, Jamil Salmi. Dotted with examples of system and institutional transformations, the book sets out to "explore *how* institutions become tops in their league to guide countries and university leaders seeking to achieve world-class status . . . [and] to explore the challenges involved in setting up globally competitive universities (also called 'world-class,' 'elite,' or 'flagship' universities) that will be expected to compete effectively with the best of the best."[16] Salmi argues that the "superior results" associated with leading ranked universities—"highly sought graduates, leading-edge research, and technology transfer" derive from "three complementary sets of factors." These are

> (a) a high concentration of talent (faculty and students), (b) abundant resources to offer a rich learning environment and to conduct advanced research, and (c) favorable governance features that encourage strategic vision, innovation, and flexibility and that enable institutions to make decisions and to manage resources without being encumbered by bureaucracy.[17]

The Challenge of Establishing World–Class Universities emphasizes that the role of government is crucial, particularly in research infrastructure: "It is unlikely that a world-class university can be rapidly created without a favorable policy environment and direct public initiative and support, if only because of the high costs involved in setting up advanced research facilities and capacities."[18] At the same time, American autonomy and an entrepreneurial approach are also seen as vital, much as Bob Clark had argued in 1998. Salmi finds that universities in the United States are the best because of their "relative independence from the state" together with "the competitive spirit that encompasses every aspect of it." In the United States "the environment in which universities operate fosters competitiveness, unrestrained scientific inquiry, critical thinking, innovation, and creativity."[19] At the institutional level Salmi emphasizes "strong," visionary, and performance-focused executive leadership with "a clearly articulated strategic plan to translate the vision into concrete targets and programs,"[20] as well as the use of internationalization strategies, especially in research.[21]

Salmi's argument shows that it is difficult for most nations to mount top-100 global multiversities because of cost. At the same time, he argues that money alone is not enough. Nations must play to their contexts, strengths, and resources. Strategies to develop WCUs should be nested in plans to augment education as a whole and in larger national strategies for economic and social development.[22] Importantly, and ironically, given that this is a how-to-do-it primer on WCUs, Salmi argues that not all should so aspire: "The hype surrounding world-class institutions far exceeds the need and capacity for many systems to benefit from such advanced education and research opportunities. . . . Not every nation needs comprehensive world-class universities, at least not while more fundamental tertiary education needs are not being met." It might be better to have sustainable polytechnic-style institutions nested in social realities and local needs.[23] No doubt this last piece of realistic advice has been scarcely noticed in the headlong rush towards imagined global status.

Salmi's version of the multiversity joins the global rankings template to the New Public Management recipe for transforming higher education using quasi-markets and entrepreneurial leadership. In this body of thought, academic creativity and corporatist competiveness are all of a piece under the rubric of business strategy and business plans. It is Bob Clark's 1998 idea but with a little less emphasis on the autonomous "academic heartland." Though Salmi discusses the Master Plan with approval, he does not tease out the virtues of the cross-campus collaboration within the University of California. On the other hand, his argument is not a pure neoliberal one. He factors in a larger role for state agency than Anglo-American states now claim, at least openly. He emphasizes that government planning and funding are central to WCU development, especially the successful cases of rapid development.

Governments pursue two broad strategies to build a stronger research subsector. One strategy uses competition to drive differentiation and concentration in existing top institutions ("rewarding quality"). The second strategy is to build new capacity in old or new institutions identified by government ("picking winners"). The first strategy allows government to evade direct responsibility for making choices between institutions, though the outcomes of competition are often predictable. At one extreme, this pathway allows government to avoid making specific additional investments and merely use quasi-market research competition for existing resources and status to create the concentration through the Matthew effect.[24] In the second strategy of capacity building, state investment is mandatory. The English-speaking countries tend to follow the first pathway. The United Kingdom, the United States, and Australia all allocate a majority of research support through competitive project and program funding. They also manage a larger framework of competition in higher education, for all resources and prestige, often including teaching-related funding. This framework tends to favor the leading institutions and enables them to strengthen their relative national position over time,[25] elevating their global position also. The United Kingdom buttresses the top layer of research universities by allocating additional resources on the basis of a census of research performance, the Research Excellence Framework.[26]

In contrast, many other countries have implemented capacity-building world-class university programs in universities identified as actual or potential WCUs. Such schemes often involve competitive bidding for inclusion in the program. Salmi identifies nine countries that have funded universities as institutions, and another nine that have funded departments or research clusters directly. In all, in the 2005–2009 period alone there were nineteen programs in Europe and twelve in East and Southeast Asia, though only one in Africa (Nigeria), two in the Middle East (Israel and Saudi Arabia), one in North America (Canada), and none in Latin America. These programs include the Excellence Initiative in Germany, which began in 2005; Operation Campus in France (2008); Project 211 (1995) and Project 985 (1998) in China; the Brain 21 program in South Korea (1999); a series of programs in Japan including Global 30, Global COE, the Program for Promoting the Enhancement of Research Universities, and the Top Global University Program; and parallel initiatives at greater or lesser levels of funding and effectiveness in Saudi Arabia, Russia, and other countries.[27]

STRATEGIES OF INTERNATIONALIZATION

In 2011, together with Philip Altbach, Salmi released a set of case studies, *The Road to Academic Excellence: The Making of World-Class Universities*. The first half of the book echoes the method of Bob Clark in *Creating Entrepreneurial Universities* (1978). It consists of four narratives of successful development in East Asia: Shanghai Jiao Tong University in China, Hong Kong University of Science and Technology, the private Pohang University of Science and Technology in South Korea, and the National University of Singapore. Other chapters cover universities in India, Nigeria, Chile, and Russia where the ideal trajectory is less apparent. Salmi identifies several "accelerating factors" assisting the successful cases, which are mostly strategies of "internationalization" that secure effective conformity with the global multiversity template. These strategies have been especially important in East Asia.[28] However, internationalization has differing meanings, governed by where the country and its universities sit in the global order. In English-speaking countries, its impact is benign: stronger cross-border relationships and growing awareness of other systems, without having to transform at home. In non-English-speaking environments, it means importing the global multiversity into the home setting. Internationalization becomes Americanization, which is not benign and is often problematic, especially for faculty not working in the STEM disciplines, for whom national language is the essential medium and sometimes also the product of their work.[29]

These internationalization strategies include research concentration in the STEM disciplines; encouraging citizens who have completed their doctoral studies abroad, mostly in the United States, to return to the nation; measures to attract foreign research talent; adopting English as the main university language; incentives for English-language publishing; encouraging faculty to spend time in top universities abroad; and benchmarking of research units and teaching programs with American, British, or Western European comparators. At Shanghai Jiao Tong University, Qi Wang, Q. H. Wang, and Niancai Liu report that about 15 percent of all discipline-based courses are bilingual. The university conducts joint degree programs in the United States, Germany, and France. A quarter of all first-degree students spend periods aboard; the target level is 50 percent of students by 2020. Selected doctoral students go abroad, supported by scholarships that cover tuition fees, travel, and living expenses.[30] Internationalization policy also implies "different concepts of university governance and management" and "international standards to improve quality in all aspects."[31] Pohang University of Science and Technology, which is bilingual in English and Korean, announced in 2010 "that it would invite 10 Nobel laureates or Fields medalists as full-time professors" for a three-year period. Each invited scholar was to be given US$1 million for salary and US$4 million for research and living costs.[32] Salmi identifies a number of "accelerating factors" that can hasten the ascension to WCU status, including bringing back the national research diaspora, using English, making the campus more accessible to foreign talent, niche focus on particular STEM disciplines, international benchmarking, and innovations in curricula.[33]

"The U.S. research university model is widely considered the gold standard and is emulated globally," proclaims Altbach in *The Road to Academic Excellence*. "The quintessential U.S. public research universities are those of the University of California system. . . . The California Master Plan for Higher Education of 1960 constitutes an effective way of organizing a differentiated public higher education system to cater to research excellence as well as to access and massification."[34] What other countries have taken from the California Idea, above all, is a layer of peak research universities above a hierarchical education system. This intellectual order is readily rendered congruent with elite formation without disturbing the social order.

GLOBAL SAMENESS

The world science system, global rankings, and the WCU movement on the basis of the global multiversity template all tend to facilitate convergence. Kishore Mahbubani states:

> All the better universities know that they have to have strong science and engineering faculties to get any kind of global recognition. Equally importantly, the language of science and engineering is a global language. The laws of physics equally apply to all corners. Hence the global spread of education in science and technology is another major driving force in the creation of one world.[35]

By facilitating open global systems, global homogenization makes it easier for all parties to communicate freely, to cooperate, and to build joint research and teaching programs. Arguably, this maximizes collective output on a world scale. However, the homogeneous systems used in universities and research are not readily nuanced and customized for each locality, and this has a number of downsides.

First, the universal rollout of the American multiversity as the iconic form of higher education, cemented in place by the normative power of global rankings, has negative implications for other institutional forms in higher education—small universities and colleges; very large universities with uneven research intensity; universities that do not pay high salaries to faculty in global demand; institutions primarily focused on teaching (including some such as American liberal arts colleges that are intellectually and socially elite, though it must be said that some liberal arts colleges do a surprising amount of non-STEM research); institutions focused on underrepresented populations; specialist universities confined to one or two disciplines in business, medicine, media, or the arts; and technical-vocational institutions focused on applied research and industry training. It also has negative implications for universities emphasizing the humanities and the humanistic social sciences or nationally specific research in professional disciplines that do not figure in the world journals (perhaps law, and some work in business and education). Despite Altbach's comment, the ranked-university universe breaks contact with the California Idea in significant ways. One difference is that each individual research university is positioned as competing with all, rather than as a member of a collaborative system in which the success of one is the success of all. Another is that, unlike the California system forms, ranking does not encompass institutional diversity. It bears down hard on nonmultiversities. It drives them upwards towards a global research-intensive form that not all can perform, not all should perform, and none can finance. All nations, rich and poor, need institutions other than science universities, but the elevation of the multiversity as the one single emblematic form undermines the status and resources of all other institutions.

Second, the uniform global multiversity tends to suppress national-cultural diversity. The global multiversity form creates a strategic dilemma in all universities, in all countries that publish in languages other than English—that is, the majority of the higher education world. The effect is felt most completely in smaller nations that are propelled into global English quickly because of the returns to scale.[36] It also undermines the potentials of larger language groupings, such as speakers of French and German, which have some claim as global languages. Across the world, national-cultural tradition is manifest also in institutional form and identity. The global multiversity discriminates against alternate configurations of high science, scholarship, and social prestige, including other long-established institutional norms.

Here the hegemonic impact of the global multiversity recalls earlier critiques of education as cultural imperialism.[37] Consider the great Latin American national universities such as the University of Sao Paulo in Brazil, the University of Buenos Aires (UBA) in Argentina, and the Autonomous National University of Mexico (UNAM) in Mexico City. These institutions, which almost parallel the church in their scope and centrality to the state and national life, are larger than the multiversity and have a broader remit. UNAM has over 300,000 students, dozens of sites, and carries out a quarter of all research in Mexico. It houses many leading research centers and is also a large provider of social access to higher education. It also sustains a significant part of Mexico City's cultural life, not to mention one of the leading football teams. Its social and cultural missions handicap its position in global rankings. A broad range of nonresearch roles, and large numbers of teaching-only faculty and service personnel tend to dissipate potential research resources and reduce faculty research performance on a per capita basis. Yet given the national expectations surrounding UNAM's role as a flagship university in Mexico, a ranking outside the top 100 hurts it in the eyes of public and government. Global rankings of the Shanghai ARWU and *Times Higher Education* type create a no-win situation for UNAM. Should it reduce its national mission to meet the global template? If it narrows mission, it loses national funding and perhaps status. If it does not narrow mission, its ranking and again its status and perhaps also its budget are depressed. Also, what happens to its extensive Spanish-language scholarship in the humanities, doubly excluded by language and discipline? The global multiversity circuit brings the world, especially scientists, together. Yet when it is regulated by ranking, this reduces diversity in knowledge, ideas and cultural forms. Higher education should expand the capacity for self-determining agency, not narrow its range and rob it of its confidence to be itself.

COMPARING SYSTEMS

The effects of the WCU movement among non-WCUs raises the question of the implications of ranking for national systems of higher education. A study by Leon Cremonini and his colleagues suggests that policies designed to create stronger

WCUs in Finland, France, and Germany have neglected the issue of benefits for the national system as a whole, which cannot be seen as automatic.[38] One ranking that tackles this issue directly is the Universitas21 (U21) ranking. This compares national systems, not institutions. The composite index used in the U21 ranking includes orthodox values for research outputs and quality. It also covers social participation in higher education and the autonomy and connectedness of institutions.[39] These additional factors are again sensibilities called up by the U.S./California experience. At the same time, the U21 ranking is consistent with a range of missions and a division of labor between research-intensive universities and the other institutions. All else being equal, it also rewards cooperation between research universities, rather than modeling them solely as competitors, as do other rankings. However, the U21 system ranking does not prevent the suppression of global cultural and linguistic diversity. No mechanism of cross-national comparison in higher education has solved that problem.

The U21 system ranking has achieved little prominence, however. It is a footnote to the common fascination with league table hierarchies based on individual research universities, which imagine the global multiversity as a stand-alone firm, with little attention to the national contextual elements that condition performance and none to the relative quality of mass education institutions. In this framing the California Idea's notion of a multilayered interdependent system slips from sight.

12

Systems and Stratification

System design and stratification have many different configurations. Except in very small systems, there is normally a hierarchy of institutions, formal or informal, associated with stratification in the social value of participation and mostly attuned also to the segmentation of incoming students. Even in the egalitarian Nordic societies, certain research universities enjoy more prestige than do other institutions.

The tendency to stratification of institutions on the basis of unequal value is inevitable where there is inequality of wealth and status and social competition for a limited number of well-paid professional jobs. When institutions and students choose each other (rather than students being allocated places on the basis of location or by government decision), the primary stratification takes the form of bifurcation.[1] A bifurcation is a binary division into separate and opposing subgroups that together constitute an interdependent system. Institutions divide between "selecting" (or "status-seeking") universities and colleges, where there are more applications than places, and "student-selected" (or "student-seeking") institutions that are easy to enter. This tendency to elite/non-elite bifurcation of institutions is ultimately driven by the absolute scarcity of highly valued social opportunities, or in the theoretical terms of social science, the zero sum character of positional competition.[2] The number of stellar careers is limited and only some university "brands" and degrees carry a high probability of such careers. This is an ultimate barrier to egalitarian higher education, unless higher education is leveled downwards and taken out of social allocation (as in China during the Cultural Revolution of 1966–1971). If higher education ceased to be an avenue for positional advancement, a large part of its social role would evaporate.

When the participation rate advances, the mass education segment of higher education grows in size relative to the elite segment. The proportion of relatively low-value places tends to grow: the base of the pyramid expands more quickly than the peak that it supports. Social access widens but the average probability of reaching the elite level is reduced. When all else is equal, the expansion of participation is associated with a tendency to steeper stratification of the system. The 1960 California Master Plan institutionalized the relative expansion of the base by largely concentrating future growth in two-year community colleges. In addition, as noted, by fixing enrollment shares between the subsectors, it blocked the downward spread of the research university role. The research sector could never reach more than 12.5 percent of the age cohort. California public higher education became "steeper" than systems in which a larger proportion of young persons experienced research universities. This formula concentrated degree value at the top of the system, protecting the University of California and enabling it to compete with the leading private universities, while sustaining a large sector with relatively low diploma value likely to decline over time.

POLICY AND SYSTEM SHAPE

As the example of the Master Plan shows, stratification is not solely a natural process. System and structure are constructed by policy, regulation, and resourcing. National, federal, and provincial jurisdictions are in play, sometimes in complex combinations. It differs by country. Private sectors are sometimes regulated together with public institutions and sometimes regulated separately, or scarcely regulated at all. Governments can modify the natural tendency to stratification. They can also enhance that tendency, in general or in a nuanced fashion. They can attempt to fix an institutional hierarchy, and they can allow it to float freely. In some countries, all places in tertiary education enjoy social status and provide a solid platform for the workforce, while in other systems it is not so. There is broad scope for policy choices.

The steepness of the hierarchy is reduced when governments move beyond mere rhetoric about parity of esteem and apply policies that actually equalize the status and resource base of institutions. A number of Western European systems, notably those in the Nordic countries, sustain unitary public systems based on the principle of institutional parity of esteem. Private higher education plays a lesser role in Finland and Norway and a negligible role in Sweden and Denmark. The commercial subsector is absent. No tuition is charged to citizen students in public institutions. Thus Nordic governments work against the grain of natural stratification and utilize higher education as a means of reducing rather than enhancing Matthew effects. These nations offer all of their citizens high-quality higher education as a matter of right. Not by coincidence, these nations have relatively high levels of intergenerational mobility in higher education[3] and relatively low inequalities of income and wealth, reflecting and facilitating an egalitarian approach to educational policy (which is not to say that social equality is simply "caused" by educational equality: see part 3). The crucial achievement is that in terms of quality, they level up and not down, within a freer atmosphere than applies in most systems. While universities such as Helsinki and Copenhagen are the most attractive places for faculty to work, it is possible to be a world-leading researcher in any Nordic university. University leaders also have scope to pursue differing paths to high performance. Their work is facilitated by Nordic school systems with high and egalitarian learning achievement and high levels of state-driven R & D investment. The Nordic model is under pressure to move to state-managed quasi markets, and there are tensions deriving from competition for research funding and managerial intervention in academic work, but it remains a more completely public policy than California.[4] It shows what public educational provision can achieve when there is broad consensus about taxation and its use for common social purposes, including education.

In Germany and the Low Countries, all research universities traditionally enjoyed parity of esteem, though as in some Nordic countries, they were distinguished from nonresearch university institutions. Germany has now moved away from parity of esteem by applying the Excellence Initiative in selected research universities. The Netherlands maintains formal parity within the research university sector. While universities such as Utrecht, Amsterdam, and Leiden stand out, the top group is much larger, a broader distribution of elite research capacity than in the English-speaking world. The difference between the positional leaders and other research universities is less than in the United Kingdom, where Cambridge and Oxford are in a category of their own, and in the United States, with the Ivy League and the flagship publics.

In contrast to the Nordic approach, in many countries the steepness of the institutional hierarchy is increased by policy—when resource levels and quality of provision are differentiated because it is too expensive to provide all students with "world-class" teaching, facilities, and income support; when nations enhance the support given to selected WCUs without boosting status and resources at other levels; and especially when competition is a principal medium for determining status and resources. As noted, competition naturally generates Matthew effects that strengthen elites. When competition is joined to unequal starting points, as is the case in nearly all systems, and/or joined to unequal resource allocations, as in the many systems that allocate research funding on a competitive basis, then the stratification of institutions is magnified. These effects reinforce the already self-reproducing nature of the university hierarchy. In higher education it is more difficult to displace the established sector leaders by meritocratic pressure from below than is the case in most other industries—for example, those that produce cars, mobile phones, or financial services.[5] Over time the leading firms in those industries tend to change. In higher education the positional leaders stay on top. Some of them have been there for hundreds of years.

Most (though not all) nations do not collect enough tax revenue to offer universal access to research-intensive teaching universities. Institutions need a threshold level of resources to be global research players. Many cannot achieve it. This generates institutional differentiation based on the research role plus resource levels. When research universities partly sustain their research on the basis of tuition, the resulting price barriers generate asymmetries in access that are based on tuition cost, reinforcing the stratification of students and hence the natural binary structure of systems. The research role is a primary marker of elite status and a mediating factor in the pairing of elite institutions with elite students. In competitive systems, institutions become strung out in a vertical status hierarchy, in which research performance, financial resources, student selectivity, and degree firepower are all more or less aligned. In the United States this hierarchical segmentation is not left entirely to the free play of market forces (money and reputation). It is regulated on the basis of classifications with separate institutional missions, generating subcompetitions of high-research universities, other doctoral institutions, four-year institutions, and two-year colleges.

American stratification is not driven just by positional competition and resource scarcity. It is sustained also by the need for definition and identity in the face of the large, open, and opaque higher education system, labor market, and society. Classifications provide a place for all. Community colleges offer locality and perhaps "community." The in-between CSUs suggest social mobility. Vocational colleges promise a job. Research universities promise the world. The overall hierarchy facilitates both some upward mobility and also Bob Clark's "cooling out" function, whereby institutions in the lower echelons help students to temper their ambitions and lower their expectations.[6] Through institutional classifications, the hierarchy of unequal institutions performs the same function as a free market in position—it aligns unequal social origins, as well as unequal academic merit, to unequal social outcomes—but in a more predictable way. The broad range of "uses" to which higher education is put encourage all-round movement towards the greater certainty and more tradable value, along with the nuanced sense of belonging and opportunity, that subsectoral categories bring. This formal hierarchy does not guarantee equality of opportunity, but it no doubt contributes to a stable social order.

SYSTEM VARIETY

The shape of systems varies according to national tradition and history, policy assumptions, social expectations, and the professions and labor markets. As noted, some societies use a horizontal division of labor between institutional types, with parallel academic and technical-vocational streams. If there are vertical implications in such distinctions, they are modest and understated. Other nations present distinctions as vertical in the manner of California. Commitment to upward transfer arrangements is highly variable. Purposes also vary. In some societies, vocational preparation is expected to dominate the sector. In other countries, such as the United States, generalist first degrees are standard practice. All other nations had different starting points from that of California. Once established, higher education structures are path dependent. People invest in them. They do not readily transform. Mergers, new subsectors, and the fall of structures are traumatic and protracted events.

In established higher education systems of Western Europe and the English-speaking countries, both elite research universities and institutions of mass education have emerged, as in the United States. Some universities combined the missions. The fact of different missions does not in itself lead to a fixed division of labor of the California type. Formal classifications are used in only some countries. Certain others, such as Russia, apply formalized classification to the leading group of research universities rather than all institutions.[7] Subsectors more often compete on the boundaries than remain quiet. Middle institutions press against the limits of their role and press upwards for status, hoping that resources will follow; yet they are dependent on resources to make the climb upwards in the first place. Though machinery for coordination takes many forms, subsectors rarely enjoy California's autonomy, and coordination is often directly controlled by the state. Long-term planning is rarer than it was, having often given way to quasi markets and principal-agent steering, but these mechanisms allow governments to maintain control. Classifications are usually regulated by government rather than by autonomous civil organizations as in the United States. Two-year colleges, for-profit activity, and online provision and certified on-the-job training are less likely to be regulated by institutional definitions and firm intrasectoral demarcations. Private provision is normally looser than public provision, especially online higher education, which by its nature is impossible to fully regulate, especially when in cross-border mode.

Many examples could be cited to demonstrate the variety of arrangements. Both Australia (1988) and the United Kingdom (1992) abolished binary systems based on the distinction between universities versus polytechnic-style institutions and teachers' colleges. In these now unitary systems, degree-providing institutions are not formally segmented but are constituted as a single quasi market. There is parity of esteem, but only in a formal sense. All can become registered as providers of full-fee international education in the global market for students (one of the rationales for the official parity) and all may compete for public research funding. Yet there are widely understood distinctions in research intensity, resources, and social standing. This plays out in the differential values attached to degrees, though government normally sustains the fiction of unitary parity of esteem—for example, by not measuring rates of return by institution and focusing on differentiation only by field of study. In the outcome, the research-oriented sector is stretched on a vertical continuum from leading global universities to institutions almost solely teaching- and service-focused, with a handful of doctoral students and a little applied research and consultancy. Thus the UK/Australia unitary system form includes universities of both the UC and the CSU type in terms of social standing and real research role. Between the selecting and the student-selected universities lies a group of middle institutions, pushing upwards, carrying some research but never enough to become elite. In Australia, policy and research funding support have aligned so as to ensure that the majority of funded universities are located in this middle group and all carry research-university credibility in the market for international students.[8] The striking differences with California are that in both the United Kingdom and Australia, as also in New Zealand, most full-time higher education students are located in universities with a formal research mission, and the system is managed through a competitively ordered market segmentation rather than in classification-based segments. American higher education is more unabashed in embracing the notion of itself as a "market," yet the UK and Australian systems are more marketized than the California Idea.

In 1963 Martin Trow criticized the report of the British Robbins committee for "making the universities with their high standards and expensive practices, the numerically dominant form of British higher education." He suggested that British higher education would be better off with a California-style pyramid rather than an inverted pyramid.[9] Certainly the pyramid makes for a more stable system. The elite is unambiguous. Yet whether there is more or less opportunity for upward university mobility in California is unclear. Nominally, the middle-level British and Australian universities can climb to positional leadership, but with the possible exception of the University of Warwick, singled out for study by Bob Clark, none have actually done so.

Both the United Kingdom and Australia also maintain a further/vocational education sector with weaker social standing than that of the degree-providing universities, as evidenced in student entry scores and rates of return data. This sector is not dignified with the title "higher education." Further education in the United Kingdom has something of a community college function.[10] It provides two-year diplomas and is moving into three-year degrees. But it is smaller and weaker than in California. Its access role is shared with lower-status universities. The sharply vertical relationship between universities and further and vocational education in the UK/Australian approach contrasts with the binary systems in Germany, Taiwan, South Korea, and the Netherlands, where the respective standing of the subsectors is more ambiguous. While the most prestigious institutions, and those where the highest paid professionals are prepared, are in the academic-research sector, Germany, Taiwan, and Korea support high-quality technical-vocational universities at degree level. These institutions service large-scale advanced manufacturing industry sectors. In the Netherlands, the *hogescholen* in the second sector are more generalist in character and focused on local employment. They have less standing than the *fachhochschulen* in Germany and seek to advance their position through a larger research role, a development so far resisted by the established research universities and the state.[11]

Unlike the system structures in the Netherlands and Germany but like those in most of East Asia, the research university sector in Taiwan and South Korea is highly differentiated. Seoul National University in South Korea towers over all other higher education institutions, enjoying perhaps more social and occupational prestige within its nation than does Harvard in the United States. This is true also of the University of Tokyo in Japan, and Tsinghua and Peking Universities in China. In contrast the Hong Kong University Grants Council pursues policies designed to ensure that most universities have similar size, mission, and status. The small island city has five universities in the world's top 500 and three in the front ranks—the University of Hong Kong, the Chinese University of Hong Kong, and the fast-rising Hong Kong University of Science and Technology.[12]

Modern Chinese higher education has been largely built in the last twenty years, in accelerated fashion and on a monumental scale, on the base of the traditional institutional landscape leveled during the Cultural Revolution. A low level of participation together with the capacity of the post-Mao state to execute long-term planning and infrastructure financing constituted a remarkable opportunity; in the 1990s China adopted a California template. Its system design joined research-intensive universities focused on global science to provincial universities, the equivalent of the CSU campuses, and to two-year colleges with a generalist mandate, the equivalent of California's community colleges. These distinctions were held in place by a classification system along American lines. The government also facilitated mergers to form comprehensive institutions, prior to the takeoff in enrollments at the end of the decade. The 211 program for one hundred modernized universities began in 1994. The 985 program, which allocated $10 billion in extra funding to thirty-nine selected research universities, began in 1998.[13] Spending per student in elite institutions has always been much higher than in nonelite institutions, but the gap has increased. In 1997 elite universities were funded per student 20 percent more but by 2007, following allocations under the 985 program, they had twice the per-student funding of nonelite institutions.[14] Although the leading research universities have grown in size, the overwhelming bulk of the expansion in China has taken place in second- and third-tier institutions, as in California. Over time there have also been divergences from California. The national government encouraged the growth of private institutions developed under the auspices of public universities as a way to broaden access to high-demand public institutions while facilitating private funding. The private sector is more closely regulated in China than in California. In addition, in 2014 it was announced that six hundred institutions would be remade as vocational institutes, creating a dual-track higher education sector parallel to Germany and Korea. China's first vocational *gaokao* (end of school examination) was conducted in June 2014.[15] Low-tier generalist institutions producing flexible credentials have lost some standing. The new vocational sector is nested in a strategy to shift part of China's export sector from middle level to advanced manufacturing. This shift from California forms to German-origin forms looks significant.

As noted, across the world, the most common elements in higher education systems are the multiversity and an accessible mass higher education sector. The social reach of research universities—their extent of coverage of the population—is varied. Credential hierarchies and institutional size, shape, specialization, and configuration take many forms. The size and scope of the ambiguous middle institutions also varies, and mass higher education is less globally standardized than is elite higher education. Some evidence suggests that stratification in systems is becoming steeper[16] because of growth effects in broadening participation at the base, WCU agendas, and the use of quasi-market competition, and increased reliance on private funding in many countries. Whether the national hierarchy is steep or not, mass higher education varies in quality. Some mass education, while nonselective at point of entry, provides solid programs and credentials that are pathways to occupations and solid graduate earnings advantages in comparison to nongraduates. At the other extreme are institutions and degrees that are fraudulent or otherwise lacking value. There is much variation in the role and quality of private sectors, and within that group, in the role of commercial providers. There are relatively few elite private universities across the world, in part because of the high cost of funding research science, which in economic terms is a public good that cannot be funded in markets. Outside the United States, the Philippines (where private universities have become de facto leaders because of the impoverishment of national universities) and perhaps South Korea, nearly every leading university is a state sector institution. In this respect the world diverges from American higher education, though not from the forms of California's public higher education.

PROBLEMS OF MASS HIGHER EDUCATION

The state underpins the research university and shows no sign of retreating from that role anywhere. Even the Ivy League is massively subsidized by research grants and student loans funding. Worldwide, the state's role in mass higher education is more variable. Some regimes take full responsibility for the quantity and quality of higher education as a whole, whether provided in public sectors or on a shared public and private basis. In some other nations, the state's contribution to mass higher education is in retreat. In a third group of nations, that role is partly or little developed.

In the English-speaking world, most of Europe, the post-Soviet zone, and parts of Asia, there are public institutions, many of them large, offering state-shaped and often state-provided mass higher education. These subsectors are akin to the community colleges in California. As in California, for the most part the system dynamic of mass public institutions is not one of buyer-seller markets. It parallels large-scale, bureaucratically driven wartime mobilization and the large state systems of basic education or public health that handle high volumes of people processing with moderate effectiveness. In contrast, nations such as India, Indonesia, Philippines, Japan, South Korea, and Brazil have large private sectors carrying most of mass higher education. In the first three cases, the private colleges tend to be small, antiquated, and poor in quality. There is also a growing commercial component in many nations, more like modern firms and similar to (and often owned by) the for-profit sector in the United States. In Peru, for-profit universities account for 38 percent of undergraduate enrollments; in Brazil they enroll 36 percent.[17] The problem for mass commercial education is that almost always, like mass public education, it is positioned as low quality in terms of use value and positional value. Subsidized research-intensive universities, public or private, remain dominant. This limits the scope for commodification in both the upper and lower reaches of national systems.[18]

Across the world, elite research-intensive universities are travelling relatively well. They have powerful social support, and states believe that research is a strategic necessity. Mass higher education is not travelling as well in many countries. As in California, the expansion of participation is often accompanied by declining resources per head, increases in tuition costs, and a flattening of the absolute earnings returns to graduates, though the average graduate retains an advantage over nongraduates. As systems move beyond 50 percent participation and approach full universality, in the lower reaches of the status hierarchy, especially in generic disciplines, there is a flattening of the status advantages that high education brings. When everyone is a graduate, this no longer confers a distinction. There may come a point when the disadvantages attached to nongraduation are eclipsed by the financial costs and opportunity costs of enrollment, especially if the actual learning experience is weak. Quality-assurance techniques are installed in most mass higher education systems. But while quality assurance encourages internal institutional reflexivities, it does not generate a broad-based momentum for measurable quality improvement. Often it is used to bed down performance management regimes and to augment marketing, enabling institutions to show they are going well even when they are not.

Some mass higher education is healthier, perhaps more like California in the 1960s than California today. There is no necessary trade-off between growth and quality when government enhances both. Foreign examples, good and bad, matter more than they did. In the global higher education space that is a function of communicative convergence, all system cases—private sector dominated and public sector led, highly stratified or fairly flat—can now be seen by every other. In a world in which higher education has converged in certain ways, particularly in levels of participation and in the forms of Clark Kerr's multiversity, it is also more apparent than it was in 1960 that higher education anywhere can be done differently. All national systems have something to learn from others.

13

American Universities in the Global Space

So this is the global setting in which American universities find themselves when they lift their sights above the domestic concerns that normally dominate the agenda. It is a setting in which all research universities are globally networked and aware and in which American research universities move with confidence, albeit with varying degrees of enthusiasm. It is a setting in which relations are both collaborative and competitive, as at home. Amid global time-space compression, the strategic possibilities are open and expanding, with scope for innovation in missions, structures, and products,[1] in contrast to home where regulations, conventions, and habits are set. But as noted, in the global setting American and non-American institutions are differentially positioned. Universities outside the United States face a dilemma about how much to Americanize and whether to displace national traditions, language, and objectives.[2] In contrast, American universities are under no pressure to conform to foreign standards, languages, or models, and as yet they are under little pressure to acquire deep knowledge abroad. Whereas all 25 million students in Chinese higher education have learned English, in 2013 only 61,055 American students in higher education were learning Chinese.[3] Likewise, the world watches American higher education, not vice versa. In the Webometrics ranking of universities on the web, MIT leads the world for impact, the number of hits on the website. Harvard leads the world in openness, the amount of data it makes available. Both universities provide courseware on a free access basis. Harvard ranks number 1 in Webometrics overall, followed by MIT, Stanford, and UC Berkeley. UC Los Angeles is thirteenth.[4] The first thirty-five universities in web impact are all found in the United States, aside from Oxford and Cambridge in the United Kingdom.

In 2006 the author conducted fifteen research interviews in a public research university in the Midwest with a large portfolio of cross-border activities and a reputation for a strong international orientation. One question was "In your view are there any universities or programs, *in any other country,* from which American universities have something to learn?" Of the fifteen interviewees, twelve ignored the reference to other countries, naming solely American examples. Three executives named the National University of Singapore (NUS). The Midwestern public university had just negotiated an agreement with NUS, and the university's executive had become aware of NUS's outstanding global strategy, in which it was ahead of all American universities in international engagement in both teaching and research, and its research output was climbing steeply.

Does it matter whether American universities are globally aware and engaged? It was not an issue at the time of the Godkin Lectures. It is now. The arguments for the spread and deepening of a global consciousness, and against continued parochialism and American exceptionalism, are fourfold.

The first is the most basic, though the most difficult to accept. All is not well in the American society, polity, economy, and education. Self-correcting mechanisms are not the only possible resource. Other countries, and their ideas, may suggest answers. Consider the more stable family in most of Asia, the higher and better-spread school achievement in Finland and East Asia, and the stronger tax-spend compacts, more moderate tuition, and more stable higher education financing in many countries.

Second, global mobility of people in higher education is growing in volume as total tertiary participation grows, and global talent is strategic to all national innovation systems. In the last half century, the flow of students from Western Europe to the United States has not increased as a proportion of all European students,[5] but the flow out of East and South Asia has become larger and more significant at both ends. Between 1980 and 2012, the worldwide number of foreign students in higher education increased from 1.1 to 4.5 million persons.[6] Between 1980–81 and 2013–14 the number of international students enrolled in American higher education increased from 311,882 to 886,052 and to 4.2 percent of the student population, though this was a low percentage by international standards. From the American viewpoint, the most important role of foreign students is at the doctoral level. Doctoral students comprise 15 percent of all international students.[7] In 2011, 34.2 percent of all American university doctoral graduates in science and engineering were noncitizens. In 2010, 28.8 percent of all doctoral graduates in full-time American academic positions in science and engineering were foreign born. Of those in postdoctoral positions, 48.7 percent were foreign born, and nearly all of that group were noncitizens.[8] The public universities play the major role in training foreign nationals at the doctoral stage. For example, in 1996–2005, foreign doctoral graduates were the majority of all doctoral graduates at Texas A&M University (2,018), Ohio State (1,945) and Purdue (1,944), and they were a large component at others, including Illinois (1,933), Texas at Austin (1,786), Michigan (1,720) and Wisconsin–Madison (1,709). The largest cohort in the private sector was the 1,639 at Stanford. UC Berkeley educated 1,608.[9]

American society has a notable capacity to absorb immigrants. Aside from the years immediately after 9/11, when immigration from East Asia as well as the Middle East was tightened, the country has long offered an open door to high-skilled foreign nationals, to its benefit. Of the foreign recipients of U.S. doctorates in science and engineering in 2008–2011, 49.5 percent had definite plans to stay, including 50.4 percent of those from Europe, 54.9 percent from China, and 57.8 percent from India. However, these percentages had fallen. Of the 2000–2003 recipients of American doctorates who were citizens of China, 63.6 percent had evidenced definite plans to stay.[10] In the eight-year span, there was spectacular growth in Chinese universities and science, and alternate opportunities for these doctoral graduates had improved.

Research universities in many nations are dependent on global talent, and American doctorates have almost universal currency. But American universities can no longer assume they have overwhelming preponderance as the favored destination: most foreign graduates retain strong affective ties to home and many will return if they can obtain attractive opportunities there, and European nations are now working harder to draw foreign researchers. To attract and hold talented people, it is essential to understand the larger world setting in which they emerge and in which they develop their careers.

PLURALIZATION OF RESEARCH POWER

Third, as noted, the majority of high-citation science is produced outside the United States. In an increasingly plural world knowledge system, the rest of the world's share will keep growing. To maximize their effectiveness and sustain a leadership role in research, American universities will maintain working networks with all other major research producers in each field via people exchange, joint projects, and publishing. It is more than a matter of self-interest. Research-based knowledge is a global public good,[11] and cross-border collaboration is central in areas such as global climate change, high-energy physics, epidemiology and public health, and urban systems.

While the United States houses most of the thirty leading research universities and half of the top 100, as measured by publication and citation counts, its share will fall over time as non-American universities strengthen their relative positions. Trend analysis of the Shanghai ARWU data shows that the number of West European universities in the top 80 has grown, and there has been much diversification of the top 500. In the 2004 Shanghai ARWU ranking, there were just three universities from East Asia, in addition to those from Japan, in the top 200. There were none from China. In the 2014 ranking, there were twelve East Asian universities outside Japan in the top 200, including six from China—Tsinghua, Peking, Shanghai Jiao Tong, Zhejiang, Fudan, and the University of Science and Technology—two from Hong Kong, two from Singapore, and one each from Taiwan and South Korea.[12] In 2004 there were eight mainland Chinese universities in the top 500; in 2014 there were thirty-two. The number of top 500 universities in Taiwan, South Korea, Malaysia, Brazil, and Chile also increased. Iran, Egypt, Turkey, Malaysia, Slovenia, Serbia, and Hungary had universities in the top 500, and Saudi Arabia had four in the top 500 and two in the top 200.[13] This parallels the sharp growth of published journal papers in many emerging systems (see above). The progress of the Asian universities in the ARWU, especially in the top 100 and 200, is retarded by the ARWU's use of the Nobel Prize indicators. Only Japan has a significant history of Nobels. China and the other East Asian systems look better in rankings based solely on publication numbers and citation counts, such as those of Leiden University and Scimago Lab.[14] For example, in 2010–2013 NUS in Singapore published almost two-thirds as many high-citation papers as the University of Oxford in the United Kingdom, though as yet NUS has received no Nobel Prizes.[15]

It is certain the pluralization of science capacity will continue, given the pattern of investments in R & D in the last decade. There is a close relationship between public investment in scientific research and ranking position, but there are lags between investment in research and increased output, between increased output and citation, and between citation and the effect in rankings (which reflect longer-term as well as short-term patterns). Universities in China, Korea, Singapore, Saudi Arabia, Iran, and other countries with accelerated investments derive their current rankings from the government funding inputs of five to ten years ago. In another decade, the present investments in R & D will show fully. There will be many more East Asian universities in the top 200 and some pushing upwards in the top 100. The United States is still the largest fish in the pond by far. But it no longer owns the pond.

Fourth, in the growth of research science in post-Confucian East Asia, there is something more at work than just the pluralization of global capacity. In 2011, total R & D investment in East Asia was $448 billion, just behind North America, at $453 billion, and well ahead of Western Europe and the United Kingdom, at $320 million.[16] By the time of writing, the investment in East Asia will have moved well ahead of North America. Asian higher education is rapidly assuming a larger role in the world.[17] In particular, university science across East Asia is both massive and very dynamic. Not only is the annual number of English-language scientific papers growing rapidly across East Asia, except in Japan, quality is also improving quickly, as will be discussed in the next chapter. There are common cultural elements at work in the East Asian region, on a game-changing scale. A transformation in global relations of knowledge power is taking place. As Kishore Mahbubani states: "There is no reason for the West to be pessimistic. The West will not lose power. It will have to share power."[18] North America and Europe will share power in science and higher education with East Asia, especially China, within the terms of a knowledge system that evolved largely in Western countries.

It is time to look more closely at the transformation in East Asia, where Clark Kerr's institution is flourishing, but as a multiversity with Chinese characteristics.

14

Enter the Dragon

Historian Charles Holcombe argues that East Asia is "a culturally and historically coherent region, deserving of serious attention as a whole," and not simply as a group of countries that happen to be geographically contiguous.

> East Asia is most usefully defined as that region of the world that came to extensively use the Chinese writing system, and absorbed through these written records many of the ideas and values of what we call Confucianism, much of the associated legal and political structure of government, and certain specifically East Asian forms of Buddhism.[1]

Though there are many differences between East Asian nations—for example, in language and politics—East Asia is a shared civilizational zone, akin to "Western Europe" or perhaps to "Europe plus America." Its origins lie in Northern China of the Shang, Zhou, and Warring States periods. The last was a creative time of great diversity in ideas, prior to the first territorial state to secure broad centralized control, the highly effective Qin empire (221–207 B.C.E.). The Qin was followed by the Han dynasty (202 B.C.E.–220 C.E.), which built on the forms established in the Qin. In the long Han period, many continuing features of the Sinic (Chinese) state and society became institutionalized, including the state approach to education. The Qin and Han dynasties developed a statecraft that combined Confucian ethics with a legalist system of bureaucratic rule. Under the Han, politics was dominant over the military and commercial sectors, a primacy maintained throughout Chinese history.[2] The Han state saw itself as responsible for the good order of society and the conduct of its members. Though the central state habitually devolved authority to the regional and local levels, it could intervene anywhere at will in the interests of social order. It was believed that at any given time only one dynasty could hold the "mandate of heaven," but the mandate was revocable: the continued survival of the dynasty depended on good government and thus was ultimately founded in popular consent.[3] This anticipated elements of European political philosophy by 1,800 years or so.

Under the Han, meritocratic selection of scholar-officials began, on the basis of an examination in the Chinese classics. By the end of the dynasty, there were thirty thousand students in the Imperial Academy. This was the beginning of institutionalized higher education in East Asia and of its role in social allocation. After the fall of the Han, literary cultivation moved to the homes of aristocratic families. During the Tang dynasty (618–907 C.E.), Sinic statecraft, social systems, and education spread to Korea, Japan, and North Vietnam, and the role of academies, examinations, and scholar-officials was expanded. Much of the academy activity took place in the private educational sector. Under the Song (960–1279 C.E.), self-learning and educational ambition became part of many middle-class families. State and private academies were opened in many parts of China. Confucian education was always ambiguous. It was an expression of hierarchical order, adherence to authority, and devotion to parents. It was also a source of individual agency and upward social mobility. Both sides of Confucian education entailed a contribution not only to self and family but the public good. These themes still shape education in the Sinic world, though its notions of scientific knowledge have modernized. Holcombe explains the two-sided "Confucian equation":

> The expectation of hierarchy inherent in this ideal of serving parents filially and not offending superiors also highlights one of the key contradictions in Confucian thought. On the one hand, Confucians idealized the memory of a highly aristocratic ancient Zhou social order and conservatively sought to perpetuate it. "I transmit but do not create" is one of Confucius's more famous sayings. Some of the most important Confucian virtues, moreover, such as filial piety and loyalty (*zhong*), can only be expressed through hierarchical relationships. This is one side of the Confucian equation. The other side of the equation, however, was a pointedly egalitarian and meritocratic strand of Confucian thought. Anyone, it was assumed, could potentially perfect himself or herself through self-cultivation and then lead the world by his or her example. As Confucius said, "in education there should be no class distinctions." China had ceased to have a hereditary aristocracy already by the third century BCE, and the meritocratic line in Confucian thinking would eventually find realization under the empire in the remarkable Chinese civil service examination system, under which government officials were selected on the basis of anonymously graded performances on written tests.[4]

The educational practices of family and school became more deeply entrenched with each dynasty. There is remarkable continuity in China. On the one hand, the rule of the Communist Party of China (CPC) can be understood as manifestation of the Leninist form of organization, applied first in the Soviet bloc. On the other hand, the CPC can be seen as yet another dynasty, one of the most successful, in

China's long history. The CPC dynasty, like its forebears, knows that its rule will be maintained as long as it provides order and prosperity—that the continued authority of the state rests on its capacity to serve the people,[5] and the right to trade must flourish but is subordinated to social conduct and order. History suggests that Chinese dynasties have deeper roots and last longer than Leninist forms. If there were equivalent continuity in Europe, the Western Roman Empire would not have vanished in the fifth century but would have returned in successive iterations for two thousand years of European history. This does not mean that East Asian civilization is tradition bound. It is also inventive and renewable, or it would not have survived. Its present dynamism, its capacity for practical innovation, is clear.

East Asian educational tradition rests on layer upon layer of practice. For example, China was the first country to develop paper, books, and printing and published more books than the rest of the world put together until at least 1500 and possibly later.[6] At the time that China, Japan, and Korea were forcibly engaged by European and American power, the literacy rate in Japan was as high as anywhere in Europe. This long Sinic continuity, particularly deep educational cultivation in the family, is the foundation on which today's East Asian higher educational systems are erected.

FAMILY AND STATE

The family and the state are relatively strong in East Asian. Civil society and intermediate institutions such as cities and professions tend to be weaker than in Europe and North America. Sinic countries do not sustain the state/society and state/market tensions that are typical of the English-speaking world, with its limited liberal states in the Adam Smith tradition, and the recurring antistatism of its political life. It is very unlikely there will be a California-style tax revolt in Asia. Whether in single-party or multiparty regimes, states in East Asia typically have broad social support, stable continuity, a long-term view, and high social status. Graduates from elite families often aspire to enter the leading departments of state. Leaving aside the closed and repressive regime in North Korea, all of modern Japan, South Korea, and China have demonstrated an impressive capacity to mobilize a high level of popular support for policies of social and economic transformation, in part because they have provided their growing middle classes with expanded social opportunities through education. Thus in East Asia, government leadership of educational reform is a given, and all modernizing East Asian states, with the partial exception of Vietnam, place higher education and science on a high priority.

Japan developed a front-rank university and research system between the 1960s and 1980s, though its dynamism in higher education has now slowed. South Korea established impressive government research institutes in the 1980s,[7] with many of their personnel moving into industry R & D in the late 1990s and onwards, at the same time as the nation expanded and modernized its universities. Taiwan, Singapore, and Hong Kong SAR also accelerated the evolution of the higher education and research in the 1990s. The takeoff in China began in the late 1990s. Through higher education, East Asian states provide their populations with social esteem and opportunity, and like many governments, they see graduates, science, and technology as keys to future productivity and industrial innovation. State interventions are strategically focused and closely linked to performance measures. Typically, the state sets targets, applies resources, achieves the benchmark, and moves on, taking policy to the next level. In every East Asian system, the state played the crucial role in triggering the rapid expansion of mass higher education: lifting secondary school enrollments, providing higher education infrastructure, reforming structures, encouraging mergers to facilitate growth, training university teachers, and expanding the budget for tuition subsidies and student income support and loans. Typically, once the state signaled its support for growth, enrollments surged in classic Trow fashion, as first the middle class and then the whole population began to seek social advantage for their children through education. As noted, in South Korea the GTER was 98 percent in 2012, Taiwan's GTER was 84 percent, and Hong Kong and Japan exceeded 60 percent.

After 1998 the growth of participation in China surged ahead of the rate of growth in per capita income, though the latter was exceptional by world standards.[8] The annual intake of new students leapt from 1.1 million in 1998 to 5.5 million in 2006, growing at 23 percent a year. The admission rate, which was 10 percent in the elite system of the early 1980s, rose to almost two-thirds of those sitting the *gaokao* at the end of school.[9] By 2012 there were 25.6 million regular higher education students, 14.3 million in four-year institutions, and 283,810 at doctoral level.[10]

State policy on education and science is especially effective in East Asia because it works in tandem with family ambition and the deep Confucian well of learning in the home. It would be difficult to transplant the East Asian educational dynamism to countries without Sinic families. The symbiosis between state and family shows itself in two ways: the financing of education and the level of measured student learning.

While government leads the development of higher education, it does not buy its role by providing most of the funding. East Asian educational effort is not sustained by large government budgets. Central government revenue in China was 11.3 percent in 2011, compared to 16.6 percent in the United States in 2012. Singapore's was a little higher, at 17.8 percent in 2012.[11] The family provides not just parental time and energy but financial resources. Unlike continental Western Europe but like North America, the typical approach is mixed public and private funding, with the private share increasing over time. The family commitment to education is so strong that many poor families invest heavily in formal education and extra schooling and tuition outside school hours.[12] In South Korea, private spending on all forms of "shadow schooling" has reached a remarkable 3 percent of GDP, more than many countries spend on their whole schooling system.[13] Shadow schooling, with its extra hours of learning, is a key factor in the exceptional PISA (Program of International Student Achievement) performance in all East Asian education systems, including Vietnam (see table 14.1). The proportion of the costs of formal schooling and higher education paid by households is high in world terms. OECD data show that in South Korea in 2011, 44.1 percent of the spending of tertiary education institutions was financed by households and 28.9 percent from other private sources, a total of 73.0 percent from all private funding. The respective figures in Japan were 50.9 percent and 65.5 percent in total. For comparison, in 2011 private funding in the United States financed 65.2 percent of all spending, and the OECD average was 30.8 percent.[14] Private funding also plays a major role in Singapore, where most enrollments are below research university level and in the private sector. In China between 1997 and 2007, the proportion of higher education revenue funded by private tuition rose from 14.9 to 33.7 percent, though it fell back to 26.5 percent in 2012. The proportion of revenue funded by public sources in China dropped from 78.4 percent in 1997 to 44.1 percent in 2007, rising again to 58.3 percent in 2012.[15] Shared state and family funding of tuition makes it all work, freeing states to invest strategically in infrastructure, research, top students, and world-class universities

In all East Asian systems, public subsidies per student are higher in elite research universities than at other levels. In the top universities, the proportion of total costs covered by government is again relatively high. This is true in most of Asia, and also Russia and some other post-Soviet systems.[16] Private costs are higher in middle universities than in top universities. Further, and in sharper contrast to social practice in California, households in East Asia pay a high proportion of costs in low-status institutions. In East Asia, high private costs at the bottom of the pyramid do not seem to subtract from participation rates. This is because strong family demand for higher education is near universal and has low economic elasticity. Families dream of achieving the highest level, a place in the leading university, such as Tokyo or Peking University. If families have discretionary money it tends to go first to the children's education.

The central role of the family shows also in pretertiary student learning. The OECD's PISA compares the learning achievements of 15-year-olds across the world in three disciplines: reading, mathematics, and science. East Asian students outperform students in the rest of the world by a large margin, with only Finland within reach.[17] As table 14.1 shows, the seven top systems in mathematics were all in East Asia. Vietnam had only 10 percent of American per capita income in 2013 but shares the Sinic educational tradition (North Vietnam was occupied by China from the early Han to the end of the Tang). It does better than the United States in

TABLE 14.1. Student achievement in PISA reading, science, and mathematics at age 15 years: Top 10 countries in mathematics, United States, and selected comparators, 2012

	Reading, mean PISA score	Science, mean PISA score	Mathematics, mean PISA score	Mathematics students at top PISA levels, 5–6 (%)	Mathematics students at low-est PISA level, 1 (%)
OECD average	496	501	494	12.6	23.1
Shanghai, China	570	580	613	55.4	3.8
Singapore	542	551	573	40.0	8.3
Hong Kong SAR	545	555	561	33.7	8.5
Taiwan	523	523	560	37.2	12.8
South Korea	536	538	554	30.9	9.1
Macau SAR	509	521	538	24.3	10.8
Japan	538	547	536	23.7	11.1
Lichtenstein	516	525	535	24.8	14.1
Switzerland	509	515	531	21.4	12.4
Netherlands	516	522	523	19.3	14.8
United States	498	497	481	8.8	25.8
Vietnam	508	528	511	13.3	14.2
Finland	524	545	519	15.3	12.3
Germany	508	524	514	17.5	17.7
United Kingdom	499	514	494	11.8	21.8
Canada	523	525	518	16.4	13.8

SOURCE: Adapted by author using data in OECD 2014b.
NOTE: SAR = Special Autonomous Region of China.

all three PISA disciplines. The 30-million-person Shanghai region has a long lead over all other school systems in the world. Even the poorest and lowest achieving provinces of China had 2012 PISA results just below the world average. These low-income zones share the social esteem for teaching that is a feature of all East Asian countries and contrasts with the relatively low standing of the teaching profession in the United States and other English-speaking countries.

However, it can be argued that the family element is more important than the school. This is demonstrated by John Jerrim in a 2014 study of the 2012 PISA performance of school students of East Asian descent who were second-generation migrants in Australia. Their average PISA score in mathematics, 605,[18] was not far below Shanghai (613) and well ahead of Singapore (573), Hong Kong SAR (561), and Taiwan (560). Despite the fact that these 15-year-olds were Australian citizens attending Australian schools, they outperformed their Australian peers by an average of more than 100 PISA points. The difference is equivalent to two and a half years of schooling. "Moreover," states Jerrim, "while PISA test scores of native Australians declined substantially between 2003 and 2012, the scores of children with East Asian heritage improved rapidly."[19] When in-school effects and between-school differences were accounted for statistically, the difference in performance was still one year of schooling, underlining the role of the home and extra tuition.[20] The East Asian–heritage students, the majority from families that did not speak English at home, spent an average of fifteen hours a week in study outside school compared to nine hours for the native students, and 94 percent expected to enter university, compared to 58 percent of native Australians.[21] The outstanding performance of East Asian–heritage students in Australia parallels the success of Asian American families in SAT and university entrance. Migrant families typically exhibit exceptional drive to achieve, and East Asian–heritage parents are often themselves relatively well educated. But John Jerrim found that when the statistical effects of these factors were eliminated, much of the superior performance of East Asian–heritage students remained, although the performance of other migrant children came back to the average.[22] The fact that the PISA performance of East Asian–heritage students in Australia is similar to that of East Asian students is striking.

East Asian countries emphasize the STEM disciplines.[23] The majority of China's school students in China are on a STEM track. Mathematics, which enjoys prestige as a selector into university programs and the basis of technology, is compulsory to the end of school. The largest cohort of South Korean graduates are not in business, as in English-speaking countries, but in engineering, though many graduate engineers go to business occupations. South Korea's "STEAM" program joins STEM to the arts, aiming to broaden the appeal of STEM studies while encouraging creativity in technology. Although East Asian professors in the humanities argue that their disciplines are overlooked, it is not wholly so: PISA reading scores are almost at high as mathematics, most university students are at least partly bilingual, and there are liberal studies in some elite universities, including Peking University and a joint Yale-NUS program in Singapore.

If East Asian higher education is not fully inclusive of the disciplines, it does better with social inclusion. Sinic societies are not highly egalitarian and have varied Gini coefficients. University hierarchies are steep, and the socially advantaged—in China this includes the children of party cadre in middle-level positions and above—dominate entry to top institutions. On the other hand, PISA performance in Sinic systems is egalitarian. The size of the highest-achieving student group is large, and few students are in the lowest achieving group (table 14.1). In Singapore, 40 percent of students are in levels 5–6 in PISA mathematics compared to 9 percent in the United States. Only 8 percent of Singapore students are in the bottom group in PISA mathematics compared to 26 percent in the United States. These systems sustain high overall performance without an equity/excellence trade-off, indicating the universality of parental desires for educational achievement, plus the fact that states organize school systems so as to facilitate learning by all. The common assumption is that hard work, not talent is decisive, and anyone can work hard. The downside of high expectations and extra work is that many students carry a heavy burden, and some are measurably unhappy. One of the questions in the 2012 PISA asked students if they agreed with the statement "I feel happy at school." The happiest students were in Indonesia, Albania, and Peru. Students in Singapore were ranked twelfth out of sixty-four systems. All other East Asian populations except South Korea were above the OECD average.[24] Students in the United States were slightly below the OECD average for self-reported happiness. Interestingly, Finland was near the bottom. Last was South Korea. Perhaps all the shadow schooling, on top of day school and anxious parents, is a bit too much.[25]

THE ECONOMIC PLATFORM

In addition to Sinic states and education-focused parents, two other conditions are at work. The first is the desire, deeply felt across East Asia, to catch up to the West after 150 years of imperial violence, economic exploitation, and relentless modernization. To catch up is to restore self-respect and protect the nation from future intervention. The desire for global parity powers the strategies of benchmarking with American higher education, especially in Singapore and China. Perhaps benchmarking would otherwise violate autonomy and identity. As noted, internationalization on American terms creates contradictions; national identity is periodically reinserted, but the tension is read differently when benchmarking is a means of building individual and national agency, rather than losing it. The outcome of the encounter between Sinic tradition and Western science and modernization is neither an imported Westernized education nor a reworking of the old tradition. It is a hybrid of the two, something new, a post-Confucian form of higher education system. As Martin Jacques remarks in relation to China, more than one kind of modernization is possible.[26]

The second condition is economic growth. Except in China and Vietnam, East Asian economies have per capita incomes at Western European levels or above (table 14.2). Singapore ($76,237) is one of the richest countries in the world, and Hong Kong SAR's income ($51,509) is at the American level. South Korea is catching up quickly. China experienced phenomenal growth after the late 1970s, at first through the abolition of collective farms in rural areas and then through export-oriented manufacturing and modernization in the cities. Between 1990 and 2013, GDP in constant 2011 prices rose from $1,689.3 to $15,643.2 billion, at an average annual rate of 10.2 percent. Its lowest rate of annual growth was 7.6 percent in 1999 amid the Asian financial crisis.[27] This has lifted China from a poor developing country to a middle-income power with GDP equal to the United States in purchasing power parity (PPP) terms. There are marked regional inequalities, but per capita incomes in the Beijing and Shanghai regions are already at European levels.

TABLE 14.2. Economy and population, East Asia, the United States, and the United Kingdom, 2013

Higher education system	Population (millions)	GDP PPP ($s billion)	GDP PPP per capita ($s)
Macau SAR	0.6	78.2	138,025
Singapore	5.4	411.6	76,237
Hong Kong SAR	7.2	370.2	51,509
Taiwan China	23.4	894.5	38,238
Japan	127.3	4,535.1	35,614
South Korea	50.2	1,642.6	32,708
China (mainland)	1,357.4	15,643.2	11,525
Vietnam	89.7	459.7	5,125
United States	316.1	16,230.2	51,340
United Kingdom	64.1	2,372.7	37,017

SOURCE: Author, adapting data compiled by World Bank 2015; CIA 2015.
NOTES: Constant 2011 US$. Taiwan data adjusted using US CPI. Taiwan population 2014.
PPP = Purchasing Power Parity. SAR = Special Autonomous Region of China.

Growth of 10 percent a year is a strong platform for advances in both public and private financing of higher education.

Most other systems in East Asia have also benefited from economic growth that is relatively high by world standards. Between 1990 and 2013, the economy grew by an annual average of 6.2 percent in Singapore, 5.1 percent in South Korea, about 5 percent in Taiwan, and 3.9 percent in Hong Kong, though just 1.0 percent in Japan.[28] With GDP growing rapidly, the East Asian nations have taken the opportunity to increase public and private investment in R & D as a proportion of GDP. Figure 14.1, which shows investment in R & D as a proportion of GDP in 2000–2013, illustrates how in three of the five East Asian systems, R & D investments have risen above the U.S. level in terms of the proportion of GDP. Singapore's proportional investment in R & D is lower than that of the United States only because Singapore's GDP, the denominator in the ratio between R & D spending and GDP, is very high in world terms. As table 14.2 shows, per capita GDP in Singapore was 50 percent higher in 2013 than the U.S. level.

Between 2000 and 2013, South Korea's total spending on R & D rose from 2.18 to 4.15 percent of GDP. In 2013 it was second in the world to Israel. Korean R & D grew by 0.15 percent of GDP per year after the year 2000, sustained by global companies such as Samsung as well as government. The rise of Korean science, technology, and higher education can be mapped against the evolution of the Korean economy as an exporter of knowledge-intensive products. The 2012 OECD review of Korea's industry development policy notes that whereas in the late 1970s 35 percent of Korean exports had medium-knowledge content and only 2 percent had

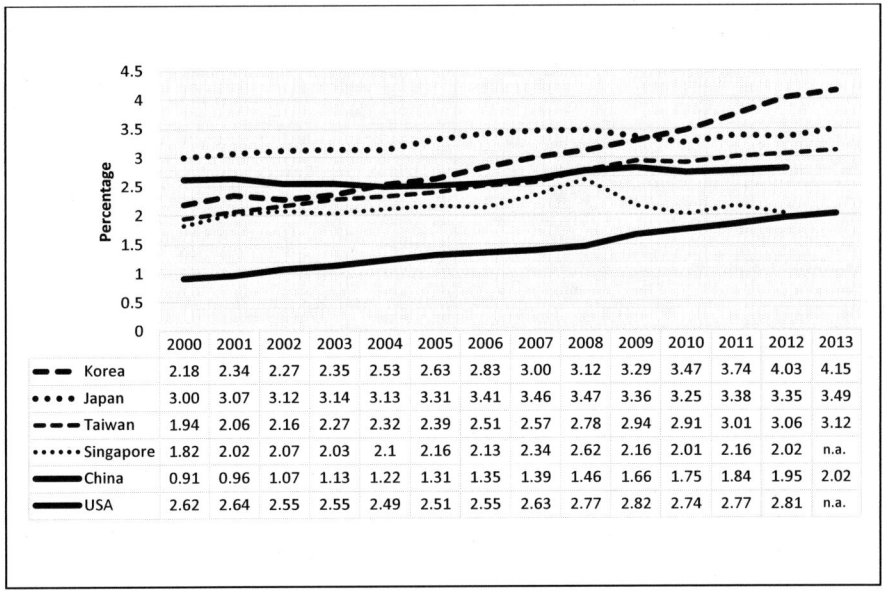

	2000	2001	2002	2003	2004	2005	2006	2007	2008	2009	2010	2011	2012	2013
— — Korea	2.18	2.34	2.27	2.35	2.53	2.63	2.83	3.00	3.12	3.29	3.47	3.74	4.03	4.15
• • • • Japan	3.00	3.07	3.12	3.14	3.13	3.31	3.41	3.46	3.47	3.36	3.25	3.38	3.35	3.49
— — — Taiwan	1.94	2.06	2.16	2.27	2.32	2.39	2.51	2.57	2.78	2.94	2.91	3.01	3.06	3.12
• • • • • • Singapore	1.82	2.02	2.07	2.03	2.1	2.16	2.13	2.34	2.62	2.16	2.01	2.16	2.02	n.a.
████ China	0.91	0.96	1.07	1.13	1.22	1.31	1.35	1.39	1.46	1.66	1.75	1.84	1.95	2.02
████ USA	2.62	2.64	2.55	2.55	2.49	2.51	2.55	2.63	2.77	2.82	2.74	2.77	2.81	n.a.

FIGURE 14.1. R & D expenditures as proportion of GDP, East Asia and the United States, 2000–2013.
NOTE: n.a. = data not available
SOURCE: Author, using data from OECD 2015

high-technology content, in 2009, 80 percent of exports were medium-technology products and 10 percent were high-technology.[29]

Taiwan has a similar trajectory. The growth of leading-edge research in electrical engineering and computing has coincided with exports in information technology. Taiwan's R & D expenditure of 3.06 percent in 2013 exceeded the U.S. GDP spending ratio of 2.81 percent in 2012, while Japan's R & D investment of 3.49 percent in 2013 was well above all nations in the English-speaking world.

In China R & D spending rose from 0.91 percent of GDP in 2000 to 1.31 percent in 2005, and then to 2.02 percent of a much larger GDP in 2013.[30] That is an increase of almost 0.1 percent a year. The policy target is 2.5 percent of GDP. The gap between China and the United States, in terms of the proportion of GDP allocated to R & D, halved between 2000 and 2013. If the present trends continue, China's total investment in R & D will pass that of the United States by 2015. Only about 8 percent of China's R & D money goes to the universities, which is half the proportion of the United States. Most of the R & D investment is settled on the state-controlled enterprises that lead the Chinese economy. It is unlikely that all of this allocation to the state enterprises is spent specifically in research. Regardless, enough of the fast-growing research budget trickles down to the research universities to power growth of more than 15 percent a year in journal papers in the English-language literature.

EAST ASIAN SCIENCE

Figure 14.2 illustrates the rapid growth of published science papers in East Asia relative to the output of the United States. In 1995 regional output was only one-third that of the United States. Less than a generation later, in 2011, total output from East Asia had almost caught that of the United States, and China alone was at almost half the number of U.S. papers. If present trends continue, China's output of published science will exceed that of the United States well before 2025. When the world's most populous country increases scientific production at 15 percent a year for a decade and a half, it is certain much of future human knowledge will come from that source.

In an overview study of the "great American university," Jonathan Cole poses this question in relation to research universities: "Is it possible to imagine that the great American university could lose its dominant position in the world of higher learning to the Chinese over the next half century?"[31] Though the withdrawal of state funding from the public research universities is a problem, this almost certainly will not happen. At present the United States is overwhelmingly the strongest nation in scientific knowledge. Its leading research universities are in a very different quality league from those in East Asia, as measured by citations per paper and per faculty, and are world leaders in every major field of knowledge. Nevertheless, in the physical sciences and engineering, the gap in quality is beginning to close.

In 2000, China produced 3.7 percent of all papers in chemistry, compared to 20.3 percent in the United States. Twelve years later, in 2012, China produced more of the world's papers in chemistry than the United States, 16.9 percent compared to 16.2 percent. This was a major change, but more significantly, China's share of the top 1 percent papers by citation rate increased from 0.6 percent in 2000 to 16.3 percent only twelve years later, in 2012. That year China produced almost half as many high-citation papers as the United States, at 33.5 percent. There was a similar pattern in engineering: from 2000 to 2012, China lifted its share of high-citation research papers in engineering from 2.5 to 12.2 percent, compared to the United States' 37.5 percent in 2012. China also produced 16.7 percent of high-citation work in computing, 8.4 percent in geosciences, 7.3 percent in mathematics, 5.9 percent in agriculture, and 5.2 percent in physics. Research is focused on fields associated with accelerated modernization, including construction, materials, communications, transport, resources, energy extraction and economy, urban systems, and ecological aspects of development. There is a bias towards physical sciences and engineering in all East Asian countries. Research in the life sciences, medicine, and social sciences is much weaker, with the exception of agriculture. In 2012 China produced only 2.0 percent of the world's most highly cited papers in biological sciences and 1.5 percent in medicine, compared to the United States' 56.0 percent in biological sciences and 51.0 percent in medicine.

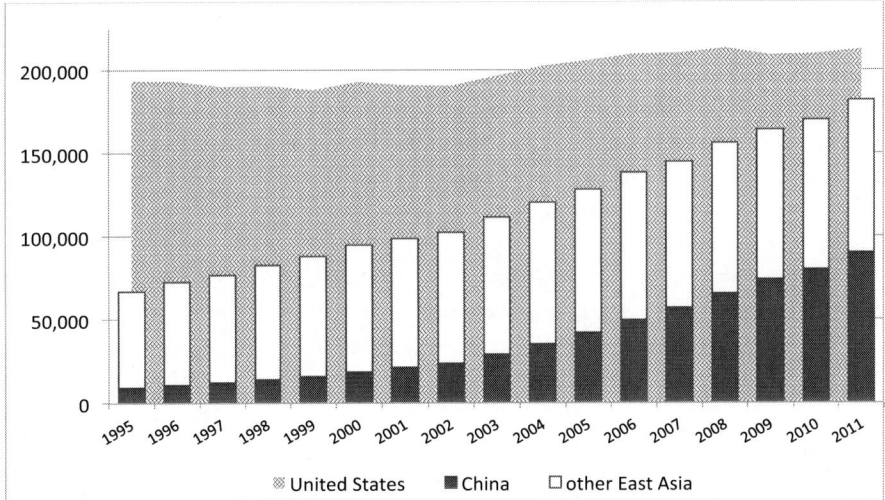

FIGURE 14.2. Annual production of published science papers, United States, China, and other East Asia (Japan, South Korea, Taiwan, and Singapore), 1995–2011.
SOURCE: Author, using published data from NSF 2014, derived originally from the Thomson-Reuters Web of Knowledge.

China was weaker in the social sciences: in 2012 it produced only 0.3 percent of highly cited papers in psychology and 1.0 percent in other social sciences. Arguably, in China, and more generally in East Asia, the social sciences have yet to establish the ambiguous role of independent public servant, critic, and instrument of the state and social order, which is essential to their functions in Western Europe and North America. Another problem is the low standing of the humanities in East Asia, despite traditional literary scholarship. There is no instrumental economic rationale for investment in either the critical social sciences or the humanities, and they contribute little to ranking performance. Yet they constitute public and government reflexivities, social language, and powerful knowledge and are indispensable bearers of national cultural identity.

THE POST-CONFUCIAN MODEL OF HIGHER EDUCATION

The post-Confucian model of higher education in East Asia has gaps. Its achievements are still in the making. All the same, those achievements are remarkable but also familiar: an older theme with new twists. Participation that grows without limit has become part of every East Asian higher education system, as Trow forecast. As in California, the premier institution is the multiversity. Much money, energy, and talent goes into nurturing research excellence. There is also a system approach. The classification-based institutional hierarchy combines a limited number of high-research institutions with middle institutions focused on professional training and an access-oriented mass sector. However, system and institution are more directly supervised by the state than in California. Though the state grants operational institutional autonomy, on the whole university leaders have less room to move (though this can fluctuate). This is true of both the democracies and of China's dynastic party-state. Unlike California higher education, in East Asia there is a conscious policy of internationalization: the templates of best practice are not all found at home.

The dynamism of the 1960 California Idea of higher education was sustained by economic growth and resources sufficient to support infrastructure and low or no tuition, a social consensus that the public good lay in expanding equality of educational opportunity, a democratic polity that responded to growing demands for access, and individual and collective optimism about the benefits of higher education. The dynamism of the post-Confucian model is rooted in Confucian educational cultivation and ambition in the home, a social consensus on the familial and national benefits of higher education, modernizing states that anticipate demand for higher education as much as responding to it, and the determination of those states to direct priorities and sustain the momentum of progress. The East Asian state is busier than its 1960 California counterpart. There is also the momentum deriving from the collective project of catching up to the West, supported by internationalization in research universities. Shared public and private resourcing and effort combined with rapid growth of the middle class and the state's capacity to increase R & D funding at a remarkable rate have enabled a faster rate of development than in California. At the same time, a similar mood of universal excitement is apparent. All these features of the post-Confucian model are especially obvious in the mainland system of China but are shared by Hong Kong, Taiwan, Singapore, and South Korea. There is a common dynamic, a recognizable spirit, across most of the Chinese civilizational zone.

This raises the question of why the same dynamism is not evident in higher education and science in Sinic Japan and Vietnam. Vietnam has some of the conditions of the East Asian takeoff but not others. It has Confucian educational cultivation and ambition at home, channeled by society-wide examinations at the end of school. Vietnam's excellent PISA results indicate that the foundations for a highly educated population are in place. The other element in the state-family dyad, the state, is much weaker. With a per capita income of $5,125 (2013), Vietnam lacks the public means to build global science while providing growth infrastructure and full access at an adequate level of quality. There is symbolic talk about world-class universities, but the state lacks not just resources but an authentic long-term perspective and the capacity to concentrate resources in high priority areas. Government needs reform. Its practitioners are underpaid, and corruption is widespread. Conduct often reflects the norms of the late Soviet era in which many leaders were trained, rather than Sinic meritocracy. Returning diasporic doctoral graduates are underutilized.[32] Time will tell whether Vietnam can follow the East Asian pathway as resource levels improve.

Japan was the first nation to implement the post-Confucian model in higher education and research, successfully turning itself into one of the world's leading nations in science long before the takeoff occurred in the other East Asian systems. Science and technology continues to feed developments in industry innovation, but in the last two decades, as noted, the Japanese economy has grown at just 1 percent a year, the public sector has been weighed down by the OECD's largest public debt as a proportion of GDP, and government fiscal policy is closer to UK austerity than to that of an investment-led East Asian polity. University funding is held down; government focuses on controlling output through plans and audit, which is conservatizing; so far, Japanese universities have been unable to fully internationalize. It is unclear whether this malaise is common to the post-Confucian model, suggesting the loss of dynamism will eventually affect China, South Korea, and Taiwan, or if it is specific to the political economy and culture of the distinctive variant of Sinic civilization in Japan.[33]

15

Higher Education in China and the United States

Will science and higher education in East Asia equal or overtake that of the United States, or even the United States and Europe together? Much is said about state authority, university autonomy, and academic freedom in East Asia, particularly China, and the implications for creativity. This is not a simple problem. China is not like Soviet Russia was in higher education and science. Kishore Mahbubani observes: "Although China is still a somewhat politically closed society, it is a closed society with an open mind."[1] The universities welcome visitors and learn freely from abroad. They publish in the global literature. Stereotyping claims that East Asian classrooms are inherently didactic, and critical thinking is absent, are not confirmed by research. Given the growth of high-citation papers in the sciences, it is difficult to argue that East Asian science in general lacks critical thought or creativity, though recurring interventions by China's officials in what should be academic peer decisions about research are a serious problem (one that is not confined to China, or to East Asia). The evolution of higher education in China is more top-down than in America,[2] but as noted in the previous chapter, universities sustain a devolved authority within the comprehensive Sinic state. At the same time, for good or ill, the central state retains the scope to intervene in individual institutions as it sees fit.

In Singapore and Japan, the university president is selected by the governing council of the university, not the state. Nevertheless, in all East Asian systems, normal operations depend on a high degree of synchrony between institutions and the state. This can be conservatizing, particularly in relation to disciplines that touch the work of government, though from time to time, state intervention may also contribute to creative output by lifting the performance bar, encouraging internationalization measures, and shaking up conservative academic cultures. In China, government appoints the two university leaders, president and party secretary. Both are invited to regular party schools. Leading research universities are never far from national purposes. This is not the California Idea based on arms-length autonomy and civil society-like mechanisms of coordination. It is closer to the regulated autonomy of neoliberal systems with principal-agent relations, but with active potential for direct intervention. Yet Chinese universities exercise local autonomy and have scope for strategy, including considerable freedom in their day-to-day dealings with American and other non-Chinese universities. There are cases of institutions advised by government to merge that have refused to do so, citing their preference for their own, different development plan, and doing so without penalty. From time to time, the state media carries sharp criticisms of policy by university presidents.[3] There are also times when the central government intervenes unexpectedly in local affairs. It is difficult to discern a permanent, clear-cut pattern. Both local autonomy and central agency are active.

However, there are two larger difficulties facing the post-Confucian model. First, education and research in North America and Western Europe benefit from an open zone of free conversation between academic research, public discussion, and the take-up of new ideas in industry and government. This zone is smaller and less stable in East Asian countries. Civil traditions are weaker, and intermediate organizations, public but not governmental, such as think tanks and foundations, are thinner than in the United States. In China the state limits the Internet as an independent space, and media are constrained. Here the post-Confucian model is both a strength and a weakness. On one hand, the universities are understood as a semiautonomous branch of state and, at best, new data and ideas readily move into government and can have real impact in policy and its implementation. Some state officials have PhDs. They value intelligent advice. On the other hand, in the absence of universities with a broad public role and adequate means of dissemination, including unimpeded access to old and new media, ideas that are not immediately potent in government and acceptable to it can sink from sight.

The second problem is the episodic repression of individual scholars, especially humanist critics of the regime. Here again the issue is more ambiguous than it may first appear. In China, more so than Singapore or Japan, feisty political debate is normal to the interior cultures of state institutions (as often the case in dynastic regimes). There is routine criticism of party decisions, sometimes of individual leaders and ministers, inside leading research universities. These universities are part of the state. Criticism behind closed doors is accepted and often welcome, part of the process of debating policy options and generating new ideas for government, a within-state version of what Jürgen Habermas calls the "public sphere," an ongoing site of reflexivity on the periphery of the decision-making core.[4] However, when similar criticisms are made in open public forums in China, that is a different matter. What was seen as constructive criticism of particular policies inside the state becomes a destructive public attack on the general authority of the state. In Chinese tradition, sharp public criticism by persons with the authority of university professors has always been seen as significant, a high-stakes challenge to the regime.

Outspoken public dissent by Chinese scholars is not read in terms of academic freedom but in terms of a second tradition in China, that of heroic challenges to the state by single scholars on the grounds that the regime has lost the mandate of heaven, the right to govern. Historically, such scholars often paid a severe price for making the challenge.[5] Thus what appears as China's heavy-handed management of individual scholarly dissidents rests not only on the Leninist instinct for political monopoly but on the longstanding beliefs, going back to the Han, that what scholars say is important, that the proper conduct of the scholar is to advance the public good and orderly social conduct, and that scholars criticize the ruler only when they believe that the regime must be overthrown. This tradition has some resonance across the whole Chinese civilizational zone. Even in multiparty Japan, South Korea, and Taiwan, public academic critics are less strident and carry more weight than in the United States (where public dissent by faculty is freely tolerated and largely ignored). East Asian professors tend to be supportive of the state and consensual in public values. Hence while networked discussion on the Internet has changed the terms of politics all over the world, the Internet's ease of trivial criticism and its quicksilver messages and data flows are particularly challenging for China. Free Internet is at odds with the state's long supervision of political conduct, as part of its duty to social order, and the Internet's style of conversation is at odds with the traditional gravity of political matters.

On the other hand, the embrace of the Internet in South Korea shows that its normal operations can be compatible with East Asian society without fracturing the flexibility of state-maintained order and the maintenance of East Asian family and social values.

In Western terms, jailing academic critics for what they say in public is suppression of academic freedom. This is consistent with the definition of academic freedom as negative freedom, freedom from constraint (usually understood as constraint by the state). No scholars in any country in the world want to be told by government what they can say. Chinese scholars are not different in that respect. However, in China academic freedom is also seen in another way. Academic freedom is understood in positive terms. In this practice of academic freedom, scholars enjoy strong traditional authority and a formative responsibility not only to their discipline but as models of personal conduct. This positive notion of academic freedom is empowering and attractive for professors and would not be set aside lightly.[6] The coexistence of the two traditions that affect scholarly conduct— the tradition of positive academic freedom, which obliges the scholar to speak his or her mind in forums in which public authority is not affected, and the other tradition about high-stakes challenges to the regime—makes it difficult to find a middle path in which critical noise is normalized. This robs China of some creative possibilities. But the point is that in China, dissident scholars are an issue not of academic freedom but of political conduct. What is at stake is the space for self-determining forms of individuality and the evolution of forms of social order and public space. China is slowly liberalizing. In the long run, that trend seems unstoppable. Urbanization, the higher education of the middle classes,[7] and the internationalization of the universities are part of the process of liberalization. This will eventually lead to the development of new customs. China is not there yet.

The party-state in China, many of whose leaders had a cosmopolitan higher education and know the United States, has set this liberalization in train itself, with unknown consequences. Nevertheless, from time to time, persons within the leadership hesitate and balk, part of the longer-term pattern of oscillation between centralized liberalization and centralized control. The regime has yet to find a way to consistently accommodate open criticism. As Qiang Zha puts it: "As long as one doesn't challenge the legitimacy or capacity of the CPC to rule China, a scholar will be free to follow the normal routines of scholarly and social life." Nevertheless, the problem of public order is always threatening to spill out from under the blanket of state order. "Ordinary Chinese people now do assume the liberty to discuss the wrongs of the CPC in the past six decades."[8] China is unlikely to move soon towards a post-dynasty contestable, multiparty polity. If this happened nearly overnight in Gorbachev fashion, it would be a recipe for chaos and national decline, which nobody in China wants. It may never happen. It is not the only possible pathway for a liberalizing system. There is scope for the evolution of a more transparent party-state, a more open public order, and richer public discourse within the terms of dynastic rule, in which the management of criticism is decentralized, and ultimately reduced or evacuated, without precipitating social fragmentation. There is a lot of water yet to flow under this bridge. Relationships between universities in China and universities in the United States are among the factors that will shape the future inside and outside China.

Robert Rhoads and Katalin Szelenyi argue that "Just as we have used our sharpest university minds to advance science and technology, we must do the same in terms of advancing global social relations."[9] If there is to be a stable world society and polity capable of handling the major challenges ahead, it is likely that it will be a hybrid between Anglo-American traditions and Chinese civilizational traditions in political culture and social organization.[10] At the global level, each bloc is too weighty to be decisively subordinated to the other. In the evolution of a productive hybrid, universities will be crucial in drawing together policy makers and intellectuals, combining projects, sustaining long-term cross-border conversations, and fostering bilingual concepts and ideas. This suggests that part of the internationalization strategy in American higher education must be the building of a broad highway for two-way exchange with universities in East Asia, especially but not only in China.

Many research universities in the United States have developed programs focused on East Asia.[11] UC San Diego's Graduate School of International Relations and Pacific Studies, founded in 1986, was an early and successful example. American initiatives within China itself are numerous and include joint programs and purpose-built branch campuses and international study centers. U.S. universities have been more active in China than those from Canada, the United Kingdom, and most of Europe. The data on research paper collaborations show that only Germany and Australia have pursued relations in China with a similar energy, while the United States is well ahead of other non-Asian countries in dealings with South Korea and Taiwan. Australia is stronger than the United States in Singapore.[12] Nevertheless, and although American higher education is well known in China, Chinese and East Asian higher education remain largely unknown within the mainstream of U.S. higher education. Flows of personnel are predominantly one-way, primarily Asian students coming to the United States. The flow of ideas and influence is almost entirely in the reverse direction. Relations continues to verge on the neocolonial, despite the fact that the East Asian systems now together constitute one of the world's three principal zones of higher education and science and deserve greater respect. Certain factors are holding back the evolution of fuller relations.

AMERICANS ABROAD

One factor is the small scale of American study abroad in Asia. In 2012–13 a total of 289,408 U.S. students engaged in study abroad, but only 3 percent stayed for the full year, with 60 percent spending just summer or eight weeks or less. This was just over one-third of the number of incoming international students, 819,664, who stayed in the United States for a full year. Of the total study-abroad group, whether involved in short or long stays, only 14,413 (5 percent) went to China, 5,758 to Japan, and 3,042 to dynamic South Korea. Much the largest group went to the United Kingdom, followed by Italy, Spain, and France in Western Europe. The 14,413 American students who spent time in China in 2012–13 compares with the 235,597 Chinese students who enrolled to study for a year in the United States.[13] To encourage American students to travel to East Asia in sufficient numbers, it is necessary to subsidize them until critical mass is reached and the flow is normalized.

Second, as noted, there is the same asymmetry in language learning. Chinese students all learn to read and write in English and many have some conversational English. Less than 0.4 percent of American students learn Chinese at university. Surveys by the Modern Language Association show that in the year of the Master

Plan in 1960, 16.2 percent of all students in higher education were enrolled in a foreign language. In 2013 that proportion stood at only 8.1 percent, the lowest level since 1998. The majority of students studying a language other than English were learning Spanish. Of the 1,522,070 students studying a language, 61,055 (4.0 percent) were learning Chinese, an increase of just 1,179 since 2009, and 12,299 were learning Korean.[14] The lack of bilingual fluency limits not only the potentials of future American graduates but also the present capability of faculty and executives. While many people in China's higher education are familiar with America, China below first-level tourist contact is a mystery to most of their American counterparts.

Third, as these problems suggest—and despite the exchange schemes, joint programs, and branch campuses—contact with East Asia remains largely peripheral to the core business of American institutions. Few universities have taken decisive steps to bring East Asia into the mainstream of American university life in the way that East Asian universities have profoundly internationalized themselves by drawing on the strengths of the American university tradition. One exception is the global strategy of New York University (NYU). NYU students spend at least a semester in each of NYU's three campus sites, in New York, Abu Dhabi, and Shanghai. NYU Shanghai is in partnership with East China Normal University, the final member of the 985 group in China and as such one of the top thirty-nine research universities in the country. NYU Shanghai entails deep engagement. It brings the formation of future leaders in China together with a parallel group of students from the United States, while also embedding NYU in the Chinese higher education system at a senior level. In this kind of prolonged encounter, many students will begin to develop language skills and knowledge of culture, society, and the economy in China. Faculty and administrators will live in China for long periods and will also develop language competence.[15]

GLOBAL SYMMETRY

It is not easy for any university to take a step as bold as NYU has done—the kind of initiative that involves setting aside customary habits and ways of seeing. Edward Said notes: "We are all taught to venerate our nations and admire our traditions: we are taught to pursue their interests with toughness and disregard for other societies."[16] John Dewey remarks that "the notion of an inherent universality in the associative force at once breaks against the obvious fact of a plurality of states, each localized, with its boundaries, limitations, its indifference and even hostility to other states."[17] People normally look at the world through the lens of "methodological nationalism," which is the idea that "the nation/state/society is the natural social and political form of the modern world,"[18] and that one's own nation-state *should* color the lens. It takes a leap of the imagination to understand all culture as multiple and relational, to understand one's own society as just another culture, albeit one's own, and to see life as others see it.

The United States is entering a world in which it will no longer be overwhelmingly dominant, though for the foreseeable future it will remain the strongest power. In learning how to navigate the new balance of power, American universities will make a crucial contribution. It is a large effort to understand life from more than one viewpoint at the same time, for Americans to cease to be nothing but American, becoming more plural in their thinking while still being American. However, in the longer run that capacity for what Amartya Sen calls "transpositional" thinking[19] is essential if we are to grapple with the challenges of a world in which diverse histories come together in a common space, and people can build on the achievements of each other's societies without setting aside the virtues of their own. As Peter Singer states: "Our newly interdependent global society, with its remarkable possibilities for linking people around the planet, gives us the material basis for a new ethic."[20] Higher education is a place where people learn to think differently and where new thinking can flourish. This is one of the principal reasons for the existence of universities—to help their nations to innovate as conditions change. In the future American universities will be crucial to the larger kind of worldwide thinking that will be needed.

NYU's framing of learning in multiple locations creates favorable conditions for the development of graduates with the capability of multiple, global thinking. The most important feature of the NYU experiment is that in it, Chinese and American students, and American and Chinese faculty, meet each other on equal terms. The suggestion that East Asian higher education and research might have something to teach American higher education, as well learning from America, would have carried little weight in 1960. The question for Clark Kerr's generation was how American educational soft power could help to install a dynamic of self-improvement in higher education and science in East Asia. The world has changed. Clark Kerr's mission has succeeded in East Asia in remarkably short time. As a result the Eagle and the Dragon now have something to offer each other. They also need to find ways of living together and to educate their societies accordingly.

In the worldwide radiation of the California Idea, Chinese universities have already drawn from America its practices of access, the multiversity, the system forms, and global science. They have yet to fully explore the creative benefits of free critical discussion and of the public discursive role of universities and to develop a rounded approach to the nonscience disciplines as well as the physical sciences. Perhaps American higher education could take from China and Korea ideas about how to strengthen student engagement in the STEM disciplines in settings in which law and finance are all too alluring and the benefits of uniting education in the home with the school and college. And there are the gains to be made by setting plain hard work, grit, and mental exercise above habits of party school "networking" and grade inflation.

Dewey also makes the point that it is an illusion to suppose that there is "a model pattern which makes a state a good or a true state" or that we can meaningfully rank states according to how close they are to our own.[21] Though it is a mark of strong organic traditions that they have a sense of certainty about themselves and see no need to open their horizons to elements which have no history in their own affairs, in reality no way of life has all the answers to the needs of the human condition. In the encounter between higher education in the Sinic and American traditions, East Asian countries might consider how American universities work the broad public space around them to engage dynamically and creatively with economy, society, and government, and how higher education is central in the advance not just of human capabilities and of technological applications, but of self-determining freedoms. English-speaking countries might think about their present difficulties in surmounting the great issues such as climate change, the fact that people in those societies seem to work together properly only in wartime or depression, and the way that East Asian states, societies, and higher education systems routinely take a longer-term view than do societies in the English-speaking world. Anglo-Americans might also consider how it is that East Asian higher education seems to be able to meet public and private objectives simultaneously—rather than defining private good as something to be achieved separately from the good of all, the public good.

Clark Kerr and the 1960s California Idea harmonized individual needs and the collective good in a society that then found it comfortable to combine the two. This is something that has been lost. In working towards a new American synergy between private interest and public goods, a synergy that is essential for the health of any society, the high points in other traditions can help to illuminate the way.

PART THREE

Bringing It All Back Home

The California Idea in a More Unequal America

*Taxation is perhaps the most important of all political issues. Without taxes,
society has no common destiny, and collective action is impossible.*
—THOMAS PIKETTY, *CAPITAL IN THE TWENTY-FIRST CENTURY* (2014),
P. 493

16

Higher Education after Clark Kerr

In the final 2001 chapter on *The Uses of the University*, in his last words on the topic, Clark Kerr remarked on "the lessened prestige and public standing of the cities of intellect since the 1960s when they were at the peak of public favor and influence." He also listed a range of issues facing higher education, especially the multiversity.

These issues included the impact of globalization, and of fluctuating American productivity, on the economy and the returns to graduates; the growth of mature student demand and the "changing demographics of state populations"; "the rise of for-profit competitors to nonprofit higher education" (of which more below); and the partial shift in governing power to trustees and state governors, coupled with external pressures to use resources more effectively.[1] Kerr was also concerned about the role of technology in higher education, which for him, as for many others, loomed larger because it was ill-formed and unknown. Among the disciplines, Kerr noted that the life sciences were accumulating ever more power and resources, while faculty in the humanities were especially unhappy. The latter problem bothered him through his career, not least because humanities faculty had a talent for grievance, and there were inherent tensions in housing the liberal arts within science-oriented research universities.[2] Jennifer Washburn reports that in 2001 Kerr was also worrying about the potential of commercial ties to undermine the integrity of research. As he saw it, the problem was that faculty and administrators who needed money might make concessions that did not trouble them but were bad for the institution. "The university ought to remain a neutral agency devoted to the public welfare, not to private welfare," he said.[3] At the time, former Harvard president Derek Bok had similar concerns.[4] Other issues that Kerr did not mention in his final list in *The Uses of the University* but which he wrote about elsewhere included the politics of diversity and the politics of gender in higher education, both of which grew in importance throughout his working career and increasingly flourished in the time of his active retirement.[5]

The issues identified by Kerr continue to play out. None are disabling, none threaten to interrupt the trajectory of the multiversity or to undermine the capacity of public systems of higher education to combine excellence and access. Differences between disciplinary worldviews and debates on the purposes and conduct of higher education are chronic. Universities have long been contested as a site of advantage, and the multiversity is always pulled in different directions: this is Kerr's point. Despite the concerns expressed in his final chapter, average graduate premiums have been maintained in the United States, and in a highly stratified labor market, they continue to be high by world standards[6] (it is the marginal rates of returns that are in question, especially the returns to community college diplomas).[7] Research science continues to gather strength. In short, higher education remains central to American society, and as part 2 of this book showed, the multiversity is growing rapidly everywhere else, along partly American lines. Yet in California, and in the United States, public higher education faces deeper problems than it did in 2001.

These problems include the state fiscal evacuation of higher education, not just in California but in most parts of the country, especially after the 2008–2010 recession; the rising cost of tuition in public institutions and the faltering in participation rates, combined with the personal and national cost of student loans; the poor rate of upward transfer between tiers and, more generally, the limitation of social access; and the growing competitiveness between institutions, the widening gap in market-determined college quality between tiers, and, more generally, the weakening of institutions below the level of the multiversity. The scarcity of resources has exacerbated ongoing problems such as the relative growth of nontenured faculty[8] and the assertion of entrepreneurial ends over educational values—for example, in the drift into a disproportionate focus on noncore activities so as to raise revenues. All is not well in the student body either. An increasing number of researchers and scholars point to undue focus on the status value and networking value of higher education rather than vocational skills, let alone intellectual curiosity, mental formation, and human capacity as ends in themselves, and to the drift into lesser cognitive challenge, lighter study, and grade inflation in settings where students-as-consumers rule on faculty, as well as vice versa.[9]

These are all problems of higher education as a status market in which the public funding of public institutions has been thinned out and the steadying influence of that funding has weakened. When its level can be confidently predicted, as in the early years of the Master Plan, public funding sustains a reassuring bedrock of values. It guarantees that public institutions belong to all, that they serve the common good and are accessible to every family, and that there is no limit to what can be expected of their quality or their care for students. Fluctuating and falling public funding, coupled with a more complete shift to a status market in higher education and public institutions beginning to resemble private institutions, has ushered in different values. The mission of public higher education that was inherited from the Master Plan era has been destabilized and partly broken. The old blueprint (merit, excellence, equality) survives, but what of the will to sustain it, especially in government, which is the only place where the public interest can be concentrated?

But what *is* the public interest, in general and in higher education? In government offices, in civil discussion, and in many university offices, the mixed economy that Clark Kerr learned about in the New Deal era and fine-tuned in higher education with precision while working at the University of California and at the Carnegie Commission has become blurred. Often it seems that public interest and private interest have been inverted, so that "private" is good, and "public" is suspected of ulterior motives. Or rather, it seems that the correct public interest action is to elevate the economic market and its play of private interests to the organizing principle of society, and universities, and government itself. Public means private.

The malaise of the public sector does not derive from higher education, it originates in politics and government. Faith in the capacity of government to pursue public goods is at low ebb. The tax base has been weakened. The mood is cynical. Politicians are seen as bought and self-aggrandizing. In a more unequal economy and society, the social goal of equality of opportunity, which provided the Master Plan with much of its charisma and sustained the Great Society, has lost much of its bite. "Public" higher education remains a function of policy and accountable government; it remains "public"—confirming that the pretense that it is a market of almost private, quasi firms *is* just that, a pretense—so it is caught in the same downward spiral as the rest of the public sector. In this setting, higher education has been re-represented as a competition in the production and sale of marketable goods: private earnings and employability and the brands of leading universities. This is a competition that public colleges, with their broad burdens, can never wholly win. But who wants them to win? Private institutions carry a special glow of common approval. The (common) public institutions have lost luster. This is not just a contest between opposing sets of symbols. The data on faculty salaries[10] and comparative research outputs suggest that top American public universities have lost ground to their private counterparts. In a 2015 paper summing up higher education in the United States, prepared for a global audience in London, Robin Helms, a research specialist with the American Council on Education in Washington, DC, stated that "increasingly, higher education is seen as a private rather than public good. . . . Concerns about accessibility for students from economically disadvantaged backgrounds persist, but momentum to address the situation is lacking due to the public-to-private-good shift in mentality."[11]

Part 3 explores the conditions in which political and fiscal support for the common public good in higher education became more doubtful and was partly fractured. There was a shift in the realm of ideas. Monetarist economics made the size of government an issue, and rational-choice political science provided an intellectual framework in which, remarkably, the "public interest" was defined as impossible. Ideas become important when they are joined to power. In this case, power had its origins in neoconservative think tanks and grassroots campaigns in the 1970s and coalesced in the antistate and antitax individualism of the New Right, which was pioneered in California and moved into the political mainstream with the presidency of Ronald Reagan (1981–1989). Underlying the politics and drawing momentum from it was a long-term historical shift in the political economy of the United States. Measured economic inequality increases from about 1980, the year that the Reagan presidency began. This seemed to confirm the potency of the new individualism, at one and the same time meritocratic and hierarchical, in politics and higher education.

Rising inequality and the political swing to the right, in association with the continuing expansion of mass higher education as forecast by Martin Trow, have altered the landscape in which the California Idea of higher education plays out. Part 3 reviews the implications of these changes for the two pillars of the meritocratic edifice that still shape our understandings of higher education: education as human capital and education as equality of opportunity and social mobility. The shift in the political economy led by Clark Kerr's nemesis, Ronald Reagan, proved to be as influential in its own way as Roosevelt and the New Deal, and it has lasted almost as long. This shift has reshaped, and in some respects decisively limited, the economic and social potentials of American higher education. If the California Idea of higher education was partly utopian, then the Reagan-era political economy has heightened the utopian element, pushing further from reach the 1960s egalitarian vision.

But at the same time, the alternative utopia, that of the market society driven by ever more unequal competition in society and higher education, has failed. In society, poverty has increased markedly, upward mobility has slowed, and the middle class faces declining living standards and declining prospects in the next generation. In higher education, on all of the indicators except high-research performance (where the multiversity has been protected from wholesale privatization by intrinsic market failure, federal research funding, and academic cultures), American higher education has declined. Higher education is less well funded and less affordable, participation is wavering, academic learning is in question, and quality below the top institutions appears to be falling without limit. Some upward mobility still occurs, but the balance of effect in American higher education favors the reproduction of inequality rather than upward mobility. Clark Kerr and his contemporaries were working on a smaller scale and with more favorable conditions than now prevail. They underrecognized gender and diversity and loaded too much of the enrollment into bottom-tier two-year colleges. Nevertheless, it is obvious their Idea was better than what followed.

17

The Impossibility of Public Good

In the 1950s and 1960s, as the California Idea of higher education emerged, within the policy framework of the mixed public and private economy inherited from the New Deal era, a different set of ideas about government and the public good was also being developed. In 1951, defense intellectual Kenneth Arrow published a paper on social choice and individual values, first prepared when he was working as a summer intern at the RAND Corporation in 1948, in which he inquired into whether it was possible to derive collectively rational decisions from the aggregation of individuals' preferences. Arrow used set theory to prove that when two or more individuals were making decisions over three or more alternatives, it was logically impossible to derive collectively rational group decisions from the individual preferences, whether through voting, social welfare policy, or markets. There was no prospect of achieving a common decision consistent with each person's individual preferences. In instances of collective decision making, one or the other assumption would have to give way: either the outcome of individual preferences would not be collectively rational or individuals would lose their freedom to determine personal ends. This conclusion became known as the "impossibility theorem." Crucially, it was grounded in Arrow's starting assumptions: that methodological individualism prevailed, meaning that all goods were individualized, and there were no collective social goods distinct from the aggregation of individual goods,[1] that individuals made rational decisions based on utility, that individuals' preferences were unrestricted and inviolable, and that individuals' preferences were incomparable.[2] Within the terms of these premises, Arrow presented his theory as universally applicable in all social sites and all cultures.[3] It was not grounded in an empirical anthropology of human social behavior. In a sympathetic commentary, S. M. Amadae concludes that "Arrow's theory of social choice was entirely normative."[4]

In the period between the 1930s and the 1960s, many intellectuals concerned themselves with how to dismantle the coercive authority of fascism and Stalinism. John Dewey and others wanted to do this via democratic collective deliberation and decision in the public sphere.[5] Arrow set himself against these strategies. His high individualist approach was radically different. He argued that only "uphold-ing individual freedom over personal preferences" could be "the basis of legitimate rule." Working democracy based on majority rule tended to infringe on liberty by violating the preferences of at least one citizen. State administration of social policy was a potential disaster and redistributive taxation was a certain disaster, as it was impossible to manage a redistributive policy so as to meet the preferences of all citizens, including those whose wealth would diminish. The impossibility theorem rendered as intellectually incoherent the very notion of "social welfare." This finding was consistent with the belief of contemporary welfare economics that there was no basis for an objective statement of collective welfare.[6]

Nevertheless, the impossibility theorem did not negate the practical possibil-ity of an agreed subjective policy determination of collective welfare through the democratic process or by government administration; it merely negated the pos-sibility of Pareto optimality—that is, a condition in which no individual would be worse off. Strictly, the impossibility theorem was not applicable in situations where individuals took the preferences of others into account, or when they started from an assumption of common preferences, or they began from the assumption that all had a minimum entitlement, or more generally, where they took into account the health or fairness of the system or other distributional norms. In other words, it did not apply when people behaved as citizens with shared social values rather than as utility-maximizing *homo economicus*. Arrow emphasized that in his con-struction, "all social choices are determined by individual desires" and are not "imposed by considerations external to individuals' preferences,"[7] which could include law, the taxation regime, or public policy. There was no place in the ideal Arrow world for principles such as social equality of opportunity in education or for taxation of inheritance designed to redistribute resources between families and provide each child with a more equal start or public economic intervention during a depression on the grounds that all persons should be able to work for a living. States S. M. Amadae: "His theorem rejects the possibility that a social consensus on ends could emerge as a result of a philosophical ideal transcending individuals' desires as a guide to collective decision making."[8] Arrow's impossibility theorem also excluded utilitarian judgments, which assumed individual utilities could be compared, dealing a further blow to classical welfare economics.

The impossibility theorem rested on unrealistic conditions: a self-centered uto-pia in which autarkic individual freedom was absolute and the shared conditions enabling that freedom to be exercised and enjoyed were taken for granted—despite the fact that such social conditions would be fatally undermined when all persons pursued their absolute self-interest without any regard for others. To quote Amadae again:

> Agents share a world of objective logic or fact, but privately determine values and ends. Arrow's social world is one in which individuals have personal preferences, and the world of things and other individuals serves as background in which individuals realize their private ends. . . . Arrow does not so much envision a shared social world as he does a collection of individuals whose identities are defined by their well-ordered set of preferences, and who strive to achieve their most preferred outcomes.[9]

However, by no means all social scientists oppose the use of unrealistic assumptions, and many set out to transform the world using normative methods.[10] The imaginative landscape of the disciplines is populated by many ideal forms and cases. Arrow's kind of individualism, absolute negative freedom without the J. S. Mill constraint (I am free only to the extent I do not infringe the freedom of others), was attractive to many.[11] The impossibility theorem became widely noticed. It evolved into the foundation of social choice theory, which in the United States, though not Western Europe, largely replaced the older tradition of welfare economics.[12] The effects in other parts of economics were less transformative. The fact that Arrow had demonstrated that markets were incapable of collectively rational decisions was not seen to undermine Adam Smith's invisible hand theorem. Markets had never been expected to achieve Pareto optimality. *Homo economicus* had no intrinsic concern about collective decisions. On the other hand, the effects in political science were subversive and generative. The most dramatic effect was that not just social welfare but the "public," the "public interest," and "public good" were rendered meaningless by the impossibility theorem once its high individualist assumptions were accepted. This was the starting point for the development of public choice theory, which described itself as "the economics of politics."

PUBLIC CHOICE THEORY

The principal leader of public choice theory, James Buchanan, set out to detonate the "normative delusion" that "the state was, somehow, a benevolent entity and those who made decisions on behalf of the state were guided by consideration of the general or public interest."[13] The foundational text of the theory, *The Calculus of Consent* (1962), written with Gordon Tullock, rested on Arrow's finding—established not through empirical observation but through logic erected on the base of Arrow's high individualist assumptions—that there is no such thing as the public good.

Again, the intent of public choice theory was normative: to change expectations about the state. Buchanan and Tullock stated that they were interested not in what the state was, but in what it ought to do.[14] What it ought to do was trade. In public choice theory, both politics and government were understood as similar to an economic market and populated by self-seeking agents. "The theory of markets postulates only that the relationship be economic, that the interests of his opposite number in the exchange be excluded from consideration."[15] Hence joint or collective interest was ruled out from the start. How then did communities determine a just social order? Buchanan believed that individuals should use politics to seek forms of justice and social organization that best uphold their individual interests. Political leaders might claim to be responsible to persons or causes other than themselves, but they were not. Those who espouse general principles did so in order to advance their self-interest, by using the mask of altruism to lift their standing and secure the trust of others so as to either more effectively pursue their self-interest or to secure a general order that will guarantee and maintain it.[16] It was not so much that there was no public interest expressed in government; rather, there were multiple "public interests," with each one conceived by an active individual. Group decisions were simply the sum of the individual decisions combined through a decision-making rule.[17]

Buchanan's notion of forms of common justice as an outcome of competition and trade contrasts with Adam Smith's views in *The Theory of Moral Sentiments* ([1759] 2004). For Smith, human sympathy was foundational to society, and sympathy was neither motivated by self-interest nor served it indirectly.[18] Adam Smith saw a world of mixed public and private goods in which humans were motivated by, on the one hand, sympathy and sociability and, on the other hand, by self-interest and self-love. He believed that it was essential that humans keep self-regard in check. Buchanan saw only self-interest and no check, and private goods that were obtained in market production and exchange. Clark Kerr and the other 1960s builders of California's higher education would have recognized themselves more readily in Adam Smith than in James Buchanan.

Public choice theory took a different tack than earlier theories that posed problems of government failure alongside problems of market failure. While the vision of self-serving politicians and bureaucrats was mobilized by Buchanan as a negative referent to weaken the credibility of government while detonating the notion of public good, this was also the mode of government that he saw as not only inevitable but desirable. The negative referent was readily switched to positive. After all, self-regarding competitive behavior was the motor of progress.

> Within the constraints that he faces, the bureaucrat tries to maximize his utility. He is no different from anyone else in this respect. He can hardly be expected to further some vaguely defined "public interest" unless this is consistent with his own.[19]

The notion of politics as another market legitimates practices that some would describe as the corruption of public values—for example, politicians who are owned by corporate interests that finance their campaigns or public servants who exchange favors for cash. However, Buchanan saw economic freedom as the basic form of human freedom, making possible other forms of freedom such as political freedom.[20] Given that public values were a mirage, nothing could be lost. When politics was managed by lobbyists working for large companies, there were no ethics to violate. These precepts in their raw form were not universally adopted, but the public choice arguments continuously seeped into the polity, so that there became more tolerance towards the role of money in Congress than there had been in Clark Kerr's time, and politics became more often interpreted in terms of self-interest than in terms of the general interest. In turn, such behaviors and such interpretations appear to confirm the core assumptions and narrative of public choice theory. Public choice theory also helped to weaken faith in the potential of public programs, including educational programs, to improve social conditions. As Buchanan notes,

> public choice theory, along with complementary empirical observation, has defused enthusiasm for collective solutions to social problems. In this negative sense, public choice has exerted, and continues to exert, major ideological impact.[21]

Nowhere did this become more apparent than in the politics of taxation. Taxation is the key to the capacity of the state to pursue its programs—as Piketty notes, without taxation there is no material basis for the common interest.[22] For public choice theory, taxation was also the soft underbelly of the New Deal–type state, the point where it was most vulnerable to political critique. Though the citizen-beneficiaries of social programs tended to like those programs, who would not want to pay less tax?

Buchanan opened up this issue carefully. He stated that for him, government embodied a dilemma. On one hand, each person was "a participant in government (a citizen)" and in that sense complicit in collective decisions and collective action. On the other hand, government by its nature forced some citizens to acquiesce to behaviors inconsistent with their preferences, such as "the confiscation through taxation of goods he treats as 'his own.'"[23] In that circumstance, "coercion is apparently exercised upon him in the same way as that exerted by the thug who takes his wallet in Central Park."[24] Buchanan argued that the state must be structured so as to protect individuals from coercion, both by other individuals and by the state itself. He devised the idea of a two-tier state, consisting of a basic constitutional framework of rights enforced by law, the "protective state," and the domain of contractual exchanges in those rights, the "productive state." Most day-to-day government activity occurred in the productive domain. The concern was to ensure that governments did not overstep the boundary and tamper with rights and liberties in the protective domain. If government intervened in this area, "its acts may be regarded as 'criminal.'"[25] Here, again, taxation could be construed as an invasion of liberty.

At the same time that public choice theory began to achieve large-scale impact in social science, in the 1970s, the world of public policy was becoming more receptive to promarket values and notions of limited government and taxation. The stagflation of the mid-1970s, in which growing unemployment and inflation coincided, led to the abandonment of Keynesian demand management as a policy tool and a partial shift from fiscal to monetary management as was being urged by Milton Friedman. The collapse of global currency coordination in 1971 paved the way for greater financial deregulation. Buchanan provided robust support to the arguments against Keynesian economic management.[26] Friedman reciprocated, endorsing Buchanan's proposition that politics should be seen as a market of self-interested individuals rather than the site of a collective public interest.[27] These views were becoming part of the intellectual and policy mainstream. Friedman's call for the strengthening of markets forces in education through vouchers and his sharp critique of state-subsidized tuition in higher education as regressive in terms of social distribution also became widely noticed.[28] Buchanan agreed with Friedman's position. Student radicalism had occurred, he argued, because students received education at a price that was well below its cost of production, especially in the public higher education institutions. Clearly, they did not value the product. The introduction of full-price tuition would empower students in a more useful way, while disciplining them to make effective use of their investment. It would also bring the universities and the faculty into lines with student-consumer needs.[29]

The new politics of limited government and taxation, and education markets, was to have a major impact on public higher education—directly, by truncating its public funds and financing private sector competitors, and indirectly, by changing the society in which it worked. The anti-Keynesian state manifested a declining interest in elevating society, for example, by fostering equality of opportunity. Such programs always led to demands for more expenditure. Consistent with social choice and public choice theory, some in government and others in think tanks, lobbying organizations, and media circles began to talk down expectations of the state. It was some time before the practical implications of these new ideas were apparent. For California and for the California Idea of higher education, they showed first in relation to tax.

18

The Impossibility of Taxation

Clark Kerr's most difficult challenge was the Free Speech Movement at Berkeley, which began on October 1, 1964. It was the first crest in the successive waves of student power, grassroots activism, and the counterculture that for a decade swept across the campus, San Francisco,[1] the United States, and much of the world. Kerr refused to use force at Berkeley, and in any situation, he always negotiated when he could. However, he never found a way to reach agreement with the New Left. The two parties lived in different worlds. If both were committed to the public good, they had contrary notions of what was in it, and they differed fundamentally on the meaning of the multiversity. Kerr saw the multiversity as the best hope of society and wanted to protect it by reestablishing civil peace on campus. For the students, whose confrontations with authority were a public amphitheater within which they were building a new and alternate society, the university was part of the system, part of the problem, and negotiations with Kerr were an irrelevant distraction. The multiversity was the incubation chamber for their sustained creative experiment—and also its collateral damage. Still, the student revolt did not stop the machine of California's higher education from working. Alongside the almost-continuous activism, the 1960s continued as a fecund building time. Through the decade, under Clark Kerr and his successors, the University of California developed its campuses and its research, and the number of community college students rapidly increased. The main political effect of the prolonged period of student activism was indirect: it weakened the standing of the multiversity within mainstream political culture in California.

The public reaction to student activism was a contributing element in the rise of the Republican right, first in California and then in the nation. This conjunction of elements showed first in Ronald Reagan's 1966–1967 gubernatorial campaign promise to "clean up the mess at Berkeley."[2] Ultimately, Reagan's political career, in which he served as thirty-third governor of California (1967–1975) and as a popular and transformative fortieth president of the United States (1981–1989), was highly consequential for public education in California, though more so in national office than as governor. In conjunction with the shift in economic and financial management from Keynesianism to monetarism and while fostering the populist antistatist individualism that took root in the country in the second half of the 1970s and the 1980s, Reagan and the Republican right broke continuity with the stream of policies originating in the New Deal era, one of which was the Master Plan. Nevertheless, the Republican right may well have triumphed in California without the stimulus provided by the student revolt at Berkeley. Kerr remarked later:

> I have observed that no other state except New York has experienced more examples of influence by the left than California: in Hollywood, in San Francisco on the waterfront and in the Haight-Ashbury district,[3] and in Berkeley during the 1960s. Also, few states have seen more spectacular flourishes of influence by the right than California: the political successes of Richard Nixon and Ronald Reagan, the support given to the John Birch Society, and the attention given to reports of the state Senate Committee on Un-American Activities. To understand modern California, however, it is more important to acknowledge the longer-run domination by the right than the shorter-run glimpses of the influence of the left in the second half of the twentieth century.[4]

There were some signs of later outcomes early in Reagan's first term as governor. Soon after taking office and following his engineering the dismissal of Clark Kerr from the UC presidency, Reagan announced that the state budget was in crisis. Taxes were too high and spending had to be cut. In the University, "there are certain intellectual luxuries that perhaps we could do without," he told a media conference. Taxpayers shouldn't be "subsidizing intellectual curiosity." Higher education was about preparing people for jobs. Dan Berrett argues that this was the moment when a more utilitarian approach to higher education began to take hold, an approach focused on career and earnings, and broad support for liberal higher education began to slip. The trend was strengthened in the economic downturn precipitated by the 1973 oil shock. Periodic polls of student attitudes allow the shift to be mapped. "In the early 1970s, nearly three-quarters of freshmen said that it was essential to them to develop a meaningful philosophy of life. About a third felt the same about being very well off financially. Now those fractions have flipped," said Berrett in 2015. Business studies commanded 12 percent of enrollments in Reagan's first year as state governor in 1967. By the time he was president in 1981, business had become the largest single major, a position it still holds.[5] Nevertheless, it would be far-fetched to claim the fortieth president was primarily responsible for the slippage in the popularity of liberal education. In the longer run, his antistate, antitax, and pro-deregulation positions would have more impact on public higher education. While in office, Reagan fostered disillusionment with the role of government and with the idea of public interest or public good, along the lines suggested by public choice theory, decisively tilting the public/private balance in policy towards the private side, and fragmenting the fiscal-social compact that had supported the Master Plan in its first two decades.

These longer-term effects were not all foreshadowed during Reagan's time as state governor. He largely managed California in 1967–1975 according to the then-prevailing Keynesian fiscal norms. Roads and infrastructure were funded. Spending and taxation rose. The University of California experienced a run of tough budgets under Reagan, concurrent with a slowing in enrollment growth because of demographic change,[6] but at the time it was assumed that its budget problems were an expression of the governor's well-known and publicly expressed political hostility to the University rather than his fiscal norms. When community college enrollment exceeded the Master Plan forecast, money was found. However, when Keynesian economic management was jettisoned and the shift in political economy occurred in the second half of the 1970s, Reagan became a leading enthusiast for the new conservative populism.

In California the politics of small government and small tax mushroomed into a vibrant mass movement. As in the works of Buchanan and public choice theory, the tax revolt made little distinction between taxation and theft. In 1978 the antitax movement succeeded in securing majority support for the California ballot initiative Proposition 13, which sharply reduced property taxes and capped property tax rates. Property taxes provided the main source of income for local counties and school districts, and after Proposition 13 was passed, the drop in revenues from property taxes was equivalent to 40 percent of total county revenues. The state moved to protect schools, cities, and local communities, but in doing so placed the other items in the budget in jeopardy, including higher education. A host of further tax cutting and tax-related measures emerged, accumulating a long-term legal and fiscal nightmare for state government. In 1980 Proposition 9, which would have halved state income tax, was defeated, though only after it had led in the polls for most of the campaign period.[7] In 1988, partly to compensate for the outcomes of Proposition 13, the state adopted Proposition 88, which allocated 40 percent of state income to schools and community colleges. This provided some protection for the mass public education institutions, but not the CSU and UC systems.

After the spending mandates and tax limitations were taken into account, only 15 percent of the California state budget was unallocated. This 15 percent, the only part of the budget that could be freely varied downwards, included higher education. Higher education found itself competing with many other priorities in a state more dependent than before on forms of taxation that, unlike property values, routinely fluctuated with the economy: income, capital gains, and sales taxes. State higher education funding became especially vulnerable during periods of recession.[8]

In 1980 Reagan campaigned for the national presidency on a slogan stating that government was not the solution, it was the problem. It was an exact reversal of themes of the Kennedy campaign of 1960 and the Johnson campaign of 1964, in which the leaders sought to raise expectations of government and draw public support for the pursuit of large, collective solutions to society's problems. Reagan diminished expectations of government in the fashion suggested by public choice theory: by weakening the intrinsic notion of a common public interest. This was an accurate indicator of what was to follow.

In 1981 the president broke a national air-traffic controllers' strike by using military personnel as substitute labor. This outcome weakened the unions, providing favorable conditions for the deregulation of wages and working conditions across the economy, including the growing emphasis on executive pay systems that were determined by individual performance rather than internal relativities within the firm or workplace.[9] In the same year, the top rate on the federal income tax scale was cut from 70 to 50 percent. In 1986 the top tax rate was reduced again, from 50 to only 28 percent. The second top rate was maintained at 33 percent, indicating that the tax package was designed to benefit the highest income earners above all. The bottom tax rate was raised from 11 to 15 percent. The reduction in the top tax rate encouraged high-income earners to press for larger salaries in the deregulated environment. The trend line in measured inequality in the United States, which dates from about 1980, the year Reagan assumed office, surges after the tax cuts. There was to be a close relationship between growth in the income shares of the top 1 percent and 0.1 percent of recipients and reductions in the rates of taxation on high labor incomes and later reductions in the rate of tax on capital incomes and inheritance.[10]

FUNDING OF THE UNIVERSITIES

The tax revolt ensured that the public funding of public higher education would never be as strong again as it had been in the 1960s. Table 18.1 summarizes the funding trend from 1960 to 2010. It demonstrates the rapid rise in total funding in the first two decades of the Master Plan as enrollment grew more rapidly than planned in the community colleges. In the 1970s the University budget slowed due to the combined effects of Governor Reagan and demography. The economy was up in the 1980s, and Governor Deukmejian made higher education a priority, granting the University of California a 30-percent increase in its operating budget in 1983. Despite the gathering fallout from Proposition 13, it was a good decade for the University. State support increased also in the other higher education sys-

TABLE 18.1. Student enrollment in public higher education and state and local government financial support, California, 1960–2010, by decade (constant 2010 prices)

	Student enrollment			Government financial support		
Year	University of California	California State University	California Community Colleges	University of California ($s billion)	California State University ($s billion)	California Community Colleges ($s billion)
1960	43,748	61,330	97,858	0.727	0.405	0.429
1970	98,508	186,749	526,584	1.852	1.601	2.058
1980	122,761	232,935	752,278	2.387	2.155	3.378
1990	152,863	272,637	818,755	3.465	2.722	4.152
2000	165,900	279,403	999,652	3.439	2.755	5.047
2010	232,613	358,063	1,161,807	2.591	2.346	5.764

SOURCE: Adapted by author, from data from Callan 2012, pp. 67–69.

tems, though the Proposition 13 limitation meant that in some years, community colleges turned away applicants.

However, higher education was declining overall as a state fiscal priority. The share of total state expenditures going to the UC and CSU fell from 11.3 percent in the Master Plan year of 1960 to 7.8 percent in 1995. Over the same span, funding for prisons rose from 2.4 to 7.1 percent of state spending, as Kerr notes.[11] The 1990s saw the end of funding growth in the UC and CSU, though the enrollment grew by 8.5 percent in the UC and 2.5 percent in the CSU. The next decade, 2000–2010, was considerably tougher than the 1990s. It saw a major reduction in fiscal support, much of it concentrated at the end of the decade, reflecting the effects of the 2008–2010 recession. State funding of the University of California fell by 24.7 percent in real terms between 2000 and 2010, while the enrollment increased by a massive 40.2 percent. There was a 14.8 percent decline in California State University funding over the same 2000–2010 period, while the enrollment rose by 28.2 percent. The funding of the community colleges increased by 14.2 percent, which almost matched the enrollment growth of 16.2 percent, but the community colleges had less opportunity to raise nonstate revenues than did the CSU and UC campuses.[12]

The 2008–2010 recession generated havoc in state revenues and was especially bad for the unprotected areas of the state budget. John Douglass reports a cut of $813 million in the funding of the UC system in 2009 and 2010.[13] Public funding, the basis of long-term planning in the early decades of the Master Plan, became more volatile and less predictable than tuition revenues and other private sources. This brought with it an ongoing danger that educational quality would be undermined by careless short-term decisions. When Stanford pioneered mass open online courseware (MOOC) programs in 2011, state governor Jerry Brown, son of Edmund G. "Pat" Brown, the governor who had ushered in the 1960 Master Plan, advocated MOOCs as the means of maintaining participation in higher education on the cheap, despite the abysmal completion rates that normally attend MOOC units.[14]

University of California campuses began to imagine a future in which state funding was negligible. In the decade between 2002–03 and 2012–13, state revenues received by UC Berkeley declined from $497 to $299 million in current dollars, a reduction in constant price terms of 54 percent.[15] Successive state governments had learned that they could reduce funding without a severe public backlash, but there was more likely to be public opposition if they sanctioned the tuition increases necessary for institutions to make up the shortfall. From the 1990s onwards, a new pattern was established in which the years of funding recovery were insufficient to compensate for years of reductions. Small cuts were not undone and tended to accumulate. In this asymmetrical policy framework, and given the continued legal and fiscal constraints on the state, California's recession-induced cuts looked largely irreversible.

Like their public sector counterparts in many other states, the UC and CSU have found it difficult to secure state support to raise tuition so as to compensate for the effects of state cutbacks. Nevertheless, tuition increases sufficient to plug the gap in spending also foster long-term political problems for the public sector. Public institutions depend on public support both to secure favorable state policies and, more generally, to function effectively in a highly networked society and economy. Public support tends to be undermined by rising tuition, and in California this also threatens the pristine access mission of the University of California. On the other hand, public support is weakened also by reductions in service quality due to insufficient funding. The access mission needs to be subsidized.[16]

In 2013, after the recession, the student-to-faculty ratio in the University of California was 24 to 1, compared to 19 to 1 a decade earlier, and 15 to 1 in the 1980s.[17] The public university campuses found themselves positioned between the Scylla of a resource decline that would undermine all objectives, including the research outputs and quality on which so much else depended, and the Charybdis of public unpopularity and mission compromise. In effect they were forced to become more like a private university so as to uphold their public mission effectively in social competition with the real private sector. They had limited options. The only potential sources of additional resources were research funding, foreign students, noncore revenues, private gifts and endowments (which had a very limited role on most campuses), and revenue bonds for capital projects (when allowed by state legislation). In this setting, the University of California campuses had no clear forward strategy.

The problem as stated here was specific to public higher education. The effects of the 2008–2010 recession differentiated between the University of California, which depended partly on the California state budget and whose tuition was regulated by the regents, and private universities such as Harvard, Yale, Stanford, and Princeton, which were free to manage their prices and carried significantly larger endowments than Berkeley, UCLA, and San Diego. Though both state funding and university endowments fell sharply in value in the first two years of recession, the trajectory of recovery differed by sector. By 2014 endowments had been largely restored in value. The state funding cuts seemed at least partly permanent.

The decline in the relative resource position of the top public universities has both short-term and long-term effects. In a study of patterns of American research publication, James Adams estimates that in the 1990s there was a slowdown in the growth of science papers in the United States. This decline was centered on the public universities. Although their share of federal research grants grew in the 1990s, the decline appears to be associated with the fall in their revenues from their respective state governments, which weakened their capacity to sustain research infrastructure and faculty time spent in research.[18] Between 2002–03 and 2012–13, the proportion of Berkeley's revenues coming from state sources dropped from 34 percent to 13 percent.[19] This was likely to have more pronounced effects in the future trend line of research outputs than had the cessation of funding growth in the 1990s noted by Adam.

PROBLEMS OF THE MASTER PLAN

However, as part 1 indicated, the larger problems of the California Idea of higher education relate to the access mission rather than the excellence mission. These problems are centered on the public schools and the community colleges. "The effectiveness of California's public schools were not an issue for the framers of the Master Plan," states Patrick Callan. Participation, spending, and teacher qualifications were high in national terms. Within two decades, the task of the schools had become more difficult, while Proposition 13 in 1978 had undercut their capacity to meet the additional demands. "Proposition 13 set school finance into a downward spiral, one that was marked with only brief spurts of recovery in peak state revenue years."[20]

California's demography changed fundamentally after the heyday of the equality of opportunity in the 1960s, when the social consensus underpinning the Master Plan was set. The population became larger and much more ethnically diverse. The data for 1960 do not distinguish white and Latino categories. In 1970 the state was 77 percent white, 12 percent Latino, 7 percent African American, and just 3 percent Asian or Pacific Islander. By 1990 the proportion categorized as white fell from 77 to 57 percent, with the growth in the Latino (26 percent) and Asian/

Pacific (9 percent) groups. Between 1990 and 2010, the size of the white population dropped by 2.1 million, while the size of the Latino and Asian/Pacific populations grew by 6.2 million and 2.2 million people respectively. In 2010, 40 percent of California was white, 38 percent was Latino, 13 percent Asian/Pacific, 6 percent African American, and 0.4 percent First Nations American, though there was a high white concentration in the wealthiest segment of the population. The age structure of the population was unevenly distributed between ethnic categories, reflecting differences in both fertility and migration patterns. On average the Latino population was considerably younger than the white population. In grade 6 in the state public schools in 2010, 51 percent of the enrollment was Latino, with 27 percent white, 11 percent Asian/Pacific, and 7 percent African American. Though the graduation rate was lower among Latinos than whites or Asians, Latinos (43 percent) made up the largest proportion of the 2010 high school graduate cohort, compared to 33 percent recorded as white.

In 2009 Latinos made up 28 percent of the enrollment in public higher education, significantly less their 43 percent share of school graduation in 2010, compared to 33 percent white and 16 percent Asian or Filipino, though there was a large uncategorized group of 15 percent, mostly located in the community colleges. At the University of California, the ethnic shares were significantly different again. While the UC campuses were more socially representative than the Ivy League, as noted, they sat halfway between that measuring stick and the California average. In ethnic terms, the UC white proportion in 2009 was 38 percent, and the Asian and Filipino share was 33 percent, outnumbering the Latino proportion at 16 percent—less than a third of the Latino presence in middle primary school in 2010—and the African American proportion, which was just 4 percent of the UC enrollment. Latinos were 30 percent of the community college enrollment, and African Americans were 7 percent in that sector. The ethnic distribution in the CSU was closer to that of the community colleges than the UC.[21] These ethnic data need to be joined to data on socioeconomic composition, but they indicate the stratified nature of participation.

Schooling in California was differentiated by a complex overlap of class, ethnicity, and regional inequalities, within a system design that discriminated in favor of families best able to help themselves. It recycled low quality, aspirations, and achievement in poor districts, and the obverse in middle-class districts. Middle-class families, many of them Anglo-American, European American, or of Chinese, Japanese, or Korean background, were statistically overrepresented in high-status higher education. Latino and African American school populations, like all ethnic groups, had mixed class origins, but they were disproportionately concentrated in underfunded schools in poor communities, and many Latino students were also affected by language barriers. National Assessment of Educational Progress (NAEP) testing found that California's eighth graders performed well below those in the strongest states.[22] In 2012 just 78.5 percent of the high school students who started in 2008–09 had graduated, with approximately 8 percent more still at school. Latinos students had a graduation rate of 73.2 percent, while that of African American students was just 65.7 percent.[23] Modest compensatory schemes changed little. Typically, efforts to broaden access to Advanced Placement subjects in disadvantaged schools were trumped by the schools serving middle-class districts, where Advanced Placement offerings rolled out at a faster rate.[24]

In this context, Proposition 13, which impacted schools directly, and other low tax measures signified the unwillingness of part of an ageing white middle class to carry the costs of resourcing schooling of good quality across all districts and all citizens and noncitizens, including cross-border migrants.[25] There was no consensus on whether the families of illegal migrants should receive free schooling.[26] Regardless, by turning their backs not only on illegal migrants but all users of public schooling, the proponents of Proposition 13 rendered it impossible for the Master Plan to fulfill its founding expectations of equality of social opportunity through participation in higher education. Patricia Pelfrey's summary of the situation is pessimistic:

> The goal of making UC a place that reflects the full diversity of the state remains unfulfilled. There is near universal agreement that it will be virtually impossible to achieve without the renewal and revitalization of pre-collegiate education—the K-12 public schools. There is little evidence that the state is capable of mustering the money or the legislative will to get its arms around this challenge, especially in light of the initiative-dominated, tax-resistant, limited-government political culture that prevails today. Where education is concerned, California, with its outsized ambitions and golden dreams, has dwindled into a cautionary tale.[27]

In higher education the weak component of the Plan was the community colleges. In the final edition of *The Uses of the University,* in 2001, Clark Kerr noted that there had been a "movement backward" in the community colleges since the 1960 Master Plan. There were "enormous discrepancies in . . . transfer programs in community colleges between low-income and high-income neighborhoods, discrepancies that increase inequality of opportunity."[28] Sheldon Rothblatt cites a 1995 range from 8 percent in Southern California to 50 percent in the Bay Area. While a small group of community colleges play a prominent role in access to UC Berkeley and other University of California campuses, many others have low transfer rates to the CSU and UC, with transfers notably lower among African American and Hispanic students than white or Asian students.[29] Because they have been asked to shoulder the great bulk of the growth in participation, without the necessary status, and increasingly denied the necessary resources, community colleges' rates of graduation and transfer have languished,[30] and patterns of student achievement have stratified on regional, social, and ethnic lines, as in public schooling.

Community colleges were pulled between the need for immediate employability and the academic requirements of transfer, which focused on a more liberal curriculum.[31] The stretch between those two different norms was as great as that embodied in the teaching-research nexus in universities, but unlike the UC, the community colleges were not fully funded to play both of their roles competently. Douglass states that just 22 percent of commencing community college students transferred to a four-year degree.[32] Often two-year diploma training was insufficient to secure much impact in the labor markets. The low marginal returns associated with the diploma probably contributed to low completion. Four-year programs in community colleges were expanding, but they were underfunded by comparison with the CSU. Tuition increases were needed to sustain and improve quality, but they threatened to reduce enrollment. The problems were long-standing ones, but they were worsened in the state budget crisis after 2008.

In the California State University campuses, also increasingly underresourced, transfer again varied by institution and region, and completion rates were low, at about 45 percent. This compared to 90 percent in the UC, which was high on the national scale.[33]

It was apparent by the beginning of the 2010s, if not well before, that the instruments of the Master Plan were no longer adequate in the face of these challenges. It could not manage growth or site new developments as required. It was stymied by the fiscal retreat of the state, which rendered irrelevant all planning issues, replacing them with a permanent problem of crisis management. Callan argues that the Plan has lacked an "adaptive capacity"[34] for at least two decades. Its mechanisms were unable to plan adequately for demographic growth in the 1990s, and the planning of new initiatives had lapsed again into local pork barreling, as was the case before 1960 (this very problem had instigated the need for a long-term, state-wide settlement in the late 1950s).[35] Callan finds that "community college enrollment for 2006 was more than 206,000 below projections of a 2000 study by the California Postsecondary Commission."[36] Douglass argues that by 2011 the Plan was "dead or nearly so" in relation to six areas: access to all who want higher education, state subsidization of student places, appropriate balance between two-year and four-year programs, guaranteed low tuition, sufficient opportunities for transfer students in the CSU and UC, and the planning and funding of enrollment growth to meet California's needs.[37]

Of these issues, the most significant was the failure of the state and of the mechanisms of the Master Plan to sustain the central social promise of 1960: the provision of access to higher education for all high school graduates who could benefit from it. The access promise was honored in full for the first two decades, as a central plank of state policy, enabling California to achieve a major increase in participation and educational attainment. It was honored intermittently in good budget years for the next two decades.[38] After that it lapsed, in practice. A common belief in universal access was maintained at the level of the state's political culture. Proposals to increase tuition in any part of public education continued to be hotly contested. All the same, for practical purposes, the 1960 promise was dead. As Callan remarks, "the egalitarian commitments of the plan were the most innovative and the most influential," but "they were also to prove the most fragile."[39]

19

Economic and Social Inequality

So far, the travails of the California Idea of higher education have been explained in terms of the declining authority of government and of the idea of the public interest, the rise of a libertarian individualism in which self-interest is untroubled by care for others, and a tax revolt by grassroots activists, joined to high-income earners and powerful financial interests, that has crippled state budget capacity. Yet the question remains: why? Why was the democratic compact in higher education allowed to deteriorate?

The larger answer, beyond education or policy, lies in the changing nature of California and U.S. society. Politics and policy are conditioned by underlying social and economic evolutions, even while they also contribute to the pattern of change, and can turn it or shape it at key moments, such as the Reagan ascendancy. Policy can set itself against the trend of the times, but this is difficult to sustain. Policy has greater potency when it taps into the mood and augments the ongoing flow of events. In the United States there has been a clear symbiosis—clear because it is visible in the economic data—between on one hand, the 1980 policy turn to diminished public goals and lower taxes for the rich and, on the other hand, rising inequality in the country. Since 1980 the growth in inequality of incomes and wealth has been remarkable, with major implications for the conditions, character, and potentials of public higher education. The rapidly growing inequality of the last thirty years, as much as anything, has pulled higher education away from the post–New Deal world, the world of Kennedy and Johnson, that Clark Kerr and his colleagues inhabited and served.

Trends in inequality are readily quantified only in relation to incomes and wealth. It is true that social mobility can be understood in other terms: for example, intergenerational patterns of occupational status or education. Status and income do not always coincide. For example, a successful public service career is more likely to bring high status than high income.[1] Nevertheless, it is difficult to define status in generic terms or to quantify status patterns over time. Income and wealth are easier to monitor. Income inequality is the aggregation of inequality of income from labor, at every level from the shop floor to the managing director's office, and inequality of income from capital in the form of financial holdings and property. More than 99 percent of people earn the majority of their incomes from labor. Both labor and capital incomes are affected by tax policy, which can both decrease and increase inequality.

The measurement of trends in income has become an active branch of economics. Thomas Piketty and others have shown that in the Anglo-American countries, the concentration of wealth and income in hands of the top 10 percent (one person in ten), the top 1 percent, the top 0.1 percent, and the top 0.01 percent (one in every ten thousand persons) has risen very considerably since 1980. The increase in income and wealth is particularly concentrated at the very top.[2] There is no debate on the empirical trend to greater inequality in the United States.[3] It is clear, dramatic, and unabated. Between 1980 and 2010 in the United States, the income share held by the top 0.1 percent of the income distribution rose from 2 percent to nearly 10 percent. Thomas Piketty finds that income from labor in the United States is now "about as unequally distributed as has ever been observed anywhere."[4] At the same time the inequality of wealth in the form of property and capital is "less extreme than the levels observed in traditional societies or in Europe in the period 1900–1910."[5] American earned incomes are now more unequal than in apartheid South Africa, or colonial India, or the slave-owning Southern states before the Civil War. This is a stunning development and one that explains much else that has happened in the country.

The analysis by Saez (2013) notes that the top 1 percent of income earners in the United States captured just over two-thirds of the total increase in incomes between 1993 and 2012, and 95 percent of the income gains made in the recovery after the recession, in 2009–2012.[6] In 2012 the income share of the top 10 percent, at more than 50 percent, was at its highest level since 1913; the income share of the top 1 percent, at 22.5 percent, had almost returned to its prerecession level of 2007, which was the highest level since 1928; the income share of the top 0.01 percent excluding capital gains was at its highest level since 1916, and its income share including capital gains was 5.5 percent, the second highest level on record, behind only the prerecession in 2007.[7] Since the 2008–2010 recession, capital incomes have only partly recovered but the salaries received by the top income earners have soared, reaching even higher levels than before the recession. At the same time, according to the 2014 OECD report *United States: Tackling High Inequalities*, between 2000 and 2010, the average income of the poorest 10 percent of Americans fell by 15 percent in real terms.[8]

In the United States the average income of the richest 10 percent is sixteen times the average income of the poorest 10 percent. This is the third highest ratio at those income levels among the OECD group of countries, behind only Mexico and Chile. The OECD average for that income ratio is 9.6. While the United States is third in average income in the OECD, it ranks only eighteenth in average income for people in the bottom 10 percent of the income distribution.[9] Piketty expects that by 2030, the top 1 percent income receivers in the United States will receive 25 percent of all income, compared to 20 percent in 2010, and the bottom 50 percent's share will fall from 20 to 15 percent,[10] greater inequality than today.

The broad trend lines in California resemble those in the nation, except that income inequality in California has become more extreme than in the nation as a whole, in contrast to the state's relatively egalitarian income distribution at earlier times. California now has the nation's largest concentration of wealth and its highest incidence of poverty. In the year 1928, the top 1 percent of income recipients in California held 20.0 percent of all income, compared to 23.4 percent in the nation as a whole. At that time the West was more egalitarian than the country. In 1979 in California, after two decades of the Master Plan, only 10.2 percent of income accrued to the top 1 percent, just above the national level of 9.9 percent. But in 2007, just before the recession, the level in California had jumped to 22.7 percent compared to a national level of 21.8 percent. The gap between California and the whole nation has now increased further. In the three years after 2009, following the recession triggered in 2008, *all* income growth in California accrued to the top 1 percent of persons in income distribution terms; this was also the case in sixteen other states. The incomes of the top 1 percent in California rose by 49.6 percent in the recession years 2009–2012, which was the fourth largest such increase in the nation. Meanwhile, the incomes of the bottom 99 percent dropped by 3.0 percent.[11] Overall, between 1979 and 2012, which were the years of growing inequality in the country as a whole, the top 1 percent in California increased their incomes by 189.5 percent, while the income of the bottom 99 percent fell by 6.3 percent.[12]

In 2008–2011 in California the ratio between the average household income for the richest 20 percent of households and the poorest 20 percent was 9.5, the third highest ratio after New Mexico and Arizona.[13] Over the three-year period 2011 to 2013, California included 8.871 million persons with an income below the U.S. Census Bureau's Supplemental Poverty Line, one sixth of all such Americans, constituting 23.4 percent of persons in the state—the highest poverty level of any state in the nation.[14] Tami Luhby compares California's Silicon Valley, where residents have "the highest level of well-being in the nation," with average incomes almost double the national average and nearly triple the average number of graduate degrees, with the state's Central Valley less than a hundred miles away, where residents have the nation's lowest level of well-being. Average incomes for single parents with two children are close to the poverty line, and nearly four in ten persons fail to graduate from high school.[15]

How do the trends in the California and the United States compare with those in other countries? In the United Kingdom between 1980 and 2010, the income share of the top 1 percent moved from 6 to 15 percent, the highest level since the 1930s. In Canada it was 12 percent in 2010; in Australia it was 10 percent.[16] The other English-speaking countries have also seen the growth of high salaries and a concentration of wealth at the top, but the top American salaries are extreme in comparative terms.

As this suggests, it is helpful to place American inequality in the larger historical and geographic contexts. In the Nordic countries in the 1970s, the most equal modern societies, the top 1 percent received about 7 percent of all income. In Europe in 2010, the top 1 percent received 10 percent of income. In the United States in 2010 the top 1 percent received 20 percent, the same level as in the aristocrat-led societies of late-nineteenth-century Europe (table 19.1). However, in 2010 the top 1 percent in the United States achieved its 20 percent of income more through labor income and less through capital than was the case in old Europe. The more modern form of salary-based inequality is legitimated by an element of merit: it is the product of hard work, not just property and capital, though as elite graduate recruitment shows (see chapter 20), competition for top labor incomes is not a level playing field.

At present, measured economic inequality is increasing in about two-thirds of countries around the world. The most striking changes have been the explosive growth of managerial salaries in the United States and United Kingdom, and to a lesser degree in other English-speaking countries, Western Europe, and Japan. In Japan the maintenance of traditional work-based relativities has been a partial brake on increased inequality. The average Japanese chief executive officer is paid sixteen times the average worker in the same corporation, whereas in the United States this ratio is now about 200 times.[17]

The earlier argument that growing wage inequality in the United States is primarily driven by technological change has fallen from favor. Most industrialized countries have undergone similar technological change, but they have divergent income patterns.[18] In the United States the main incidence of inequality is at the top end of the wage structure and centered on managers, especially in certain industries.[19] Piketty calls the United States a "hypermeritocratic society," or at least, "a society that the people at the top like to describe as hypermeritocratic. . . . This is a very inegalitarian society, but one in which the peak of the income hierarchy is dominated by very high incomes from labor rather than by inherited wealth."[20] Almost two-thirds of the top 0.1 percent of income earners are managers. Only about 5 percent are actors, artists, or athletes.[21]

Much of "supersalary" development is taking place in the finance sector.[22] Finance has double the proportion of very high salaries that its growing share of economic production would suggest.[23] Managers often set their own performance-related

TABLE 19.1. Income shares of top 1 percent and bottom 50 percent, United States and Europe

	Europe 1910: High inequality	Scandinavia 1970–80s: Low inequality	Europe 2010: Medium-high inequality	USA 2010: High inequality
TOP 1% BY INCOME				
share of labor income	6%	5%	7%	12%
share of capital income	50%	20%	25%	35%
share of total income	20%	7%	10%	20%
BOTTOM 50% BY INCOME				
share of labor income	n.a.	35%	30%	20%
share of capital income	5%	10%	5%	5%
share of total income	20%	30%	25%	20%

Source: Adapted by author from data from Piketty 2014, pp. 247–249.
n.a. = data not available.

remuneration, including bonuses, or negotiate that remuneration with boards of like-minded folk and on which they themselves may sit.[24] Again, this is inequality in a more modern, quasi-meritocratic form, centered on control over work rather than on property and inheritance, legitimated by the performance pay concept,[25] and normatively grounded in the "shareholder value conception of the firm" in which managers are seen to contribute disproportionately to value.[26] With part of their remuneration usually tied to stock options, cementing the association between management and shareholder value, supermanagers can be both supermanagers and medium rentiers at the same time.[27] In the next generation, when today's supermanager salary and managerial stock holdings have metamorphosed into tomorrow's inheritance, more traditional forms of inequality will return to front rank. The 1960s vision of the educated-selected meritocracy will recede further. Inherited inequality is more difficult to challenge and change.

In the United States, salary inequality is partly balanced by the patrimonial middle class, especially by widespread middle-class home ownership. However, the middle-class share of wage and salary income is down, savings ratios have fallen, and debt has risen;[28] moreover, the market value of many homes fell sharply in the 2008–2010 recession. Joseph Stiglitz states that average value declined by more than one-third as a result of the recession, and between 2005–2009 the average African American household lost 53 percent of its wealth, while the average Hispanic household lost 66 percent.[29] The overall position of the "middle-middle" and lower-middle classes seems to be declining, with implications also for social mobility. This decline reduces the number of positions in the middle of society that the upwardly mobile can occupy, and with less opportunity in the middle of society, it is harder to move through to the top. Socially, the United States is now less democratic than Europe. "The chances that a poor, or even middle class American will make it to the top in America are smaller than in many countries of Europe," says Stiglitz.[30] In the future, American society will almost certainly become more closed at the top, with less mobility into and within the elite, while income shares continue to decline at the middle and bottom of the pyramid.

Piketty's argument is that inequality is not self-correcting. The tendencies to inequality and to the attenuation of social mobility are endogenous to the capitalist economy, so that inequality increases over time—unless the state uses education policy, income distribution and taxation policy, welfare and spending on social programs, and infrastructure to sustain a democratic balance, as in the Nordic world:

> A market economy based on private property, if left to itself, contains powerful forces of convergence, associated in particular with the diffusion of knowledge and skills, but it also contains powerful forces of divergence, which are potentially threatening to democratic societies and to the values of social justice on which they are based.[31]

PLUTOCRATIC CAPTURE

In the Ronald Reagan years and after, instead of maintaining a balance between the endogenous trend to inequality and the state-protected value of each individual, U.S. policy allowed inequality to let rip. The trend was political as well as economic. The two aspects reinforced each other. Government not only stopped compensating, through its tax and spending policies, for the natural tendency to inequality, but it deliberately nurtured the high-income earners, moving policy and regulation decisively in their favor. In turn, by deregulating financial management and cutting taxation, government more fully released endogenous market forces. These processes became self-reproducing. The resulting lopsided accumulation of wealth further strengthened the constituencies that supported deregulation, low tax, and the lesser expectations about government.

The 1980s triumph of the rich in the political sphere turned into something more permanent. Societies that are relatively static in terms of social mobility, in which social elites are concentrating their economic power, are vulnerable to the plutocratic capture of politics. Plutocratic capture brings with it the more permanent adoption of political ideologies and fiscal and monetary policies that are crafted to advance the interests of the elite. Arguably, this is what has happened in the United States, as also in the United Kingdom.[32]

The effects of the 1980s transformation of polity and policy have continued to accumulate. The mid 2010s United States is radically different from the country in which Clark Kerr did his work and higher education was unequivocally defined as a public good. The problem of plutocratic capture of the American polity is now routinely discussed in scholarship and research on inequality.[33] It is noted by mainstream global policy agencies such as the OECD,[34]which seek a reduction in inequality on the grounds that high levels of inequality undermine economic growth and also social cohesion.[35] Plutocratic capture also preoccupies global non-governmental agencies, such as Oxfam, whose work is focused on development and poverty reduction:

> A recent study presents compelling statistical evidence that the preferences of wealthy Americans are overwhelmingly represented in their government, compared with those of the middle classes. By contrast, the preferences of the poorest people demonstrate no statistical impact on the voting patterns of their elected officials. If this trend continues, public policies will most likely reproduce the conditions that are worsening economic inequality and political marginalization.[36] . . .

Oxfam notes that in 2010, President Obama signed into law the Wall Street Reform and Consumer Protection Act (known as the Dodd-Frank Bill). The objective was to regulate financial markets to protect the economy from a future crash. "However, the financial industry has spent more than \$1 billion on hundreds of lobbyists to weaken and delay the Act's full implementation. In fact, in 2012 the top five consumer protection groups sent 20 lobbyists to defend Dodd-Frank, while the top five finance industry groups sent 406 to defeat it." By 2014 only 148 of the 398 Dodd-Frank rules had been finalized, and the financial system remained just as vulnerable to crash as it was in 2008.[37]

Plutocratic capture explains why economic outcomes and economic policies that are deeply unpopular are maintained. Stiglitz cites poll evidence which suggests that "there are large discrepancies between what most people want and what the political system delivers";[38] that 61 percent of Americans believe the economic system favors the wealthy, and only 36 percent think it is fair;[39] and that while few have a clear picture of the current extent of economic inequality, when offered a range of differing descriptions of the economy, people overwhelmingly prefer the Swedish income distribution to that of the United States, by a ratio of 92 percent to 8 percent.[40] Research by Jeremy Reynolds and He Xian on attitudes towards the social order in the United States found that young upper-class whites were the most likely to see the nation as a place where meritocratic relationships determine social outcomes. Older people from low-SES ethnic minorities were more likely than others to believe that family and social networks determine outcomes, rather than study and hard work. Between the 2009 and 2011 surveys, faith in the meritocratic domain declined.[41] It can be confidently predicted that such faith will decline further in future.

The process of plutocratic capture has been linked to financial deregulation and the reciprocally associated "financialization" of the economy, meaning the quantitative and qualitative increase in the economic weight of the finance sector.[42] According to Jon Wisman, "financial stocks grew from six percent of the stock markets' total value in the early 1980s to 23 percent by 2006."[43] Finance received

40 percent of total profit in the Unites States just before the 2008 crash.[44] The political sway and regulatory role of private banks and other financial organizations have been advanced in a symbiosis between central government regulation and private finance. Stiglitz argues that the Fed and parallel regulatory agencies such as the Bank of England are too close to the private banks.[45] With a handful of exceptions, such as Lehmann's in 2008, the leading financial players are protected at almost any cost. This neatly encapsulates the social priorities of the post-Reagan public authorities. Stiglitz notes that the $180 billion used to bail out AIG during the recession was greater than the total federal allocation to the welfare of the poor for the whole period 1990–2006.[46]

The ongoing effects of plutocratic capture of the polity are well illustrated by tax policy. As noted, the dominant aspect of tax policy since 1980 has been to advance and protect the position of higher-income earners. The debate has not been about whether to do this; it has it has been about how far to go. The top marginal income tax rate in the United States moved from 70 percent under President Jimmy Carter to 28 percent under Ronald Reagan, back to 39.6 percent under Bill Clinton, and down to 35 percent under George W. Bush. It rose again under Barack Obama but only to the Clinton level of 39.6 percent. The lion's share of the Reagan reduction in the top rate remained in place. Nor have all the tax reductions taken place under Republican administrations. Clinton's tuition tax credits, which were maintained by all his successors, are socially regressive. As a proportion of income, they benefit high-income earners more than low-income earners. In addition, the tax rate on unearned income such as property and equity, once greater than the tax rate on earned income, has been reduced below the income tax rate. This is a another gift for the wealthiest 0.1 percent, who draw the majority of income from this source.[47] Capital gains tax was taken down to 20 percent under Clinton and 15 percent under Bush.[48] Across the world, countries are competing for capital by lowering taxes on capital income or exempting it altogether,[49] separating the wealthy from the tax/spend/services economy that engages other citizens. The objective is to stem the flow of monies into the offshore havens that now absorb at least 10 percent of the world's wealth, and probably much more.[50] However, the procapital stance has been taken further in the United States than in many nations. For one year, George W. Bush even abolished the estate tax.

In the United States, market-generated inequality as such is not appreciably greater than in many other OECD countries. It is only when taxation and government transfers are included in the comparison that the full extent of comparative American inequality is revealed.[51] The change is manifest not just in income distribution but in the political culture. Since 1980 the Republican Party has been closely shaped by an antistatist and antitaxation position, with candidates for office differing only in the extremes to which they will take that position. Though the Democrats are seen as the party of government and maintain a formal commitment to ideas of redistribution and welfare, the parties are not as far apart as this would suggest. Both sides of politics are disciplined by lobbyists, campaign funding, and the potential for capital flight. A less aggressive version of the antitax posture of public choice theory and the tax revolt is mandatory in mainstream American politics. It would seem exceptionally difficult for any political party to take government without conforming to the finance-sector policy template, including continued financial deregulation and low taxation.

Given the elite capture of the polity, the main directions of education policy are easier to understand. Social elites mostly do not use common public services and have no intrinsic interest in their improvement, still less in paying for those services (unless members of the elite are altruistic, contradicting public choice theory).[52] Genuine equality of opportunity would broaden the pool of competitors for position. Elite families have an intrinsic interest in a controlled form of educational competition and the ranking of educational institutions, providing that this competition rewards families with starting advantages. When higher education is a positional competition, wealthy families can better protect their interests within a segmented hierarchy in which the direct competitors are limited. They can advance their position though tailored and selective investments while protecting their children from all-inclusive mixing. The downward pressure on state spending and neglect of public schools in poor districts; the federal subsidization of for-profit colleges despite low quality and poor student completion rates and the support for the for-profit corporations on both sides of the aisle while community colleges are neglected[53] (the exception is the Obama presidency, which struggled with Congress to promote community colleges and limit for-profit subsidies); the student loan policies tailored to the interests of commercial lenders, not students or access objectives; the tuition tax breaks; the legislative protection of Ivy League universities that service the richest 0.1 percent—these are all minor aspects of the much larger elite political project.

Yet these developments in higher education not only violate the goal of equality of opportunity, they undermine the meritocratic potential of 1960s human capital theory. Part I reflected on the important part played by higher education in American society in the more meritocratic 1950s–1970s era, when relatively open social structures were combined with growing social opportunities. Since 1980, amid the conditions of a reduced role of government, an increasingly cynical and commercialized polity, and a more unequal social order, the economic and social potentials of public higher education have been more limited.

20

Unequal Opportunity

The Dream Is Over will now look more closely at the mechanisms of social distribution in higher education, particularly at the relationship between economic and social inequality and inequality in and through higher education—and the way in which the equality-inequality equation has worsened since the era of the Master Plan in the 1960s.

The primary intrinsic limit to equality of opportunity objectives in any era is the persistence of irreducible differences between families in their economic, social, and cultural resources. Policy can partly compensate for economic differences but can scarcely eliminate the potency of the family in cultural capital and social networks,[1] and as competition intensifies, these effects are heightened. The impact of inequalities in family position could be fundamentally reduced only by shifting the locus of social selection away from educational merit and the education/career nexus, switching the efforts of families into a new domain of social competition. (No doubt modern education is preferable to warrior rituals and simulated battlegrounds.)

Economist John Roemer finds that parents influence outcome for children in three ways: social connections that facilitate access to education and jobs, family culture and investments affecting skills and motivation/aspirations, and the "genetic transmission of ability."[2] The last is arguable, but the first two are supported by a large body of research that points to the impact of inequalities in the family on patterns of school performance prior to higher education, on access to selective education, on the transition to labor markets, and on career performance. The broad effect of post-1980 policy has been not so much to create inequality in these domains as to exacerbate that potential and diminish the compensating factors.

In mid-secondary school, aspirations to enter higher education are very broadly spread, but the capacity to enter and graduate is socially differentiated, especially the capacity to enter selective institutions. Students from low socioeconomic-status (SES) backgrounds or in remote locations tend to underestimate their academic potential. They are also less willing to take risks, more likely to focus explicitly on secure and highly paid employment, more concerned to secure a predictable pathway from study to job, and more likely to be concerned that they may be lacking the necessary cultural capital. They are also less familiar with performance and application strategies. These problems arise not just in countries where there are tuition barriers and lofty elite universities; they arise also in free Nordic higher education systems, where all college degrees carry significant status.[3] In the United States these difficulties could be partly overcome by extensive identification and tailored assistance to ensure that no bright, hard-working student from a poorer background is allowed to miss out. Instead the practical operations of American higher education tend to magnify family inequality, and more so now than in the heyday of the Master Plan.

As noted in part 1, Soares reports that in 1988 to 2000, 64 percent of the students of Tier 1 institutions in the United States were from the richest 10 percent of households.[4] Given the potency of Tier 1 institutions in American society, this is a primary indicator of inequality. Socially unequal entry into Tier 1 is not due solely to unequal preparation at school level. First, it is affected by prior economic inequalities. Access to elite private universities is moderated by high tuition, which since 1990 has risen much faster than inflation. The average income of Harvard parents is $450,000, corresponding to the top 2 percent of Americans. Admissions decisions are also affected by the legacy factor (children of Ivy League alumni inherit a quasi right to enter) and parental donations. Piketty notes that such donations peak during the college years. "Such a finding does not seem entirely compatible with the idea of selection based solely on merit. The contrast between the official meritocratic discourse and the reality seems particularly extreme in this case. The total absence of transparency regarding selection procedures should also be noted."[5]

Second, as this suggests, socially stratified entry is also affected by the use of nonacademic criteria at the point of entry into elite institutions. In Ivy League institutions, the use of nonacademic criteria that favor the white upper-middle class, such as culturally specific extracurricular activities and evidence of leadership qualities, is well documented and a source of recurring controversy and debate, in part because it weakens the academic mission.[6] Equality of opportunity is further stymied by informal quotas limiting the number of Asian Americans in prestige universities, despite superior performance and, in many cases, possession of the required extracurricular attributes as well.[7] Even within the upper strata, merit is not necessarily honored, however defined. Nevertheless, private colleges are under less pressure than public institutions to honor principles of social access and fairness. Equality of opportunity is a public charge, and, if necessary, public institutions must compensate for inequalities generated by investment in the private sector and by the manipulation of its criteria and processes for entry in favor of certain families.

Third, the larger problem, affecting entry to public research universities as well as select private institutions, is inequality of information and aspiration. On the basis of a census-level study of all applicants to higher education in the United States published in 2013, Caroline Hoxby and Christopher Avery identify high-achieving school students and track their application behaviors.[8] "'High-achieving' refers to a student who scores at or above the 90th percentile on the ACT comprehensive or the SAT I (math and verbal) and who has a high school grade point average of A− or above. This is approximately 4 percent of U.S. high school students."[9] They find the vast majority of low-income high achievers at school do not apply to any selective college, although selective colleges offer them lower tuition prices than many nonselective colleges, due to the availability of generous financial aid packages.[10] Hoxby and Avery note that there is a large talent pool of low-income high achievers at school: "We estimate that there are at least 25,000 and probably about 35,000 low-income high achievers in each cohort in the United States."[11]While school achievement is not distributed proportionately across the population, 22 percent of all high achievers are in the second family-income quartile and 17 percent are in the bottom quartile. Ensuring that these low-income high achievers are identified and supported should be a central concern if equality of opportunity is to be upheld.

The researchers found that the application behavior of most low-income high achievers differs greatly from that of their high-income counterparts with similar achievement. The latter generally follow experts' advice to apply to several "peer," a few "reach," and a couple of "safety" colleges. Most low-income high achievers opt for more uniformly safe choices.

Hoxby and Avery separate the low-income high achievers into those whose application behavior is similar to that of their high-income counterparts ("achievement-typical") and those who apply to no selective institutions ("income-typical"). Income-typical students are not more disadvantaged than the achievement-typical students. However, in contrast to the achievement-typical students, who are often concentrated in poor districts of large cities, the income-typical students tend to come from districts too small to support selective public high schools,[12] are not in a critical mass of fellow high achievers, and are unlikely to encounter a teacher, a counselor, or a student who has attended a selective college. Widely used policies to recruit such students, such as college admissions recruiting, campus visits, and college mentoring programs, are mostly ineffective with the income-typical students.[13] However, it can be argued that the selective colleges should not be expected to solve the problem of "under-matching" by themselves[14] and that it is the responsibility of states, public schools, and higher education to identify and nurture these students.

Once students apply, "there is no statistically significant difference" in the probability of high-income and low-income students enrolling "or in their progress toward a degree."[15] So it is likely that high-achieving students who do not apply for flagship universities and other selective schools simply miss out on any learning and labor market benefits that would follow. Hoxby and Avery also make the point that on the basis of the data in their study, if a student is from an underrepresented minority, such as African American, Hispanic, or First Nations American, that "is not a good proxy for his or her being low-income." Therefore, "if a college wants its student body to exhibit income diversity commensurate with the income diversity among high achievers," it would not necessarily attain this goal simply by recruiting students who are members of underrepresented minorities. This would create a student body diverse in terms of ethnicity but not necessarily as diverse in terms of income.[16]

In another large-scale study in 2013, in the United Kingdom, Vikki Boliver[17] finds continued and dramatic differences in social group access to elite universities: "Applicants from lower class backgrounds and from state schools remained much less likely to apply to Russell Group universities than their comparably qualified counterparts from higher class backgrounds and private schools." Those "schooled in the state sector remain just half as likely to apply to a Russell Group university as those from private schools."[18] UK students must file applications before their final school results are known, which tends to increase what Hoxby and Avery call "undermatching."[19] Boliver refers to widespread perceptions among the underrepresented groups that prestige universities belong to the privately educated white upper-middle class. When education is seen to belong to someone else, aspirations and agency are automatically diminished.[20] In addition, "Russell Group applicants from state schools and from Black and Asian ethnic backgrounds remained much less likely to receive offers of admission from Russell Group universities, in comparison with their equivalently qualified peers from private schools and the White ethnic group." That is, students from underrepresented groups are less likely to get in when they have the same marks as students from overrepresented groups. As with Ivy League admissions in the United States, factors other than academic merit affect entry and render more unrepresentative the social makeup of the student body in the elite subsector.[21]

STRATIFICATION OF OPPORTUNITIES

As discussed in part 2, all national higher education systems are structured hierarchically, based on formal and informal distinctions between institutions, though the steepness of the hierarchy, the vertical stratification between institutions, varies by country. As systems expand, institutions tend to become further differentiated between or within subsectors on the basis of unequal value. System structures—such as the American classification system that demarcates research-intensive universities and elite liberal arts colleges from other institutions—act as a framing device in allocating people to opportunities. This operates as a second limitation to the potential for equality of opportunity, additional to and intersecting with the inequality of starting position in families.

A number of recent studies find the positional structure of American higher education is being further stretched vertically. The difference between the value of higher education in a highly selective college and in a nonselective college is greater than before. This difference shows in the levels of resources that support the different kinds of institution, the levels of esteem in which the respective institutions are held, and the power of the credentials in later life. There seems to be more at stake in decisions about where students are placed. As in the national structure of income distribution, so in higher education: value is being concentrated at the top end, increasing demand for the leading institutions, alongside a hollowing out of value in and demand for access to middle-level institutions and growing problems of low demand or noncompletion at the bottom end. In 1996 Robert Frank and Philip Cook published a book on winner-take-all markets, markets in which a small number of players dominate the game, commanding much higher revenues than the overwhelming majority of players. They described elite American higher education as one such market.[22] In 2011 Hal Hansen found that selectivity was becoming more intense in top-level institutions and declining below them. In resources, there was a nearly ten-to-one, and still widening, differential between the highest and lowest ranking schools on annual per capita student-oriented resources: "spending on instruction, student services, academic support, and operation and maintenance of facilities." The gap was mostly due to "spending growth by the top ten percent of schools . . . rather than dramatic changes in the rest." There was also "a growing hierarchization and homogenization of schools' student bodies." The "educational and networking advantages that accrue from peer interaction at schools in the top ten percent" were rising, and those advantages were falling in other schools, indicating stratification of outcomes and value.[23]

The observations about increased vertical stretch and the concentration of status and resources at the top were confirmed by Scott Davies and David Zarifa. They used Gini coefficients, Lorenz curves, and other measures of inequality to compare "the level of stratification in financial resources across four-year institutions in Canada and the United States over a 35-year period (1971–2006)."[24] Like Hansen, they found that the vertical stretch of higher education in both countries has increased. Davies and Zarifa report moderate to strong associations between resource concentration and selectivity in both the United States and Canada.

"Resource-rich institutions are . . . likely to use their resources to attract higher-ranked students through scholarships, financial aid, teaching quality, and general reputation. While these data cannot determine causal direction, they suggest that financial and cognitive resources co-vary across institutions in both countries."[25] Davies and Zarifa also found that in both countries, competitive markets are driving this increased vertical stretch, signified by resource concentration.[26] "Change in stratification may be triggered by policy environments that are subjecting universities to greater competition for revenue, whether in the form of tuition-paying clients, fund-raising, or research grants, and that are offering less bountiful and reliable government support."[27] They note that policy makers in both countries want universities "to remake themselves into highly differentiated, competitive, responsive, and entrepreneurial hubs of activity" by competing for research funds, fund-raising, seeking corporate partnerships and building tuition revenues. "These pressures are particularly acute for public universities, for whom the "golden years" of large and untargeted government subsidies are receding into the past."[28] New survival strategies are emerging.

> Established universities are competing ever-more tenaciously for "star" researchers. . . . Relative newcomers are devising strategies to move up the ranks. At lower levels in the hierarchy, institutions are seeking niches in vocational programming in order to survive, a process resembling the "anticipatory subordination" pursued earlier by community colleges. And, near the bottom reaches, for-profit and online colleges have emerged as major competitors for non-traditional students.[29]

The competition for status and resources is articulated through a tendency to cumulative advantage, a Matthew effect. Over time, top institutions leverage their advantages in resources and status to compound their relative position, all else equal. "Universities that are already older, established and wealthy enter new competitions for resources with prominent alumni networks, sizeable endowments, favorable locations, and strategic corporate ties," observe Davies and Zarifa. "These near-exclusive assets each offer an edge for attracting new corporate partnerships, lucrative research contracts, and donors with deep pockets." Colleges unable to compete with the strongest "brands" often devise niche strategies or develop new products and new markets, occupying a subordinate niche that confirms system segmentation.[30] One example is the market of working people who were school dropouts, which has been cultivated by the for-profits. This is happening in the flatter Canadian system as well as the United States. In Canada, "as elsewhere around the globe, Canadian policy makers are using market language to urge universities to expand, differentiate, compete and innovate. . . . Most provinces now permit private universities and colleges to operate, and some may push for a more explicitly tiered system. The leaders of top research universities have openly expressed their wishes to emulate elite U.S. schools."[31]

The study also found that the United States system is much more unequal than the Canadian system: "Along key measures such as total income and total expenditures the U.S. system is strikingly more stratified. Some American coefficients more than double their Canadian counterparts. . . . The Canadian system has a modicum of parity across institutions."[32] (One exception is the degree of inequality in U.S. public universities in income from tuition and spending on scholarships, prizes, and student grants. In these areas, inequality in U.S. public universities is similar to the pattern in their Canadian equivalents.[33]) U.S. higher education is "a hierarchical system dominated by a small number of super-resourced, elite institutions that are highly distinct from the masses." In contrast, "Canadian distributions are clearly stratified, but are far less skewed and more normally distributed." In the United States, "the private sector is much more skewed and contains a longer trail of upper outliers compared to the public sector." The U.S. public sector is also clearly more stratified than the Canadian equivalent. Over time, "the U.S. figures show an increasing separation of upper outliers from the rest. . . . Elite institutions have not only maintained their advantages, but have pulled away from the pack."[34]

Davies and Zarifa conclude that "these findings provide new and compelling evidence of increasing structural stratification in higher education. They are a likely outcome of a combination of social forces, including new competitive strategies among universities, academic capitalism, the spreading influence of rankings, and greater concentrations of top-ranked students among universities, among others."[35] The growing inequality of value between high-tier institutions and other institutions in itself worsens inequality of social opportunity in education. Elite higher education is a prize largely out of reach of students from poor backgrounds. The relative value of the prize has grown. In zero-sum social competition, the more social value that is centered on the top institutions, the less value that is left to be carried by mass higher education institutions, and the benefits of mass access start to empty out. It is only when the total sum of social opportunity is growing, as amid the high economic growth and more open class structure of 1960s, that enrollment in both elite and mass institutions seems to bring with it growing benefits.

In short, since Clark Kerr's leadership in California, equality of opportunity has advanced in one respect and diminished in another. The expansion of participation in American higher education has coincided with the evolution of a steeper and more competitive educational hierarchy. On one hand, there is much greater social inclusion than in the 1960s and in that respect enhanced equality of opportunity. On the other hand, there is less equality of opportunity because of the exclusionary effects of stratification and the tendency for the value of two-year college diplomas to empty out. Greater social equality at the boundary between participation and nonparticipation has become combined with lessening social equality inside higher education. The first effect tends to mask the second, but in the longer run, the reduction of value in mass higher education—which, as shall be discussed, affects both public institutions and for-profit private institutions—tends to undermine participation itself. It reduces the desire to enter higher education and weakens the rate at which students complete.

This tendency for value to concentrate at the top of higher education systems is not just an outcome of policy or rankings or the behaviors of entrepreneurial university presidents. It is partly a product of the growth of participation itself—or more specifically, the inevitable manner in which expansion interacts with the use of higher education by social groups with unequal resources. As noted in part 2, as participation grows, elite enrollments expand more slowly than total numbers. Ultimately, this is because the number of leading positions in society grows only slowly. The ratio increases between "client-seeking" mass higher education institutions and "status-seeking" elite higher education institutions, as in the growth projections of the 1960 Master Plan. With the shrinkage in the proportion of student places with high value, social selection becomes more fiercely concentrated in the elite sector, in the winner-take-all effect, and also plays out in the feeder schools that are strongest in entry to the top universities. Only some families can readily play this game. The fact that American expansion in itself has not led to greater equality of opportunity is not particularly surprising. This is not a unique product of America's highly unequal society and education. Though structural configurations vary across all countries, the great bulk of the research on the growth of participation suggests that expansion has not been associated with a reduction in class (socioeconomic) inequalities in rates of access to or graduation from high-value institutions unless policy forcibly intervenes.[36] This is because everywhere, strong social groups work educational structures in their favor. In addition, in the United States after 1980, and more so after 2008, in the recovery from recession, the natural tendency of the socially stronger to become educationally stronger was exacerbated by the political economy.

As systems grow and reach universal levels of participation in schooling and later, in tertiary education, "qualitative differentiation replaces inequalities in the quantity of the education obtained."[37] First, the key moment of social selection moves up, from schooling to access to higher education or from first degree to second degree. Second, at this key moment, the population passing through unequally ranked institutions undergoes social sorting through such mechanisms as the capacity to pay tuition. These structures differentiate the population along unequal social lines. This is the nearest thing to an iron law in the sociology of education: whenever there is a structured hierarchy of value—for example, between state and private schools, between different tiers or types of institutions, between high costs and low cost institutions, or between fields of study—families with prior social advantages are best placed to compete for the places that carry the most positional advantages.[38] This is the inexorable logic of competition. As Davies and Zarifa showed in their study of institutions, when the competitors are unequal at the start of the game, the game favors those in the strongest starting position. Samuel Lucas states that "socioeconomically advantaged actors secure for themselves and their children some degree of advantage wherever advantages are commonly possible."[39] Therefore, "meaningful inequality reduction is elusive because qualitatively different types of education maintain consequential inequality, even at universal transitions."[40] In the words of Arum and colleagues, structural differentiation allows the elite status of those families "born into privilege" to be protected.[41] Social differentiation is matched to structural differentiation in education, unless public policy intervenes to alter the matching process by spreading resources, evening up the starting position of poorer families. This creates an obstacle to "would-be egalitarian reformers."[42]

In any society, when socially advantaged groups are free to compete with all the political and economic resources at their disposal, they always play the structures to their further advantage. This not only shapes the pattern of social access to higher education, it also affects the pattern of outcomes in the graduate labor market. In general, as Triventi argues: "All else being equal, the higher the stratification of higher education, the more important is the role of social background in the occupational attainment process."[43] However, this general rule can be modified by various factors. For example Borgen notes that when college credentials are relatively generic, as is the case in the United States and Norway, all else being equal, that makes the hierarchy of institutions more important as a distinguishing factor in sorting the graduate population.[44] It is significant that the point applies to both the market-driven, highly stratified, and mixed-funded U.S. system and the publicly financed and relatively "flat" Norwegian system, indicating that it functions as another general rule across systems. A third general rule relates to financial barriers to entry. Tuition systems tend to accentuate prior social differences, as do private higher education institutions, which are free to pick and choose their clientele:[45] indeed, for some of these institutions, social selection is part of their mission. Note that the use of the income-contingent tuition loans mechanism (see the final chapter of this book), as in the United Kingdom and Australia, tends to soften the socioeconomic bias in tuition. Nevertheless, even free higher education would not resolve all problems of inequality. As Piketty remarks, "social and cultural selection" can do the same work as financial selection.[46]

The various national case studies provided by Yossi Shavit, Richard Arum, and Adam Gamoram in their 2007 collection illustrate the interplay between system structure and social opportunity.[47] In relation to the United Kingdom, Sin Yi Cheung and Muriel Egerton state that although students from unskilled and semiskilled parental backgrounds have made access gains, these have largely been manifest in the second-tier institutions, and "class inequalities were especially persistent in the more selective forms of higher education,"[48] which confirms the separate findings by Boliver.[49] The independent private school sector in the United

Kingdom and stratification between state schools are primary in maintaining social inequality in access.[50] In Israel, second-tier institutions are disproportionately occupied by less privileged students, allowing the universities "to maintain exclusivity."[51] In South Korea also, expansion has been concentrated in lower-tier institutions.[52] The study of Sweden makes the point that, as also demonstrated by Hoxby and Avery, national populations are not only differentiated by structures; they also tend to self-differentiate through them, whether deliberately or inadvertently. In Sweden there has been a dramatic expansion of total tertiary participation but only a modest improvement in the social equality of odds of enrollment. "The reason for the limited effect is that new educational opportunities are to a large extent used by middle-class students with mediocre grades but high educational aspirations."[53] As in the United States, Swedes from disadvantaged backgrounds have lower sights in relation to both the propensity to enroll and the tier that they occupy.[54] The Swedish case finds that "social forces" other than educational expansion are more efficient in reducing social inequalities in educational attainment, including "developments towards greater equality of condition and reforms that made the Swedish educational system less stratified."[55] But a threshold level of trust and equality of respect is needed to establish and maintain such educational and social systems.[56]

In the same collection of papers, in their case study of the United States, Josipa Roksa and colleagues focus on the combination of firm segmentation in the classified higher education system and the "increased enrollments in lower status institutions." The "solidification of institutional hierarchies has produced a highly stratified system."[57] Expansion plus relative growth in community colleges may increase inequality in degree-level higher education even as it improves equality in access below that level.[58] "The benefits of attending community colleges remain contested. They enroll disproportionate numbers of working class, female, minority and older students and they are accessible in local areas. Only about one-third of traditional age community college students earn an associate or bachelor's degree within eight years of completing high school." The channeling of enrollment into community colleges may hinder overall educational attainment by working class, female, minority and older students, "particularly the opportunities for earning bachelor's degrees."[59] From the point of view of equality of opportunity, the most positive American development is that African Americans and women have mobilized and gained recognition as "protected groups" in the nation's political discourse. They have made gains in access to higher education. Yet within these categories and also outside them, the poor and working class have not made equivalent gains in access.[60]

Roksa and colleagues confirm that while socioeconomic differences in total access have been fairly stable over the succeeding cohorts in their study, social stratification within higher education is increasing. In access to all four-year institutions and selective institutions, the advantages associated with a high socio-economic status (SES) background have been greater for recent cohorts. Whereas the influence of family background on educational opportunity decreased in the first half of the twentieth century, that trend stopped and reversed from the late 1970s onwards.[61] Again, it is apparent that the change towards increased inequality of opportunity coincided with the Reagan revolution's alteration of the balance between the free play of market forces and the common social good secured by public policy.

STRATIFICATION PLUS NETWORKS

Inequality of opportunity is not driven by structural forms alone, and does not have single causes. It involves agency, values, behavior, and relationships. Inequality in education is manifest where a number of the factors discussed above—family background, cultural capital, institutional stratification, social networking within elite structures, and networking between higher education and professional work—intersect with each other. Recent empirical studies explore these intersections.

In a series of papers, Lauren Rivera has summarized her doctoral research on the hiring practices of leading banks, consulting firms, and law firms in the Northeast United States.[62] The work is also published in *Pedigree: How Elite Students Get Elite Jobs* (2015).[63] Rivera argues that "understanding how elite employers recruit, assess, and select new hires can not only provide more nuanced understandings of the relationship between education and socioeconomic attainment but also inform broader debates about contemporary elite formation and reproduction."[64] She observes the movement of socially elite students into high-income-earning, elite labor markets, highlighting the role of elite educational credentials, cultural capital, and social networks. The world of elite professional recruitment, in which starting salaries are in the top 10 percent of total household incomes in the United States,[65] is far from equality of opportunity, or even educated merit as commonly understood.

Rivera's research is largely based on 120 interviews with those who sort the short lists, conduct interviews, and make hiring decisions. This includes human resource management professionals and the corporate professionals, partners, and managing directors who work with those they hire. Though they made some use of grades to establish thresholds, and some evaluators saw high grades as a sign of the capacity to successfully manage stress,[66] the firms studied by Rivera did not generally recruit on the basis of grades. Nor were their doors open to graduates from any walk of life. They recruited from selective colleges, but not just any selective college. Mostly they recruited solely from Harvard, Yale, Princeton, sometimes Stanford, and also Wharton at the MBA level. It was not the content of Ivy League education that they valued, but its prestige. They attributed superior qualities to these graduates simply because they were selected into top universities, regardless of academic performance once there.

> They largely believed that the status of a candidate's educational affiliation was a reflection of his/her intellectual, social, and moral worth, attributing superior cognitive and noncognitive abilities to students who attended super-elite (e.g., top four) institutions and assuming that those at merely "selective" (e.g., top twenty-five) schools had deficits in one or more of these areas.[67]

The second-level schools included Columbia and NYU,[68] while "so-called 'public Ivies' such as University of Michigan and Berkeley were not considered elite or even prestigious in the minds of evaluators (in contrast, these 'state schools' were frequently described pejoratively as 'safety schools' that were 'just okay')."[69] Rivera finds that "participants overwhelmingly believed the prestige of one's educational credentials was an indicator of underlying intelligence. Evaluators believed that educational prestige was a signal of general rather than job-specific skills, most notably the ability to learn quickly,"[70] and possession of the necessary "polish." Some evaluators also saw Ivy League graduates as likely to become "somebody" later in life, and hence more useful to the firm, whether working for it or not.[71] Rivera concludes that "these firms have created a stratified market for elite jobs based on institutional linkages between schools and employers that was previously thought to be minimal in the United States; one that serves to exclude the vast majority of degree holders nationally." Hence, she states, "contrary to scholarship and public discourse depicting the possession of a college degree as the gateway to economic mobility in the United States, the monetary conversion value of a degree varies by the status of the institution conferring it."[72] Ivy League admission as such is not enough. "A super-elite university affiliation was typically insufficient on its own for succeeding in resume screens. Importing the logic of elite university admissions, firms performed a strong secondary screen on the status and intensity of candidates' extracurricular activities, believing that leisure pursuits were valid markers of applicants' social and moral worth." In an era in which there is growing competition for places in higher education "the prestige requirements for elite jobs have intensified, and extracurricular activities now serve as a new credential of candidates' social and moral character."[73]

The focus on extracurricular credentials matched the use of a similar criterion in Ivy League selection. "Without significant and appropriate involvement in formalized leisure pursuits, candidates were unlikely to move to the interview stage." Such activities were used more often and more consistently to evaluate candidates than more traditional signals such as "grades, standardized test scores, prior employer prestige, or prior work experience." Candidates with such involvement were seen as "more interesting, enjoyable, and socially graceful people," rather than "bookish," solitary, or "nerdish," and also possessed of "superior time-management skills."[74] The recruiters "tended to favor those sports that had a strong presence at

Ivy League schools as well as pay-to-play 'club' sports such as lacrosse, field hockey, tennis, squash, and crew over ones that tend to be more widely accessible and/ or are associated with more diverse player bases such as football, basketball, and soccer."[75] This disadvantages poorer students who make it into elite colleges and have not spent a lifetime in the pursuits of the white upper and upper-middle class. "They favored activities that were time- and resource-intensive because the investment such cultivation entailed indicated stronger evidence of "drive" and an orientation towards "achievement" and "success." It was better to be a varsity college athlete, preferably a national or Olympic champion, rather than merely participating actively in sport, better to have "traveled the globe with a world-renowned orchestra as opposed to playing with a school chamber group," better to reach a Himalayan peak than engage in recreational hiking. "The former activities were evidence of 'true accomplishment' and dedication, whereas the latter were described as things that 'anyone could do.'"[76]

Final decisions were made in interviews, where notions of "fit" and "chemistry" were reported to be very important, and shared colleges and extracurricular interests tended to structure the conversation.[77] Rivera argues that these hiring practices, especially the narrow definition of prestige, do not reflect a close focus on efficiency and effectiveness—for example, little effort is made to gather data about the track record of candidates—but are about "similarity and culture."[78] Hiring is "a process of *cultural matching* between candidates, evaluators, and firms. Employers sought candidates who were not only competent but also culturally similar to themselves in terms of leisure pursuits, experiences, and self-presentation styles. Concerns about shared culture were highly salient to employers and often outweighed concerns about absolute productivity."[79] Cultural similarities operate as "more than just sources of liking; they are also fundamental bases on which we evaluate merit," states Rivera.[80] In a larger, more competitive, more stratified, and winner-take-all professional labor market, top-end recruitment is less about open and formal meritocratic competition and more about technologies that are used to assemble a coherent work group in which merit is reworked in terms of a common lifestyle, identity, and biography, without altogether losing its original connection with academic selection. Here merit is about reproduction of an elite tribe. "In essence, they evaluated candidates in a way that validated their own identities and legitimized their own educational trajectories and conceptions of success."[81]

In another paper, Rivera focuses on the limited impact of the diversity criterion in the hiring practices of these elite firms. She notes "widespread cultural beliefs among decision makers that university prestige is an essential signal of merit but that diversity is not."[82] Though most of her interviewees believed that their hiring processes were "race-neutral," blacks and Latinos were severely underrepresented compared to their presence in the population at large. A perceived lack of cultural capital was key, even for applicants with Ivy League credentials.

"Evaluators described how they felt many black and Latino candidates fell short on the dimension of 'polish,' or communication skills required in these client-facing jobs."[83]

Likewise, in a qualitative study of students at the University of Oxford and at Sciences Po in Paris, Gerbrand Tholen and colleagues show how the students use networked connections to secure entry to the upper echelons of the graduate labor market. One student distinguished between "good" and "bad" networks. Good networks are grounded in smarts and academic merit; bad networks are solely about family and ambition. "If the networks can be associated with hard work, the advantages supplied by it are morally acceptable, and thus the role of the elite university stays hidden."[84] The merit principle is still normative to some degree, but now it operates within restricted circles and is invoked selectively, where it legitimates elite trajectories, rather than underpinning whole-system organization. Once again we see the malleability of merit, the way it can be detached from formal processes at will and joined to various power structures and social arrangements. The idea of merit as ability plus hard work, once used to justify the displacement of leisured aristocrats, is now inscribed on the banners of a nouveau riche in formation, becoming as wealthy in turn. Here, educational merit is not the enemy of class. It has been annexed by class.

Gregory Wolniak and colleagues find that "education attainment mediates the effects that individuals' background characteristics have on their abilities to obtain high-paying and prestigious jobs." However, they suggest, "the mediating role of education attainment may differ by college major." The greatest status advantages go to graduates in fields "quantitative and scientifically oriented, fields that are more functionally linked to jobs, and fields that have traditionally been over-represented by men."[85] Majors affect not just placement on the social ladder but the degree of mobility and flexibility in graduate work, including later movement up the ladder. Majors also interact with family background in varying ways. "Our results suggest that, when viewed along a continuum, college majors are more or less meritorious based on the net effects of socioeconomic background characteristics (particularly family income) in comparison to the net effects of education attainment." The majors for which "pre-college family income had the greatest direct effect on earnings were Math/Computer Science/Engineering, and Science. . . . Majors for which education attainment had the greatest direct effect were Business, Science, and Education." In the case of Education majors, "socioeconomic background characteristics have uniquely small effects, while education attainment has a uniquely large effect on status."[86]

In a study published in 2015, Nicolai Borgen used Norwegian administrative data to map the intersection between parental background, institutional stratification, and career outcomes in creating unequal social outcomes through higher education. Borgen's contribution was to show that the role of family background is not momentary and partial—for example, operating at the point of access to higher education—but is holistic and continuous across the education and career continuum. He finds that students from advantaged families benefit most from elite colleges because they "are not only more likely to attend a high-quality college (the first filter), but are also more likely to convert their high-quality college education into success at the labor market (the second filter)."[87] This double-filter idea also helps to unlock the scholarly debate between "positive selection" and "negative selection" in higher education.

In research on higher education and social stratification, the economic positive selection hypothesis, which is close to orthodox human capital theory, states that students from socially advantaged backgrounds participate at the highest rate because they benefit the most from higher education. The negative selection hypothesis[88] says that students from underrepresented social groups—in the American context, low SES, remote location, African American, Hispanic—gain the most from higher education, compared to their compatriots who do not participate, even though these groups participate at the lowest rate. They do not earn more in the labor market than socially advantaged students, but they earn much more than their compatriots who do not attend.[89] The negative selection hypothesis helps to explain the continuing growth of participation in higher education at the margin in most countries, and it also explains why higher education is often unsatisfying for people from groups that habitually participate. They appear to gain less from it. "Advantaged young people place a uniformly high value on college,"[90] but "the decision to go to college among children from high-status families is dictated less by rational choice and self-selection than it is among children from low-status families."[91] Advantaged students participate out of routine social expectations and cultural habits.

While this helps to explain why advantaged students, once enrolled, might focus on the positional value of higher education rather than its content, it is not enough to explain their consistently high rates of participation. Borgen concludes that the positive selection hypothesis applies (and only applies) when it is supplemented by the double-filter idea, which acknowledges both advantaged students' need for credentials and their superior capacity to turn credentials into jobs. The negative selection hypothesis assumes that socially elite students can obtain jobs without educational credentials. "The sociological positive selection hypothesis," however, "depicts a world where attending a high-quality college is a prerequisite for gaining access to high-paid jobs, for both privileged and disadvantaged students."[92] At the same time, "students having few cultural and social resources to start off with have low labor market prospects and need to rely more on educational credentials than their privileged counterparts."[93] All young persons need credentials (though young people from very wealthiest families might be an exception, as chapter 21 will discuss). The poor student needs elite credentials the most. For that student, higher education can play an especially important role in social allocation and upward mobility. Yet on average, in the long run the poor student gains less in absolute terms from attending and graduating from elite higher education. Social disadvantage continues to play out at the point of entry to work and in the long-term evolution of the subsequent career.

21

Higher Education and the Economy

In higher education across the world, and the American sector in particular, in the present era there is overwhelming emphasis on the economic benefits of higher education. It is the legacy of the optimistic human capital narrative that evolved in the 1960s. If Clark Kerr did not buy into the full implications of the economic narrative, with its notion that everything in life could be usefully modeled in terms of scarcity and rational choice, in the first decade of the Master Plan he rode with the easy harmonization between educational, social, and economic outcomes that typified the time. Since then that easy harmonization has fractured, but the emphasis on the expected economic benefits of higher education has increased—despite the nagging sense that for some, education does not deliver those benefits.

Research finds that graduates mostly continue to be optimistic about their prospects.[1] This optimism is accentuated by higher education marketing, in which many institutions oversell themselves.[2] In reality, graduate vocational prospects are often unclear—more so perhaps in the United States, where higher education is less closely coupled with the labor markets,[3] than in some other countries, such as Germany with its tradition of early streaming into advanced vocational education. While Martin Trow's observation still stands, in that graduates are always better placed than nongraduates (with the exception of nongraduates from very wealthy backgrounds), American higher education is far from providing either certainty or financial security for all, whether at the two-year level, the four-year level, or above.[4] Higher education is only one of the elements at play. The transition between higher education and work is complex. These are two different social sites with very distinctive requirements, rhythms, and drivers.

Average graduate returns, in the form of salaries, occupational level, and rates of employment, are widely used as measures of educational outcomes, but this is often misleading. Averages hide from view dispersed graduate experiences. As the rate of participation expands, dispersion also advances. Snapshot comparisons of outcomes, especially in early graduate years, miss changes over time, which are by no means uniform across graduate populations and between fields of study. In the later years of the career, factors other than education, such as on-the-job learning, have a growing influence on outcomes. It becomes harder to trace the effects of education and almost impossible to separate the effects of schooling from those of higher education. Outcomes vary for graduates depending on whether the institutions they attended were selective or nonselective and on the different fields of study. Outcomes vary between different categories of graduates from the same program, with same educational achievements, and regardless of the quality of teaching and learning—though human capital theory implies that learned merit alone determines graduate productivity and earnings.

In addition, as the above discussion showed, social stratification and structures of education affect relations between higher education and the labor market at many points via a complex feedback process. So does geographical location. These problems have pushed the analytical framework of human capital theory to the breaking point.

DOES EDUCATION "CAUSE" EARNINGS?

Human capital theory assumes that education determines marginal productivity and that marginal productivity determines earnings. With some caveats, the value of investment in education is a function of lifetime earnings. It must be said that these are heroic assumptions. First, the determinants of productivity are a black box. As Hal Hansen remarks: "Human capital theory in its various forms rests almost entirely on financial returns to education, with virtually no direct empirical evidence on how schooling enhances productivity."[5] Second, the methodological individualism[6] of human capital theory is a problem. It can be difficult or impossible to accurately attribute enhanced value to individuals who work in a combined workplace, as do most employees.[7] Third, as the OECD emphasizes in *Education at a Glance, 2014*, "a host of education-related and context-related factors . . . affect the returns to education."[8] Richard Arum and Josipa Roksa take the point further, arguing that "colleges have little control over wage outcomes."[9] There is a very considerable literature on factors that can affect earnings, additional to higher education.

As noted, graduate earnings are affected by social background beyond what is mediated by education,[10] including family support in child development, such as whether children are read to at a young age.[11] Different research studies have found earnings to vary with family income,[12] type of secondary school attended, social and family networks at the point of entry to higher education, family and parental influence and social networks in the choice of and the transition to work,[13] social nesting and networks throughout the career,[14] field of study, level of qualification, and the differential status and resources of higher education institutions. Earnings are affected by custom and hierarchy in professions and workplaces, by the system of wage determination, and by the industrial balance of power,[15] as well as by the configurations and macro-fluctuations of national and regional economies. There is also the signaling role of credentials. For example, business graduates in the United States on average are relatively successful in the labor market in the early stages compared to graduates in most other fields of study, despite the relatively low levels of studying during the degree that characterize the business disciplines and the relatively low levels of graduate competency as measured in standardized tests. Arum and Roksa comment: "Some majors serve as better signals of employability than others, regardless of whether those degrees are underpinned by actual field-specific knowledge and skills."[16] Most human capital economists treat human capital narratives and signaling narratives as either-or explanations, but in the real world, human capital effects do not necessarily exclude signaling. The point is that more than human capital effects are at play.

Quantitative studies of the effects of higher education on earnings attempt to control statistically for other factors. After other factors are taken out, the residual education-earnings relationship often appears statistically as weak rather than strong. It is especially difficult to deal with selection effects, which can contaminate the relationship between education and outcomes. For example, Theodore Gerber and Sin Yi Cheung attempt to trace the effects of "college quality" on earnings. Does attendance at a selective college tend to boost earnings? If so, by how much and why? "Attendance at a higher-quality institution could be associated with higher earnings because exogenous variables like cognitive ability or social background both increase the probability of attending a high-quality institution and exert positive effects on earnings independently of institutional quality," they state. To the extent that additional earnings results from selection effects, "the association between college quality and earnings is not causal because by implication graduates from high-quality institutions would have higher earnings even if they attended lower-quality institutions."[17]

Personal characteristics such as determination and drive are also in play. Attempts to account for selection effects can generate results that vary sharply from study to study. There is no research consensus on the effects of institutional status or selectivity on graduate outcomes. For example, the study by Scott Thomas and Liang Zhang concludes that "despite significant variation, . . . graduates from more prestigious, more selective, and higher academic quality colleges enjoy small but significant wage premiums relative to peers graduating from less academically distinctive institutions, and this early advantage also increases over time—though earnings growth "varies significantly by the graduates' major field of study, with Engineering and Business graduates doing well.[18] These results are replicated in other studies. They accord with common sense. But common sense is not always right about social relations. Stacy Dale and Alan Krueger identify small returns to college selectivity but are bedeviled by selection effects.[19] Hongbin Li and colleagues note that while some researchers identify significant returns to college selectivity when selection effects are accounted for, other studies find the returns disappear.[20] For new graduates in China, gross returns to elite colleges of 26.4 percent diminish to 10.7 percent once ability, major, college location, individual characteristics, and family background are accounted for.[21] These results, also, are assumption driven.

Gerber and Cheung are skeptical about the effects of elite institutions: "Recent studies that employ more sophisticated methods cast serious doubts on the argument that elite colleges yield a greater return than non-elite colleges. These studies each indicate that the apparent effect of elite college attendance results largely or completely from the effects of a complex set of variables that influence whether or not one attends an elite college in the first place."[22] They cite varied findings by field of study and gender, move between screening and human capital hypotheses, and conclude that the role of "college quality" in relation to selection effects remains a problem unresolved. "We need better data," they state.[23] The problem is that much of the variation between the findings of the different studies is not due to variations in material relationships in the real world under observation but is generated by differences in the handling of selection effects by the various researchers.

INCOME AND STATUS

A further limit of human capital theory is that earnings are not the only potential individual benefits of education and are not always the most important benefits,[24] especially for graduates from certain fields of study. As Arum and Roksa state: "Rewards to occupations are related not just to income but also to occupational status and prestige. In social settings, individuals are typically asked about what they do, not how much money they earn."[25] Research also shows that the role of factors such as gender, field of study, and the selectivity or status of the institution play out differently, depending on whether the graduate outcome is status or income. Studies that focus on the relationship between earnings and education alone tend to provide an impoverished picture. In her research of the medium-term (thirteen-years out) outcome for graduates, Josipa Roksa finds that especially for graduates from prestige institutions and for those with generic degrees working in the public and nonprofit sectors, prospects of a managerial role are important relative to earnings.[26] Gender stratification also affects the respective roles of incomes and status: "Graduates of female-dominated fields are disproportionately employed in public and nonprofit organizations which offer lower monetary rewards but facilitate access to professional and managerial positions. . . . College major and employment sector interact in ways that reduce income penalties and enhance the occupational location of graduates of female-dominated fields."[27]

In addition, the passage of time can affect income outcomes and status outcomes in contrasting ways. Comparative returns to the different fields of study in the early years differ from those in the later stages, such as ten or twenty years.[28] Elish Kelly, Philip O'Connell, and Emer Smyth note that the early returns to vocational degrees in the field of teacher training are higher than to generic degrees.[29] Roksa and Tania Levey point out that studies of graduate returns that conclude in favor of occupational specificity tend to focus on early returns rather than long-term trajectories. However, "occupationally specific degrees are beneficial at the point of entry into the labor market but have the lowest growth in occupational status over time."[30] Graduates that acquire general skills begin work with the lower status but report greatest subsequent growth in status, they state.[31] Graduates from fields with high occupational specificity start with relatively high occupational status but experience less growth in status than graduates majoring in fields with low occupational specificity. Earnings exhibit a similar pattern, though between the fields a larger gap remains in relation to earnings than in relation to status. However, in the comparison between graduates from fields with moderate occupational specificity and those with low occupational specificity, low occupational specificity catches up in status and almost catches up in earnings.[32]

There are marked variations in findings about the effects of social background on both graduate status and graduate incomes. Gregory Wolniak and colleagues found that family incomes have "a positive and persistent effect on graduate status, while parent's education has relatively weak effects.[33] On the other hand, in their study of graduates twelve years out, Roksa and Levey found that family background has no effect on occupational status.[34] Findings also vary between countries, undermining generalizations. "Educational systems have different relationships to the labor market in different societies," states Roksa, noting differences in the nature and scale of state sector employment.[35] In an eleven-country study, Moris Triventi argues that the effects of social background on occupational outcomes vary by country in four areas: "(i) social selectivity of education system, (ii) level of higher education expansion, (iii) degree of institutional connections between higher education and labor market, and (iv) degree of institutional stratification in higher education."[36] The probability of obtaining a degree from a leading university is always greatest for graduates both of whose parents have degrees, but of the countries in Triventi's study, the effect is most marked in Norway and least in Spain. Triventi finds that overall, the effect of parental education is greater on graduate occupational status than on wages In addition, he finds that as with parental education, institutional stratification is more likely to be associated with entering a high-prestige professional occupation than entering the most highly paid occupations.[37]

In research on social stratification in China, both David Goodman[38] and Wei Zhao[39] note that social status is especially important in the context of China, opening the way to jobs and income, and also that status is closely associated with level of education. This does not mean education "causes" status/jobs/income in China any more than education "causes" earnings in the United States, because a complex of other factors affect both. In China, wealth, political power, and status tend to reinforce each other,[40] like Bourdieu's different capitals, weakening intergenerational mobility.[41]These findings again emphasize that relations between higher education, graduate earnings, and graduate status are subject to national-cultural variations.

OECD data on earnings suggest that the respective roles of credential signaling and human capital capacity also might be nationally variable: in some countries, returns to qualifications exceed the returns to measurable skills, while in other countries, the ratio is reversed,[42] though as noted, there are many other factors at play. A relative increase in the role of signaling may have implications for equality of opportunity. Wildhagen comments that if credentials operate as cultural markers rather than as reliable signs of distinct competences, they are open to manipulation, so they become more valuable for some social groups than for others.[43]

NONLINEAR RELATIONSHIPS

Though the human capital narrative implies that higher education and employment are in lock-step progression—and if it is not so, something is wrong with the graduate or with the education—in many cases this notion of linear progression is misleading. In the real world, the progression and the match between learning/qualification and work/occupation are not always clear-cut, especially for graduates with generic degrees. A 1999 study by Barbara Schneider and David Stevenson found that only 44 percent of students had "aligned" educational ambitions, meaning that they planned to complete the amount of education required by their intended occupations.[44] Not only do many students keep vocational options open, but many study for more reasons than just vocational planning, studying subjects that they are good at or they enjoy, while hoping that their future will work out. It is a strategy that embodies uncertainty. Nevertheless, because all graduates have a positional advantage in the labor market vis-á-vis nongraduates, their confidence is not wholly misplaced. John Robst notes, "The eventual match between degree field and occupation is uncertain when selecting a major."[45] He finds that 55 percent of respondents report a close relation between their work and their field of study, 25 percent report that they are "somewhat related," and 20 percent report they are not related.[46] However, this study has difficulty defining the work-relatedness of general degrees. Roksa and Levey observe that many first-degree graduates in the United States are not specialists.[47]

> Many educational credentials have no obvious matches in the labor market. This includes the majority of high school graduates in general and academic tracks and a large portion of college graduates majoring in liberal arts and sciences. Consequently, finding a job in one's field of study is not only an individual dilemma, it is a process that reflects the relationship (or lack thereof) between the educational system and the labor market.[48]

Among specifically trained graduates, many work outside their field of training, a "mismatch" that often but not always generates income penalties.[49] This is not deliberately perverse. It reflects the messy way that labor markets work. Many graduates take whatever job provides them with the best pay and career prospects, as it appears at the time of application and selection. At this point some graduates move away from the contents of their qualifications. For their part, employers select the "best" person for the position, and the specificity of training and qualifications is only one of the factors in play in determining who is "best." Many jobs are general jobs capable of being filled by graduates from any field, so that level of education reached may be more significant than field of study. More remarkably, some highly specialized positions become filled by persons trained in a different field, because employers believe they can "do the job" (or because no specialist is readily available). Not only is selection influenced by time-place contingency, by the pool of local opportunities available, and the pool of potential applicants before the employer, but recent studies of job selection and graduate networking behaviors indicate that many factors influence selection, additional to qualifications or academic performance, including the educational institution attended, the graduate's extracurricular activities as a student, subjective perceptions of "fit" between graduate and workplace, and personal ties.[50] Job selection, like degree selection, often fails to follow any clear logic.

Students and graduates keep failing at being the *homo economicus* imagined by human capital theory. Jens Peter Thomsen and colleagues report that at the point of enrollment some students do not take forgone earnings into account.[51] John Robst found that at the point of decision, prospective students often know earnings only in their chosen occupation, not in related fields.[52] Many students believe that contacts and networking are more important than skills or credentials.[53] Nicolai Borgen found that many students do not "self-select into colleges based on expected gain,"[54] especially students from affluent backgrounds.

Nonetheless, although many educational behaviors are not linear human capital behaviors, and relations between higher education and work defy single-cause explanations, this does not mean all statistically based inquiry in this domain is futile. Aggregated studies are rarely as conclusive as researchers want and often fail to satisfy orthodox human capital theory, but such studies can still identify suggestive patterns, especially on the basis of differentiation of large populations and trends over time. It is often where the expected linear patterns break that the findings become most interesting, though they contradict the orthodox narratives.

For example, Paul Bingley, Miles Corak, and Niels Westergård-Nielsen researched the intergenerational transmission of employers between fathers and sons, which is a common feature of all labor markets. They found that in both Canada and Denmark, 30–40 percent of young adults are at some point employed by a firm that also employed their fathers. Suggestively, they find that in both countries the transmission of employers is positively associated with paternal earnings, "rising distinctly and sharply at the very top of the father's earnings distribution."[55] At the top end of the income distribution also, Iftikhar Hussain, Sandra McNally, and Shqiponja Telhaj found that the income effects of attending a selective institution seem to inflate, and those returns seem to be increasing.[56] Kelly and colleagues note that in the longer term, field of study differences in earnings tend to fade away, except in medicine.[57] Borgen also identifies nonlinear economic returns to higher education. "Students who are most likely to attend a high-quality college benefit the most from attending such colleges, in line with the predictions of the positive selection hypotheses . . . but the findings support the positive selection hypotheses only at the upper half of the wage distribution."[58] The returns to college quality are five times larger at the 90th quantile compared to the 10th quantile. Borgen also notes that statistical averages mask "important heterogeneity across the wage distribution. The question is less whether college quality matters, but for whom and in what type of jobs."[59] Further, as in the work of Bingley and colleagues, Borgen notes that the family background effects are greatest at the top end of the wage distribution.[60]

Together, these findings are consistent with the data from Thomas Piketty, Emmanuel Saez, and others on the growing income inequality at the top of the distribution. Likewise, research by Thomas Lemieux over thirty years found that in the United States "within-group inequality grew substantially among college-educated workers, but changed little for most other groups," and that "the median, the tenth, and the ninetieth percentiles are remarkably stable for up to 12 years of education. Above 12 years of education, however, the return to education at the ninetieth percentile increases much more than the return to education at the tenth percentile, leading to a large increase in the 90–10 gap." Lemieux concludes: "Changes in wage inequality are increasingly concentrated in the very top end of the wage distribution . . . . [and] postsecondary education plays a crucial role in explaining this phenomenon."[61] The empirical data are consistent with other studies, but Lemieux's interpretation is more questionable. Is the measured concentration at the top end of the income distribution an effect of higher education, as Lemieux suggests, or due to something else?

The fact that field-of-study differences weaken at the top of the income scale suggest that higher education loses rather than gains determining power at that level. Very-high-income-earning graduates often have social characteristics, such as wealthy family backgrounds, that also affect graduate outcomes. As Bingley and colleagues suggest, factors such as family connections and supermanager salaries affect high-income returns at the top end. This not only underlines the point that factors other than higher education are causal in what are conventionally called "graduate outcomes," but it suggests that the ratio between the different causal elements is itself variable within the graduate population. The data imply that higher education has less effect on the employability, earnings, and status of high-income earners than it does on graduates in the middle of the social distribution. It also raises a historical question about the role of higher education in the surge of inequality since 1980.

IS HIGHER EDUCATION RESPONSIBLE FOR INEQUALITY?

In the United States, as in the rest of the English-speaking world, the rapid growth of economic and social inequality is occurring in societies in which formal participation in higher education is at or near an historic high. According to UNESCO data, in 2013 the gross tertiary enrolment ratio (GTER) in the United States was 89.1 percent, after reaching a historic highpoint of 95.3 percent in 2011.[62] If education produces human capital, which determines marginal productivity, and marginal productivity determines rates of return (the assumptions at the core of human capital theory), then growing income inequality must be grounded in a corresponding growth of inequality of skills and productivity. Higher education must be responsible for the growth of inequality, especially given that most of the age group is now entering it. Yet in reality, observes Piketty, higher education seems largely separated from the surge in top incomes.[63] "The theory of marginal productivity and of the race between education and technology is not very convincing, . . . The fact that income inequality in the United States in 2000–2010 attained a level far higher than that observed in the poor and emerging countries at various times in the past—for example, higher than in India or South Africa in 1920–1930, 1960–1970, and 2000–2010—also casts doubt on any explanation based on objective inequalities of productivity." If inequality in individual human capital was driving inequality on this scale, "it would be bad news for U.S. educational institutions," but while they "surely need to be improved and made more accessible," they "probably do not deserve such extravagant blame."[64]

Piketty emphasizes that the theory of marginal productivity, human capital theory, cannot explain the large variations in graduate incomes over time, nor does it explain "the diversity of the wage distributions we observe in different countries at different times,"[65] including countries that have similar higher education systems. Likewise, Caroline Hanley finds that "rising inequality in the United States is driven by increased high-wage earning levels that cannot be adequately explained by economic productivity-based explanations."[66] This again confirms that there are factors other than higher education that affect graduate earnings, status, and employability. Taking this further, it can be argued that the social and economic meanings of higher education are primarily determined not by the quality of human capital it produces (that is only one part of the equation) but in the interactions between the higher education system and the constantly changing social, economic, and political context in which it takes place. The 1960 Master Plan shaped the future of education in California for the three decades. It was not a blueprint for remaking the whole of California society. In the potentials and limits of higher education, in the long run the contextual factors are decisive.

22

Higher Education and Society

In *The Price of Inequality* Joseph Stiglitz notes that while higher education cannot guarantee social success for students from poor backgrounds, in terms of social averages it continues to make a difference. Between 2000 and 2010, the average household income of American men with bachelor's degrees fell by 1 percent, but the average income of those with high school diploma fell by more than a quarter.[1] "Among those with a college degree unemployment is 4.2 percent, among those with less than a high school diploma it is 12.9 percent."[2] Higher education provides better odds of social protection, as Martin Trow stated, even when it cannot always provide the leap upwards in society. However, whether it provides protection or advance, its benefits are largely confined to the richer half of the United States' population.

THE DREAM IS OVER

Figure 22.1 shows that at a national level, the long struggle to establish equality of opportunity to graduate from higher education has failed. The data combine selective and nonselective enrollment. In 2013, a near-universal 77 percent of persons in the top family income quartile in the United States had completed a bachelor's degree by age 24 years. In this quartile, the graduation rate had almost doubled since 1970, increasing from 40 percent to 77 percent in 1970. In the bottom family income quartile, the graduation rate had again risen, but from 6 percent in 1970 to only 9 percent in 2013. In the second bottom quartile, the graduation rate was 17 percent in 2013.[3] The overwhelming majority of the bottom half of the population in income terms had not achieved graduation by age 24 years, but most top quartile people had done so.

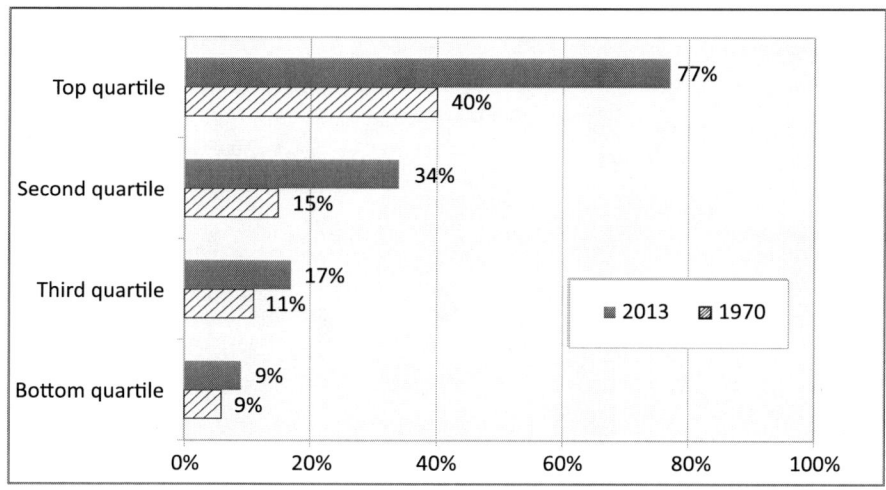

FIGURE 22.1. Social inequality in college degree attainment in the United States, 1970 and 2013: Graduated with bachelor's degree by age 24 years, by family income quartile.
SOURCE: Author, using data from Pell Institute and PennAHEAD 2015, p. 31.

The 1960s dream is over. Higher education continues to make an important difference to some individual graduates, and this matters. At the same time there are other graduates whom higher education does not help, and some of them do worse than their parents. At the level of overall social aggregates and averages, not only does higher education fail to compensate for prior social inequalities, it helps to confirm, legitimate, and reproduce those inequalities into the next generation. In *Degrees of Inequality,* Suzanne Mettler states: "Over the past thirty years . . . our system of higher education has gone from facilitating upward mobility to exacerbating social inequality." Higher education fosters a society that "increasingly resembles a caste system: it takes Americans who grew up in different social strata and it widens the divisions between them and makes them more rigid." It "stratifies Americans by income group rather than providing them with ladders of opportunity."[4]

The issue is not just access but completion, which is increasingly affected by the rising costs of both public and private higher education. Stiglitz also notes that "poor kids who succeed academically are less likely to graduate from college than richer kids who do worse in school."[5] The other problem is the quality of graduation. If figure 22.1 contained data for graduates from selective colleges rather than graduates from all colleges, the socioeconomic stratification would be more extreme.

However, for most of the lower 50 percent families, selective colleges are not on the radar. In future, as social inequality grows further, their educational aspirations will decline. Structural inequality of this magnitude, combining inequality in

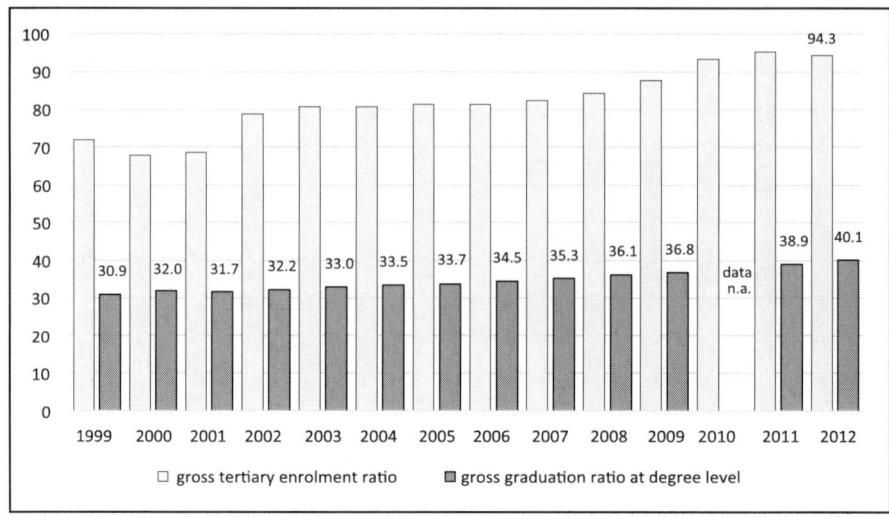

FIGURE 22.2. Comparison between gross tertiary enrolment ratio and gross graduation ratio at degree level, United States, 1999–2012.
SOURCE: Author, using data from UNESCO 2015.

society with unequal engagement in higher education, becomes self-reproducing. In its report on inequality in the United States, the OECD argues that when overall economic and social inequality are high, people from low SES backgrounds tend to invest less rather than more in education and skill development. Their aspirations are low, supporting resources are low, and even if they graduate, the barriers to success are still formidable. Over time their relative position further deteriorates.[6] The United States retains a very high rate of participation by international standards, but as part 2 showed, completion is weaker in comparative terms. Figure 22.2 illustrates the gap between participation at the two-year level or above and graduation at degree level.

Figure 22.2 shows that U.S. participation at tertiary education level is exceptionally high, reaching 95.3 percent of the age cohort in 2011. Yet because many of those students drop out before completion and others stop at two-year diploma level, in the year the participation peaked, the rate of graduation at degree level was only 38.9 percent. There was a 56.4 percent gap between the participation rate and the graduation rate at degree level. Given the data in figure 22.1, it is certain that the social composition of the gap between participation and degrees was heavily weighted to the bottom two quartiles. Given the deteriorating economic position of the bottom 50 percent in the United States, if the present trends continue into the future, the completion rate in higher education is more likely to fall than rise.

FOR-PROFIT FAILURE

It is also now clear that where the public higher education sector falters and fails families from the bottom half of the income distribution, the commercial higher education sector cannot provide, not even when it is massively subsidized by Washington. In the last two decades, the federal government applied public choice theory's foundational assumption of "private good, public bad" to higher education policy and funding. Instead of boosting the declining position of four-year and two-year public colleges—strengthening their educational potency, lengthening their programs, enhancing the confidence and abilities of their graduates, and inserting more backbone into the social value of their credentials—the federal government channeled a growing volume of total public subsidies for postsecondary education into the for-profit sector. For many families in the lower 50 percent, the old dream about universal opportunity and social mobility through free public education became temporarily replaced by a new dream about loan investment in a brighter graduate future. The choice was clear, or at least the widely spread (and publicly subsidized) for-profit marketing made the choice seem clear. The public colleges were offering rising tuition, funding cutbacks, large classes, enrollment quotas, and high dropout rates. The for-profit dream promised graduate jobs, respect for its student-consumers, and support for them while studying. And like the high-priced mortgages that were oversold to low-income families before the 2008 crash, the for-profit version of the educational dream turned into a nightmare.

Between 1995 and 2010, the for-profit colleges were the fastest growing subsector of American higher education. Their enrollment moved from 240,363 to peak at 2,018,397, multiplying by 8.4 times while the total postsecondary enrollment multiplied by a factor of 1.5[7] (see figure 22.3). The for-profits cultivated a niche market of working people who had left school or college early and wanted to progress their careers with a diploma. Given America's relatively high school dropout and postsecondary noncompletion rates, this is a large potential market. The for-profits also had growing recruitment opportunities among school leavers shut out of public colleges. They marketed more aggressively than public and private nonprofit institutions, promising greater vocational certainty. They also rapidly expanded online modes of higher education. With state governments unable to adequately support public colleges, it seemed that many in government saw the for-profit sector as the new frontier for mass higher education in the future: more exciting, more customer responsive, more flexible, more innovative. Both its enrollment growth and high profitability seemed to confirm its market success. Between 1994 and 2003, the revenues of the Apollo Group, owner of the University of Phoenix, the largest private university in the United States, expanded from $12 million to $1.34 billion.[8]

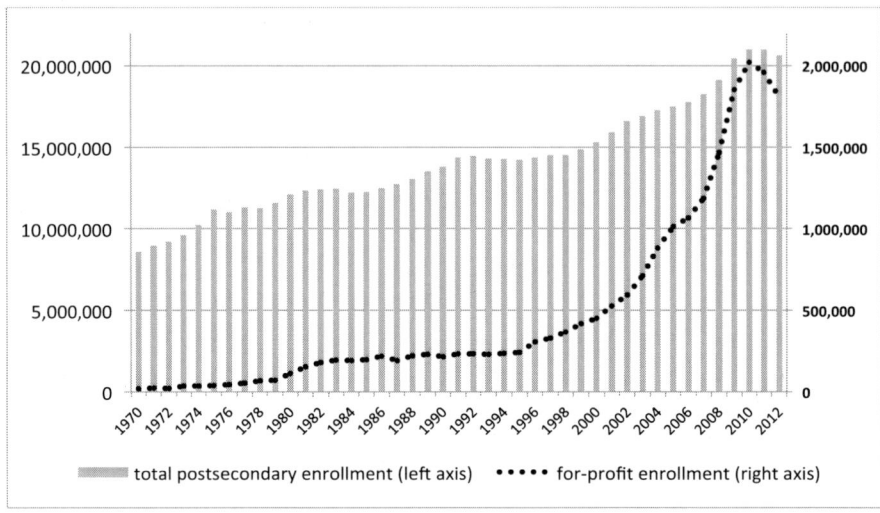

FIGURE 22.3. Enrollment in postsecondary institutions, and enrollment in for-profit institutions, United States 1970–2012.
SOURCE: Author, using data from NCES 2015.

The for-profit sector had not carved out the new territory in the wilderness entirely through its own effort. Its business model was totally dependent on federal subsidies. For example, in 2010 the Apollo Group received 88.7 percent of all its revenues from the federal government, including 85.3 percent from student loans and Pell Grants, and 3.4 percent from military educational programs.[9] In 2009 the for-profits enrolled 10 percent of postsecondary students but absorbed 25 percent of all Pell Grant dollars,[10] indicating both their success in fastening onto the most disadvantaged component of the population and their mastery of Washington. The for-profits were nurtured by supportive legislation and protected their position with a high-powered lobbying operation in both sides of the aisle. The Apollo Group donated $11 million in the 2007–2008 presidential election campaign. Remarkably, President George W. Bush made a lobbyist for the for-profit sector his Assistant Secretary for Post-Secondary Education.[11] In addition, the finance sector lobbied successfully to make student loans nondischargeable at bankruptcy, so for-profit providers were under little pressure from lenders to deliver on employability.[12]

This federally fed business model was so strong that in 2008, while the S&P index declined by 39 percent, the nine major for-profit companies saw 4 percent growth in their stocks. According to Mettler, the chair and CEO of Strayer University received $41.9 million in 2009–2010, twenty-six times more than the most highly compensated president of a traditional university.[13] Who could argue that in business terms the salaries paid to for-profit executives, parallel to those received by "superman-agers" in the finance sector, were not worth it? The total federal subsidy of for-prof-its, estimated at \$32 billion a year in 2012,[14] guaranteed shareholder value.

However, the for-profit business model had an Achilles heel: the quantity and quality of outputs. With much of the revenue outlaid on recruitment or drawn back into the corporations, there was less for teaching and learning—Mettler es-timates \$2,659 per student, compared to \$9,418 by public colleges and \$15,289 by private nonprofits.[15] Aggregate completion rates are difficult to obtain, but they are lower than in public colleges and probably below 20 percent in the first six years. Among bachelor's-level graduates in 2008, average debts were \$32,700 compared to \$22,400 in public institutions, but for-profit graduates had higher unemploy-ment rates than graduates from public institutions. For-profit graduates now ac-count for nearly half of all loan defaults, a cost again borne by Washington.[16] In its first term, the Obama administration attempted to tie continued federal subsidies to a satisfactory rate of graduate employment and loan repayment. In its original form, the bill would have forced half of all for-profit loan recipients to improve their outcomes or lose federal funding. The for-profit lobby spent \$11 million in lobbying against the proposed changes, enlisting the support of all Republicans and many Democrats. The Administration was forced to water down the provi-sions of the bill, so that in the outcome only one in twenty for-profit schools were affected.[17] However, Obama continued to work on reining in the for-profits. It is apparent that the high-water mark of the industry has passed. It is difficult to jus-tify public gifts on this scale, even in a country in which taxpayer-funded corpo-rate bailouts are the new normal, inequality in education is seen as the fault of the family, and the common faith in upward social movement through educational merit might be fading.

So where do poor families go? The dream of upward mobility through public education has faded. The dream of upward mobility through vocationally smart private colleges has been a bigger, costlier, and more deceptive disappointment.

SOCIAL MOBILITY

What then is the extent of the remaining upward social mobility in American so-ciety, and what role does higher education play in it? Societies with high inequality normally exhibit both high private returns to graduates compared to the returns to school leavers—as is the case in the United States and the United Kingdom at present—and also high intergenerational income elasticity.[18] The latter refers to the extent to which relative parental incomes are reproduced in relative children's incomes. The higher the level of intergenerational income elasticity, the lower the level of social mobility. Whereas a century ago social mobility was higher in the United States than in Europe, this is no longer the case. Miles Corak finds that the

United States and the United Kingdom have an intergenerational income elasticity of 0.4–0.5. This means that 40–50 percent of the difference in parental incomes is passed on to the children. The corresponding figures for Canada, Denmark, Norway, and Finland are 0.15–0.2. Sweden and Germany are at about 0.3.[19]

Likewise, Thomas Piketty states that while it is more difficult to measure and compare intergenerational mobility than incomes at a given point of time, available data indicate that "intergenerational reproduction is lowest in the Nordic countries and highest in the United States (with a correlation coefficient two-thirds higher than Sweden). France, Germany, and Britain occupy a middle ground, less mobile than northern Europe but more mobile than the United States."[20] Stiglitz cites data showing that in Denmark, 25 percent of the children born into the bottom one-fifth of households in income terms remain in that bottom fifth. In the United States, 42 percent of those born into the bottom fifth stay there, and nearly two-thirds stay in the bottom two-fifths. In the United States, a higher proportion are trapped in poverty.[21]

The OECD has prepared data that measure comparative intergenerational mobility of enrollment in higher education.[22] Note that these data focus on educational mobility rather than social mobility. (Note also that in the last generation most countries have greatly expanded the rate of participation in tertiary education but the social power of average degree status may have fallen, affecting the meaning of cross-generation comparison). Again, American intergenerational educational mobility is low compared to most other OECD countries. The OECD compares the odds of getting to tertiary education for two groups of students: those with one or both parents who attended tertiary education and those whose parents did not. In the United States, students from tertiary-educated families were 6.8 times as likely to access tertiary education as students from nontertiary families. This number is consistent with the income-based distribution of graduation in figure 22.1. Intergenerational mobility was almost as low in England in the United Kingdom (6.3). Only Poland and Italy (9.5) had lower mobility than United States and United Kingdom. Australia (4.3) was in the middle of the table, and Canada (2.6) had a high level of mobility. The Nordic ratios ranged from Finland (1.4) to Denmark (3.0). South Korea was at 1.1.[23]

Low social mobility is one thing, worsening social mobility is another. In a 2014 National Bureau of Economic Research Working Paper, Raj Chetty and colleagues found that American children who enter the labor market today have much the same chance of moving up the income ladder relative to their parents as did children born in the 1970s or 1980s. For children born between 1971 and 1986, they measured "intergenerational mobility based on the correlation between parent and child income percentile ranks," while for more recent cohorts, they measured mobility "as the correlation between a child's probability of attending college and her parents' income rank." They also calculated "transition probabilities, such as a child's chances of reaching the top quintile of the income distribution starting from the bottom quintile." However, Chetty and colleagues noted that because inequality has increased, there is more at stake for each child in the "birth lottery" than before.[24] This suggests that while Mettler was not as yet wholly correct in her statement about lessened social mobility, it is only a matter of time before the dramatic enhancement of American inequality translates into reduced American social mobility overall.

ALLOCATIVE POWER OF HIGHER EDUCATION

History underlines the point that higher education has the potential to contribute either to greater equality or greater inequality. Part 1 showed how higher education was associated with rising equality of opportunity and social mobility in a society becoming more open, in the 1950s–1970s United States. Higher education has been also associated with economies and societies that are becoming more unequal and more closed, with higher education part of the closure, as in the United States today. This does not mean that higher education *itself* is the main driver of social and economic equality or inequality, whether inside the sector or beyond it.

History also suggests that the autonomous allocative power of higher education, for good or ill, itself can vary in strength. The specific influence of higher education might be greater when opportunities are opening up than when they are closing down. It seems that the capacity of higher education to make a difference can be magnified by enabling government policies in conjunction with a social consensus about the value of education and equal opportunity, as in the case of the 1960 Master Plan. There is another example of this positive, transformative role of higher education on a large scale, in a society very different from 1960s United States: China today. In China the party-state emphasizes higher education as an allocative mechanism. Education has been positioned as the source of opportunity and the positioning and selecting device for the fast-growing middle class. At the same time, China's government uses higher education to strengthen its own position. By providing educational and social opportunity on a larger scale, it hopes to strengthen its own political position, as was the more or less case with Governor Pat Brown in California at the end of the 1950s. The limits to this strategy in China are the continuing deep divide between rural and urban areas[25] and the likelihood that as the growth of the middle class slows down while higher education continues to expand, the family payoffs from higher education will decline. Graduate unemployment is already a sensitive issue in China. China is having its 1960s–1970s moment in higher education. Only the continuation of exceptional levels of economic growth can sustain that moment. There has been exceptional growth for almost forty years but everything ends eventually. It is unlikely that higher education in China will always be as powerful a factor in social sorting and

in governmental strategy. It is possible that the allocative power of higher education in China is peaking now.

The Nordic countries maintain free access to institutions of uniformly good
quality in education systems that are even more open and egalitarian than society overall. No doubt this approach to education moderates the tendencies to
labor-market and income inequality natural in societies with economic markets.
However, the Nordic countries provide this kind of education system as part
of an egalitarian social consensus about tax, transfers and social spending, and
balanced industrial relations. Society shapes higher education rather more than
higher education shapes society; it is social and political developments that made
the educational reforms possible.[26]. Nordic education is a necessary but not sufficient condition for the Nordic egalitarianism that often fascinates other countries.
Education alone has not made Nordic societies more equal over time, nor has it
prevented them from becoming somewhat more unequal over the course of the
last two decades.

In all societies, whether they are becoming more unequal or not, higher education has fallen short of the full expectations created in the 1960s. The limits to the
allocative power of education have been concealed by the narratives of educational
merit and human capital in which responsibility for more equal social outcomes
become displaced downwards from the level of social order and government policy to educational institutions and to graduates themselves. However, the lesson
of the post-1960 period is that education ministers and university leaders should
set aside the hubris that higher education is the principal maker of society. Both
Clark Kerr and Martin Trow were careful to avoid this kind of claim. What happens with incomes, wealth, labor markets, taxation, spending, social programs,
and urban and rural development is much more important overall. Calling society
a "knowledge economy" or "innovation society" does not change this. Yet despite
the lesson of history, the capacity of higher education to move whole societies is
still fundamentally and frequently overstated. Piketty asks:

> Did mass education lead to more rapid turnover of winners and losers for a given
> skill hierarchy? According to the available data, the answer seems to be no: the in-
> tergenerational correlation of education and earned incomes, which measures the
> reproduction of the skill hierarchy over time, shows no greater trend toward greater
> mobility over the long run.[27]

This is right. All the same, old habits die hard: Piketty and Stiglitz, as well as
the OECD, are among those who continue to overstate the social allocative power
of higher education. They do not see education as responsible for the trend to
income inequality, but they see education as the central driver of the solution.[28]
This is equally implausible. Stiglitz, urging the reversal of the U.S. trends to higher
tuition and decreased public support for public education, states that "opportunity

is shaped, more than anything else, by access to education."[29] Piketty is convinced that broad access to high-quality training and advanced education would be the most effective method of lifting lower-tier wages.[30] The OECD argues that in cases of countries where inequality is reducing, such as Brazil, and countries with high growth without growing inequality, such as South Korea, education policy has been a principal driver. Oxfam makes a similar argument.[31] In part the global agencies focus on education for practical reasons. Education remains under government control in most countries and more open to policy and regulation than the other levers that affect inequality. It is easier to change education than to increase corporate tax or more closely regulate the globally connected finance sector. Yet egalitarian reforms in education, even when underpinned by public spending, can have limited impact in the absence of changes to domains such as tax and transfers, welfare, job creation, minimum wages, and executive pay regimes. And in any case, there is unlikely to be a sustained increase in public spending on education while tax constraints, large supermanager salary hikes, and financialization strategies remain in place. Comparing a range of countries, Richard Wilkinson and Kate Pickett note that the level of public spending on education tends to be negatively correlated with the degree of income inequality.[32] This cuts both ways. Income inequality and the prowealth tax regime reduce the social resources for education spending, and constraints on public investment in education narrow the scope for opportunity reproducing inequality.

If higher education is unable on its own to secure a significant redistribution of opportunity, what then can it achieve? What is the outer limit of its social allocative power and formative effect in the present setting? Higher education acting alone may not change the balance of social power, but it nevertheless touches the lives of more than twenty million American students a year. It also allocates social opportunities within that large group. First, as William Deresiewicz and Roger Geiger each argue in different ways, while American higher education provides little upward mobility overall, it plays an important sorting role in the upper middle class. Elite higher education, public and private, fine-tunes the social destinations of those nestling between the top 0.1–5 percent of the family income distribution. Among them are some who will become supermanagers, carrying the MBAs that stamp them as meritocratic. Today's more meritocratic form of inequality is partly tied to elite universities, as Rivera shows.[33] Elite programs also partly separate students and families in the upper-middle-class group from the more beleaguered American "middle-middle" class.[34] Second, mass higher education in two-year and four-year institutions and the for-profits helps to differentiate the middle of the job market. Credential holders are more likely to secure full-time jobs and are better placed for self-employment. In the narrow upper-middle band, selective investments, entry, and outcomes are calculated with precision. In the larger and more inchoate middle zone below, the fact of participation is more important than field, and credentials are more generic than precise. It is in these two middle layers of American society, which roughly correspond to elite and mass higher education respectively, that the principal allocative function of higher education continues to play out.

In relation to these two middle layers, American higher education is becoming more socially regressive. In the absence of an absolute growth in opportunities—or what has always been more unlikely, a redistribution that would reduce the opportunities of some families from the middle and/or upper layers of the SES distribution while promoting others from below—the competition into and within higher education must become increasingly intense, as middle-class families jostle for position and bring every possible asset to bear on the competition to secure advantage in the most selective colleges and programs. Positional competition in higher education will strengthen the families with the most assets, not weaken them. "The idea that unrestricted competition will put an end to inheritance and move towards a more meritocratic world is a dangerous illusion," as Piketty remarks.[35]

Above and below those two middle layers of society, the allocative role of higher education is not as important as it is in the middle. American higher education has long been a device for defining, motivating, shaping and sorting the middle class. Figure 3.1 shows that for the majority of Americans located in the bottom two income quartiles, higher education's role in social allocation is limited. The cost of tuition has risen at twice the rate of inflation since 1980,[36] and unlike students in Australia and the United Kingdom, U.S. students are not supported by income-contingent loans. They must take mortgage-style student loans with commercial repayment regimes. When they enter the lower reaches of higher education, they find they have more limited mobility and choices than many others.[37] For the most part, higher education does not offer them a precise vocation and still less a guaranteed career. Some stay out. Many do not complete. The lack of traction in community college and for-profit education coupled with rising private costs, the breakdown of access in California and elsewhere, and perhaps the aftermath of recession together may explain the recent fall in postsecondary enrollment in the United States. Total enrollment peaked at 21.016 million in 2010, falling by 1.8 percent to 20.643 million in 2012. Student numbers fell by a quarter of million in both the public sector and the private for-profit sector.[38] Public higher education is failing the poor. Private higher education is also failing the poor and its failure is more spectacular.

At the top of society, above the upper middle class, higher education is again less determining of social outcomes. In fact its social allocative power may be receding. Though apparent returns to higher education are maximized for affluent families, much more than higher education is at work in their strong career trajectories and high wages. As private fortunes grow and inheritance returns to a primary role, university will become less essential in achieving a place at the top, notwithstanding the continued need of some new supermanagers for meritocratic legitimation and networks and regardless of the continued prestige consumption and cultural sheltering functions of Ivy League degrees. Joseph Soares found that in 1988–2000, only 22 percent of the children of high-income professional families and 14 percent of children from other high-income families attended tier 1 institutions. In fact, 19 percent of the children of all high-income professional families and 36 percent from other high-income families attended no college at all.[39] These members of the social elite are decoupled from higher education. They have no stake in it as a social project.

However, while some young people from privileged backgrounds will be successful in life whether they attend elite higher education institutions or not, for some other young people, from less affluent backgrounds, higher education makes a large difference. Though elite institutions remain upper-middle-class dominated and American higher education overall fails to redistribute opportunities on a social scale, it continues to create new prospects for students from low SES backgrounds who lack family capital. Without higher education, these families would be worse off. The business world could not alone provide comparable social opportunities if higher education was withdrawn. The paradox is that the persons least likely to aspire to higher education, least likely to participate in it, and least able to translate graduation into high earnings and lifelong supportive networks gain on average the most from higher education relative to nonparticipants.[40] Geiger argues that higher education still offers poorer Americans their best opportunity for upward mobility, though the odds are more uncertain than they were. A threshold problem, however, is that studying hard—which provides poor students with their best odds for upward social mobility through education—is increasingly out of favor on American campuses.[41]

NONCOGNITIVE NETWORKS

Higher education is potent in transforming the lives and livelihoods of people from any background for the better, as Clark Kerr knew. However, the effect is not automatic and the student must become an active agent to secure it. Higher education goes deeper and is more likely to be transformative when students immerse themselves in their programs, enabling the academic and professional disciplines to do their work of honing technique and cultivating the imagination. Inescapably, the extent to which higher education can build confident agency, generate intellectual payoffs, and secure occupational ability is a function of how much work the student does. Study time does not affect the capacity of students to use higher education to build social status, position themselves for the future, and network to advantage. However, it directly determines the potential for cognitive benefits and, through those benefits, more robust intellectual agency and higher measured performance. This is crucial for first-generation disadvantaged students, for whom the cognitive worlds of higher education are often largely new. The majority of affluent students bring with them cultural capital of tertiary-educated households. For the average first-generation student, all else being equal, higher education has more value to add.

However, data on student workloads and time use indicate that in the United States study time is falling and is low compared to most countries for which data are available. Arum and Roksa cite survey data showing that students in all European countries except Slovakia spent more time in academic pursuits than did American students. A 2006 American study found that students spend thirteen hours a week studying and three times that amount in recreation.[42] Arum and Roksa tracked 1,600 students in twenty-five different four-year colleges. They found that in the sophomore year, half of the students had no class requiring more than twenty pages of writing in the whole semester, and a third had no class that required more than forty pages of reading a week. Using generic academic competency tests, the researchers find that after two years, 45 percent of students improved by less than one percentage point on a standardized achievement scale. After four years, the average student had moved from the starting 50 percent to the 68 percent mark, and 30 percent of students still failed to improve by even 1 percent. Nevertheless, these students had graduated successfully though graduates with higher competency-test scores tended to have lower unemployment. On average, students in high-selective institutions learned more than did others, though many had low-intensity reading and writing requirements.[43]

In Arum and Roksa's study, seniors spent an average of twenty-six hours a week in all academic pursuits, including twelve hours of study outside classes. This compared with forty total hours a week in the 1960s.[44] Just as worrying as the lost time is the alleged displacement of intellectual rigor. This shows also in the widespread tendency to grade inflation. Despite the falloff in hours of academic work, average GPAs are rising in most colleges. Deresiewicz found that the energy of Yale students is absorbed by extracurricular learning rather than formative intellectual pursuits and argues that the treatment of students as consumers—"people to be pandered to instead of challenged"—compromises teaching and learning.[45] Steven Pinker pins part of the blame for the decline in intellectual focus on the use of extracurricular criteria in determining entry into Ivy League institutions. He argues that "at most 10 percent" of Harvard students are selected on academic merit per se. The remainder are selected "holistically" on the basis of participation in athletics, arts, charity, community activism, or travel experiences. This feeds the "anti-intellectualism of Ivy League undergraduate education" with too much time spent on a frenetic round of extracurricular, social, and networking activities and not enough in study.[46] As with Arum and Roksa, Pinker's remedy is to step up standardized generic competency testing, to impose the discipline of a cognitive regime and thereby bring institutions and faculty back to the academic mission. Though generic testing can provide some data on cognitive capabilities, it misses the larger part of intellectual formation, which takes place in knowledge regimes. If testing was institutionalized at every stage from school to work, the remedy would reduce intellectual development as much as enhance it. But the need that these scholars address—to find a way back to cognitive formation—is clear. In his account of the limitations of contemporary universities, Peter Murphy in Australia emphasizes the same point.[47] It resonates with faculty everywhere.

In two book-length accounts, *Academically Adrift* and *Aspiring Adults Adrift*, Arum and Roksa offer an explanation for the retreat from intellectual formation. They point to a partial shift in the locus of authority on campus between faculty and students. Student assessment of teaching and curricula affects faculty standing and can shape careers. Rather than students being empowered as strong agents, however, they are being provided with a more comfortable life. The partial shift in the locus of authority is associated with less challenging teaching, lighter study loads, grade inflation, and increased plagiarism.[48] It all erodes cognitive formation. The emphasis on student satisfaction is part of the almost universal shift to a customer orientation in dealing with students, consistent with the idea of higher education as an increasingly competitive market, and with the professionalization and expansion of campus services that foster student adjustment, activities, and successful passage. Colleges focus on students' "personal growth and well-being," including their participation in group relationships, rather than academic and moral development, which were the principal focuses at earlier times. Higher education institutions are "academically adrift but socially alive, active and attentive. Correspondingly, students—and their families—also focus on networking and team-based activities, including parties, believing that "it's not what you know, it is who you know."[49] The core purpose of college becomes collapsed into student social life.

In *Paying for the Party: How College Maintains Inequality*, Elizabeth Armstrong and Laura Hamilton provide cases studies that illustrate the socially differential effects of the reduction of the main purpose of higher education from intellectual formation to social networking.[50] At the flagship public university studied by Armstrong and Hamilton, the central role of the "Greeks" and a middle-class social life, sanctioned if not actively encouraged by the institution, weaken the prospects for disadvantaged students, unless they are strong enough to stand aside from the peer culture. Disadvantaged students benefit least from higher education as a position and network and mating game, in which material advantages and cultural cunning tend to determine the outcome. These students stand to gain the most from higher education when it is practiced as hard work and cognitive formation and augments their knowledge, skill, confidence, and professional sensibilities. That higher education provides them with the best odds of moving up after graduation.

Higher education is essentially a process of student self-formation.[51] It always has been. All learning is a process of self-formation, albeit with most of it situated in relational social settings.[52] Traditional pedagogy models higher education as other-formation, but a moment's thought shows that its self-forming character is obvious: even didactic modes of learning work only when the techniques and knowledge they demand are absorbed by the student as an act of will and become part of the mental apparatus. One of the irretrievable cultural changes since the Free Speech Movement at Berkeley in 1964 is that students in higher education have become openly positioned as self-determining adults. This is part of the larger modern shift to a self-determining individual form of freedom, which the student and counterculture movements that so plagued Clark Kerr at Berkeley helped to create. There is no intrinsic reason why student self-formation should be trapped within the antisocial form of individuality proposed by public choice theory. Individual freedom without sociability undermines its own conditions of existence. But replacing high-individualized consumption with shared individual consumption in social networks does not constitute much of a step forward either, though it is apparent why this has developed.

Essentially, the semisanctioned "party" lifestyle at college has emerged as a necessary social compensation for the lacuna in individualist rational choice and public choice theories, without jettisoning the consumer market approach to higher education. However, the better alternative is to move beyond the market paradigm. In renovating approaches to public higher education, one task, difficult but necessary, is to shift the self-forming student out of consumption and into an intellectual paradigm in which personal empowerment evolves not through choice of friends and leisure activity but through activities that are explicitly designed to hone mental capacity.

What higher education can do is maximize students' cognitive and social capabilities, including their agency, confidence, knowledge, and imagination. "Networks" are further down the list of significant benefits. If universities and colleges are doomed to educate a society dominated by a new aristocracy of money in a political economy becoming more unequal, their best contribution to their public mission is to form a graduate population that is more intelligent, more informed, and more confident within a society in which socially nested human agency is broadly distributed. That kind of society is less likely to tolerate the loss of the commonweal and more likely to renew the forward-looking democratic spirit embodied in the best hopes of the 1960s and the starting forms of the California Idea of higher education.

After the Dream

The California Idea of higher education, as embodied in the 1960 Master Plan, the implementation of the Plan, and the societal consensus that supported it, was in some respects utopian. All the same, it was managed with skill and foresight and was sufficiently practical to record great achievements in both access and excellence. Clark Kerr expected the Master Plan to last for only about twenty years. For that period it was unquestionably successful. Some of its benefits, especially those in the realm of excellence, lasted longer than that and continue to the present day. As part 1 described, the University of California is an extraordinary research university sector, little diminished despite the times, quintessentially public in the benefits of its research and as an engine of upward social mobility. On the campuses, the UC Office of the President is felt as an encumbrance and the size of its staff is often questioned, but the system model has been essential in holding these campuses to the public mission. In some other states, amid the pressures of the times, flagship public universities have moved closer to the missions and modus operandi of the leading private universities. But Berkeley, UCLA and UC San Diego have not started to converge with Stanford, Caltech, and the University of Southern California. If that has been the price of the encumbrance, it has been a price that is worth paying.

As part 1 indicated and part 3 explained in detail, the history of the access mission has not been as happy as that of the excellence mission. For the first 20–25 years, the California Idea successfully underpinned open access to higher education for all. This achievement was ahead of its time, though as part 2 showed, the world is now catching up. After that, the capacity of all public planning in California was conclusively undermined, first by Proposition 13 in 1978, then by

Ronald Reagan's antitax and anti–public good policies after 1980 and the thirty-five years of growing inequality that followed, and finally by the plutocratic and corporate capture of Congress, so that Washington poured subsidies into dysfunctional for-profit colleges while the states could no longer fund the public community college sector. The 2008 recession made it clear that within the present fiscal-political framework, mass public higher education in California would never meet its basic public goals. The long bipartisan consensus on building higher education, in which Clark Kerr's leadership in California and his years at the Carnegie Commission after 1967 played a signal role, has now evaporated.[1] The Obama administration sensed the problem but could not effectively address it, largely because the interests that controlled the Congress had no intrinsic commitment to either overcoming gridlock or rebuilding public higher education.

The underlying problem is in political philosophy and political culture. Once government ceases to be a repository of the general will and the taxation that supports it ceases to be an instrument of the collective good. Once government is seen as the enemy, less trustworthy than market actors, though they are responsible only to themselves, then society has set aside its principal means of reflexively improving itself. John Dewey argued vigorously against the cynical belief that the state, the public interest, is "a mask for private desires for power and position."[2] James Buchanan's aphorism was that "strangers make market exchanges" and thereby bind a society together; Herbert Bowles's equally pithy reply is that "markets make strangers."[3] Markets in education have advanced the scope for individual choice and initiative, but unregulated market forces in education tend to fragment the common educational infrastructure—and values—on which everyone depends. In the public choice society, everyone is in their private bunker with guns facing outwards in all directions, ready to blaze away when provoked. But public goods and private goods do not have to be locked into a zero-sum game in which they are set against each other. The key is to identify the public interest, and its conditions, so it can be harmonized with individual rights and needs. We should expect the public and private good to be optimized together. Rather than abandoning the idea of mutual benefit, it is better to treat the public good as a source and condition of private good, thereby holding governments accountable for the extent to which they advance our lives and our freedoms.

The United States continues to lead the world in the high-research mission of universities. This is an essential resource in enhancing the engagement with China and the world, as discussed in part 2 of this book. Yet in other respects the United States is no longer the unquestioned higher education leader that it was when *The Uses of the University* was first published, in 1963. The Reagan-era policies and what came after put paid to that. America now may have as much to learn as to teach. Certain higher education systems abroad combine high levels of initial enrollment, as in the United States, with high completion among all social groups, research excellence in the universities, and mass teaching institutions of good quality. The countries that are hitting excellence and equity goals simultaneously, much as the Master Plan imagined, include the Nordic countries, South Korea, and Taiwan. Significantly, these are also societies that rank highly in *Forbes* magazine's surveys of good countries in which to do business, and they all have strong creative cultures in both arts and industry. In Denmark the highly trained creative sector (design, architecture, fashion, jewelry, furniture, cinema, research, and higher education itself) now constitutes about 10 percent of exports.[4] Korea also has a vibrant and productive design culture. Societies in which nearly all people are educated to a high level have a great pool of resources and ideas from which to draw. In this group of countries, there are varied rates of taxation, but without exception taxation is sufficient to support excellent and accessible higher education at near universal levels of social participation, and mass higher education is of good quality. An equitable high-quality system of higher education does not necessarily depend on high levels of taxation if families share tuition cost, as in East Asia, and/or tuition is covered by income-contingent tuition loans (see "National Reform of Tuition" below). However, a public higher education policy cannot achieve excellence and equity goals together unless there is consensus on the mission of education as a servant of the public good, and this is sustained by public leadership in government and higher education and by broad agreement on public financing.

Clark Kerr understood that social leadership involves responsibility as well as opportunity. The public good consists in social structures in which elite families want to contribute to the good of all, so that the private freedoms and benefits are rendered universal. Higher education ought to be be one of the structures that enables that kind of public good, on the local, state, national, and global planes.

NATIONAL REFORM OF TUITION

California is often ahead of the country and the world. The trends of the time often emerge there first. California once led the nation in education but now trails the pack. The state's malaise in public higher education speaks to a larger malaise in the public mission of American higher education. Perhaps California could lead the recovery.

The Dream is Over has pointed to the problem. It is not the purpose of the book to suggest political solutions to the malaise of public education, which will come, but only by evolving in organic fashion from within the states and communities that need solutions. However, it is clear that everything turns on the establishment of a new sense of the public good in education and social policy. The public good is something that Clark Kerr's generation, coming out of depression and war, understood very well. It is now less well understood. It can be retrieved. As Joseph

Stiglitz states, "the real solution to the inequality crisis lies in focusing on community rather than self-interest."[5]

There is one change that might provide a way forward for American higher education. That is a wholesale change to tuition, the most contested aspect of higher education, using a scheme that was first developed outside the United States. Tuition can be grounded in a less politicized and more stable system that preserves social access while improving educational resources. Tuition loans can be transformed into a public good rather than a private burden. However, it must be done on a national basis. The solution is too big for any one state.

The problems are affordability, default, and the spiraling total cost of debt. The United States still uses commercial loans based on mortgage-style timed repayments. Graduates who cannot generate loan repayments are in jeopardy. Graduates from poorer backgrounds are more likely to be in this position, as are women. This in turn tends to deter the future participation of others from those groups. The high level of default is ultimately carried by government, a considerable public subsidy. What is needed is a tuition-loans regime that works across a range of tuition charges but has minimal deterrent effect at the point of entry, and minimal socioeconomic bias: that is, a regime in which no student from any background is deterred on financial grounds. The tuition-loans regime should use public subsidies to support access rather than to compensate loans companies. To meet these objectives, a number of countries have moved or are moving to tuition-loans schemes based on income-contingent repayment arrangements, with repayment through taxation system. The United Kingdom adopted such as scheme in 2012. Australia has had one in place since 1988. Other countries include Hungary, South Korea, Thailand, and New Zealand.

In the United Kingdom in 2012 public university tuition was initially fixed at a maximum of £9000 per annum ($14,500). Almost all institutions charge at the maximum, which operates as a standard cost, though this is not essential to the scheme. Students pay tuition at the point of enrollment using government-backed loans, with the transaction taking place between institutions and government. Students handle no money at this point. The loans are described as "income contingent" because they are repaid through the tax system on a percentage-of-income basis. Repayment begins when income reaches a threshold level. Prior to that, the graduate carries the debt without the obligation to repay, though the debt slowly increases on the basis of subcommercial interest charges. In Australia, tuition debt is indexed to the cost of living; in the United Kingdom, interest is slightly higher. In both Australia and the United Kingdom, the threshold that triggers repayment is just below average full-time earnings. Most new graduates do not begin to pay immediately on graduation. Not all graduates repay their loans, particularly those who work for low rates of pay and those who spend long periods outside the workforce. In the United Kingdom, all unpaid tuition debt is retired after thirty years, while in Australia, it remains until death but is not passed on to the graduate's heirs.

Instead of subsidizing income-contingent tuition loans by picking up the cost of default, the UK and Australian governments subsidize them via the subcommercial rate of interest on tuition debt and the nonrepayment of part of the debt. In Australia, nonrepayment has been variously estimated at 25–40 percent of total student debts, no higher than the subsidies for default in the United States. In the United Kingdom, estimates have varied across a similar range, between 30 and 45 percent.

Income-contingent loans have several advantages. First, the extent of public subsidy can be tweaked by altering the terms governing the loans, including the interest rate on debt, the income threshold for repayment, and the rate of repayment (the percentage of income). Second, in the context of a modest level of total taxation revenue, income-contingent tuition loans enable the United Kingdom and Australia to expand enrollments knowing graduates will eventually pay the majority of the costs. Third, and most importantly, income-contingent loans remove socioeconomic and gender bias from tuition charges. At the point of enrollment of full-time students, the tuition regime functions like free education. Students continue to pay nothing until they graduate: completion is not deterred by accumulating tuition costs. Repayment through the tax system is less painful than commercial loan repayments. In the case of most graduates, the money is forwarded by employers to government, along with other income tax. The graduate does not make direct payments. On average, students from poor backgrounds pay less than affluent students, and women pay less than men. Students from affluent backgrounds and men are more likely to repay their debts in full over the course of their lifetime. The level of tuition charges has been increased several times in Australia. Each time the change has been socially neutral; that is, there is no evidence that following the policy change, students from low socioeconomic status backgrounds were more deterred from enrolling than were others. The only category of students unduly affected by income-contingent loans are part-time working students who are required to repay during the year of study because their income triggers the repayment threshold. The part-time working student was also the most affected by the introduction of the £9000 income-contingent, loan-based tuition regime in the United Kingdom in 2012. This is a design flaw in the income-contingent loans schemes in the United Kingdom and Australia that is yet to be addressed.

Income contingent tuition loans contribute markedly to the public good. They restore the basis for universal access. They enable high participation in higher education with no direct cost and no social bias at the point of entry, and they provide a basis for affordable public education of good quality. Under this system, tuition can be increased to the level needed to sustain agreed quality without reducing access at the point of enrollment, cutting into completion rates, or discriminating against poor students at any point. Better, income contingent tuition loans are economically progressive, in that wealthy families pay more on average than poor families. From the viewpoint of equality of opportunity, a scheme that provides for universal access and completion and discriminates economically in favor of those with least capacity to pay, who gain the most from participation in higher education, is superior to the present American student-loans system.

Income-contingent loans can be confined to the public sector or offered to all students in all sectors. Income-contingent loans can be set at any chosen level of tuition charge, but it would be unwise to offer these loans without a ceiling, especially if the tuition-loans scheme was extended to private colleges. Unlimited subsidies would encourage higher education institutions to increase charges freely, knowing that government rather than the student would carry the initial cost and the cost of unpaid debt. The ceiling on subsidies can be varied by field of study, institutional type, or particular categories of students, such as poor students. Conditions can be attached to eligibility of programs for the loans. It is a flexible policy instrument.[6]

Only the federal government could introduce income-contingent loans. It would need to absorb existing commercial loans. It is a transformation almost on the scale of health care reform, and like health care reform, it would invite fierce opposition from vested interests. But it would be the most important move the federal government could make to stabilize costs, bring tuition increases under control, and underwrite accessibility and affordability. From the point of view of federal government, it is a more affordable reform than free college education. Ultimately, graduates and government would share the cost. At the same time, income-contingent loans would not reduce the net resources available to public colleges, as free tuition would tend to do. Equally importantly, it ends the cycle of recurring state-induced fiscal crises in the public higher education sector. Federally driven income-contingent tuition loans could replace state subsidies altogether if that is what the two levels of government wanted. It would be the best move Washington could make, coupling sound public finance with equality of opportunity in higher education.

AND FINALLY, IN CALIFORNIA

Federal income-contingent tuition loans would help in California. By stabilizing tuition and access, enabling improved resources, and solving the state budget crisis, they would establish favorable conditions for going back to the drawing board. Under such conditions, where would the California Idea go? That is for Californians to say, and not foreign scholars of higher education systems. Though clearly, there will be no new Master Plan until the state is again ready to take the long-term view.

If so, what would Clark Kerr do? Of course, only he could say, but we can be certain that he would consider both excellence and access, and he would fasten onto the declining quality and affordability of mass higher education as a problem that must be addressed. He might want to extend the regulatory coverage of the new Plan to include the for-profit colleges operating on state soil, which are part of the postsecondary environment in the state and significant recipients of public money.

Kerr might also revisit the balance of enrollment and qualifications, within and between the higher education sectors. Two-year qualifications now lack weight in the labor markets. In most countries, the majority of higher education students are in three- or four-year programs. In some countries, most students are in doctoral universities, yet that is the case for only 12.5 percent of the age cohort in California. Arguably, the number of California universities with recognized research capacity is too low given the size of the state population and the need for broadly distributed capacity in advanced technologies. California needs more four-year places and more graduates that have been exposed to a research university environment.

Four-year places can be increased by expanding the enrollment of the California State University and University of California campuses and by developing more community college programs at a four-year level.[7] The research university experience could be broadened by creating new research and doctoral campuses in selected CSU sites, not funded at the same level for research as is the UC but funded for research and doctoral training nevertheless. In the longer term, other CSU sites could merge with community colleges, thus creating four regulated sectors in the interdependent and mutually responsible and networked California system: two sets of doctoral universities, the public community colleges, and the private colleges.[8] With the lower tiers upgraded, the vertical stratification of state public higher education would be less "steep," the level of education in the lower tiers would be lifted, and the state's research capacity would be increased. The 1960 Master Plan would be modernized.

For those of us outside California, it would be satisfying to again see the state's public higher education system moving forward. It would resonate around the world.

With that hope, it remains for this author to express his warm gratitude for the opportunity to explore the California Idea of higher education, and to wish its practitioners well.

London
February 26, 2016

NOTES

PREFACE

1. Douglass 2000.

1. AN EXTRAORDINARY TIME

1. Callender 2014, p. 164.
2. Rothblatt 2012a, p. 17.
3. Piketty 2014, p. 374.
4. Kennedy's image of the city, which derives originally from the Sermon on the Mount, was used by Puritan John Winthrop in 1630 prior to the settling of the colony in Massachusetts Bay that became Boston. In some other uses of the image, the locus moves from virtuous government or community to the United States as God's chosen city, thereby annexing it in the cause of American exceptionalism. For example, in the close of his farewell speech on 11 January 1989, Ronald Reagan, citing Winthrop, referred to America as "a shining city on a hill" (Reagan 1989).

2. CLARK KERR

1. Rothblatt 2012b, pp. xiii–xiv.
2. Rothblatt 2012a, p. 3.
3. Gonzalez 2011, p. ix.
4. Smelser 2001, pp. xxiii–xxiv.
5. Rothblatt 2012a, p. 12.
6. Pelfrey 2004, p. 39.
7. Rothblatt 2012a, p. 4.

8. Ibid., p. 14.

9. Ibid., pp. 7, 4.

10. Keynes 1972, p. 108, cited in Carabelli and Cedrini 2014.

11. Carabelli and Cedrini 2014, p. 31.

12. Rothblatt 2012a, p. 13.

13. Ibid., p. 14.

14. Rosenfeld (2012, p. 50) reports that while working as a professor of industrial relations at UC Berkeley, Kerr handled more than five hundred labor disputes and "became the top arbitrator on the West Coast."

15. Rothblatt 2012a, pp. 7–8.

16. Kerr 2001b, p. 27.

17. Rothblatt 2012a, p. 8.

18. Levine 2012, p. 48.

19. "I have kept that message all my life, but not without some disappointments. After my later experience with industrial relations, I came to add 'but it takes me longer to find it in some people than others.' After experiencing academic administration in-fighting, I came to add, 'and with some people I am still looking'" (Kerr 2001a, p. 14).

20. Smelser 2001, p. xxvi. Hanna Holborn Gray (2012, p. 9) refers to Kerr's "capacity for disinterested commentary and generous judgment."

21. Kerr 2003, p. 14.

22. Ibid., p. 23.

23. Smelser 2003, p. xxiii.

24. Kerr 2003, p. 36.

25. Ibid., p. 22.

26. Rothblatt 2012a, p. 6.

27. Rosenfeld 2012, p. 48.

28. Rothblatt 2012a, p. 6.

29. Rothblatt 2012a, p. 14.

30. See Buchanan and Tullock 1962, and the review of public choice theory in Amadae 2003.

31. Washburn 2005, p. 2.

32. Ibid., pp. 1, 14.

33. Sheldon Rothblatt, personal communication, 20 August 2015.

34. Rosenfeld 2012, p. 48.

35. Kerr 2001a, p. 287. According to Rosenfeld (2012, p. 496), Kerr said to a reporter, in relation to Vietnam: "I have the impression that opportunities for negotiation were not fully exploited."

36. Rosenfeld 2012, p. 229.

37. Kerr 2003, pp. 278–279.

38. Rosenfeld 2012, pp. 228–231.

39. Ibid., pp. 372–378; Kerr 2003, pp. 288–311.

40. Gonzalez 2011, p. 1.

41. Mettler 2014, p. 6; Rosenfeld 2012, p. 497.

42. Kerr 2003, pp. 316–317.

3. CLARK KERR AND THE CALIFORNIA IDEA

1. Levine 2012, pp. 45–47.
2. Cole 2009, p. 145.
3. Ibid., p. 134. Martin Trow stated that Kerr was "the most distinguished university president of the twentieth century" (ibid., p. 138).
4. Humboldt (1909–1810) 1970; Newman (1852–1858) 1996.
5. Rothblatt 2012a, p. 14.
6. Callan 2012, p. 63.
7. Douglass 2000, p. 248.
8. Kerr 2001a, p. 178.
9. Ibid., p. 184.
10. Douglass, 2000, p. 316.
11. Ibid., p. 105.
12. Piketty 2014, p. 241.
13. Ibid, p. 385.
14. Hennessy 2014.
15. Gray 2012, p. 22.
16. Kerr 2001a, p. 173; Rothblatt 2012a, p. 17.
17. Kerr 2001a, p. 177.
18. Callan 2012, p. 64.
19. Douglass 2000, pp. 287–289.
20. Rothblatt 2007, p. 258.
21. Douglass 2000, pp. 311–312.

4. THE USES OF THE UNIVERSITY

1. Kerr 2001b.
2. Newman (1852–1858) 1996.
3. Kerr 2001b, p. 106.
4. Ibid., p. 31
5. Gray 2012.
6. The 1960s recall those few months of 1936 in Barcelona or early 1790s Paris and that strange decade in England, the 1640s–early 1650s, with millennials breaking out everywhere and kingdoms of justice and virtue almost within reach. The 1960s were about belief, but secular humanist and democratic like Barcelona: a postreligious celebration of ideas about individual and collective self-determination. These prolonged historical moments of collective self-made freedoms tend to destabilize all certainty and order. In the long term they leave deep social imprints, both productive and negative. Both Clark Kerr and the radical student movement at Berkeley that triggered the loss of his university presidency were engaged in utopian thinking, though the context, content, and scale of their respective utopias were different. Each kind of utopianism helped to shape the evolution of later society, and each triggered a robust and, on the whole, successful reaction.
7. Smelser 2013, p. 12.

8. Kerr 2001b, pp. 17–18. "The three major sources of accretions in the twentieth century have been philanthropic activity among foundations, directed research funding on the part of federal agencies, and investment and collaboration from corporate sources in the university" (p. 70).

9. Ibid., pp. 22–23.

10. Slaughter and Leslie 1997; Slaughter and Rhoades 2004.

11. Kerr 2001b, p. 90.

12. Kerr 2003, p. 21.

13. Kerr 2001a, p. viii.

14. Smelser 2013, p. 3.

15. Bowen and Tobin 2015, p. 87.

16. Kerr 2001b, p. 31.

17. Ibid., p. 15.

18. Scott 2015, p. 27.

19. Kerr 2001b, p. 15.

20. Ibid., p. 81.

21. Ibid., pp. 41–42.

5. MARTIN TROW: HIGHER EDUCATION AND GROWTH

1. Trow 1973, pp. 1–2, 7.

2. Ibid., p. 7.

3. Ibid., pp. 7–8.

4. Ibid., p. 18.

5. Ibid., pp. 23–24.

6. Ibid., pp. 9–10.

7. Ibid., p. 8.

8. Ibid., p. 9.

9. Ibid., pp. 10–13.

10. Ibid., pp. 13–15.

11. Ibid., p. 20.

12. Ibid., p. 18.

13. For example, Trow 1970.

14. Ibid., pp. 5–6, 40.

15. Trow 2000.

16. Becker 1964.

17. Ibid., pp. 41–42.

18. See also Fred Hirsch (1976) on the character of "positional goods."

19. Trow 1973, p. 40.

20. Ibid., pp. 40–41.

21. Ibid., p. 41.

22. Ibid., pp. 42–43.

23. Reported in Rothblatt 2012a, p. 11.

24. Teichler 2009, cover.

25. Ibid., p. 28.

26. Baker 2011, p. 8. Despite the large number of studies, human capital theory's economic claim is also insufficiently grounded. Human capital studies focus largely on earnings and rates of return, with little evidence of the productivity-inducing effects, whether these are seen as grounded in schooling or the selection process (Hansen 2011, p. 47).

27. Trow 1973, p. 25.

28. Trow 2000, p. 6.

6. BOB CLARK: THE ACADEMIC HEARTLAND

1. *Creating Entrepreneurial Universities* (Clark 1998a) is much cited for its ideas about proactive university mission and organization.

2. Clark 1983, p. 2.

3. Ibid., p. 26.

4. Ibid., p. 30.

5. Ibid., pp. 2–3.

6. Ibid., p. 276.

7. Ibid., p. 275.

8. Ibid., p. 6.

9. Ibid., p. 13.

10. Ibid., p. 275.

11. Ibid., p. 2.

12. Ibid., pp. 137–145.

13. Ibid., p. 169.

14. Ibid., p. 169.

15. Clark 1998a; 1998b, p. 5.

16. Ibid., p. 8.

17. Ibid., p. 9.

18. Marginson and Considine 2000, chapter 4.

19. Clark 1998b, p. 11.

20. Clark 1998b, p. 6.

7. WHITHER THE CALIFORNIA IDEA OF HIGHER EDUCATION?

1. Rothblatt 2012a, p. 31.

2. Ibid., pp. 30–32; Scott 2015, p. 27.

3. Scott 2015, pp. 25–26.

4. The quote comes from Eliot's "The Hollow Men" in *Poems: 1909–1925* (London: Faber and Gwyer, 1925).

5. Shanghai Jiao Tong University 2015.

6. Leiden University 2015.

7. Pelfrey 2012, p. 59.

8. Douglass 2013, pp. 4–5.

9. Rothblatt 2007, p. 272. "First generation" means that neither parent enrolled in higher education.

10. Soares 2007, pp. 166–167.

11. Douglass 2013, pp. 4–5. In 2014 Berkeley enrolled 9,742 students in receipt of Pell Grants compared to 10,106 at Cornell, Columbia, Pennsylvania, Harvard, Brown, Yale, Dartmouth, and Princeton combined (Wilton 2014).

12. Bowen and Tobin 2015, pp. 226–227.

13. *Sacramento Bee* 2013.

14. Douglass 2013, p. 10; Callan 2012, p. 71.

15. Ibid., p. 29.

16. Douglass 2013, p. 12.

17. Kerr 2011b, p. xi.

8. THE IDEA SPREADS

1. Hazelkorn 2011.

2. Liu and Cheng 2005; Liu 2009; Huang 2015.

3. Huang 2015.

4. Smelser 2013, p. 28.

9. PARTICIPATION WITHOUT LIMIT

1. Trow 1973, pp. 5–6, 40.

2. Trow 2000, pp. 7, 14.

3. In the GTER, *tertiary* includes degree-length programs and two-year full-time equivalent programs.

4. The GTER tends to overstate participation rates because the numerator in the ratio includes mature-age students as well as students in the school-leaver age cohort. This effect varies by country, according to the size of the mature-age entry. The numerator of the GTER also includes international students and longer-term migrants additional to the birth cohort. This leads to a further overstatement of participation rates in those nations, such as the United Kingdom, Australia, and Switzerland, that enroll large numbers of international students. The number of these countries is small, however. In the United States the effect is modest because only 4 percent of students in higher education are international. In Australia in 2012 the inclusion of onshore international students increased the apparent rate of entry into tertiary education by 26 percent and the apparent age cohort graduation rate by 18 percent. The overstatement of entry was 23 percent in United Kingdom, 12 percent in Austria, and 11 percent in the Netherlands and Switzerland (OECD 2014a, pp. 81, 338). Note also that in some countries, such as the Philippines and Malaysia, net outflow because of high emigration or large numbers of students going abroad tends to reduce the GTER. In 2012 the proportion of all onshore tertiary students who were international students was 18 percent in Australia, 17 percent in the UK, 16 percent in New Zealand and Switzerland, and 15 percent in Austria (OECD 2014a, p. 354).

5. UIS 2015.

6. Ibid.

7. Ibid.

8. UNDP 2013, p. 165.

9. UIS 2015.

10. Yang 2014.

11. UIS 2015. There were no UNESCO Institute for Statistics data for Botswana, Lesotho, Nigeria, Sierra Leone, South Africa, Tanzania, and Zambia.

12. Sen 2000.

13. Carrington 2014.

14. UIS 2015; Clotfelter 2010, p. 11. See also part 3.

15. UIS 2015.

16. Brand and Xie 2010.

17. UNDESA 2012. Urbanization has grown more steadily than participation in higher education. Between 1970 and 1990, urbanization moved ahead of the GTER. After 1995, the GTER increased much faster than urbanization, although the latter also quickened.

18. Kharas and Gertz 2010.

19. UIS 2015.

20. Task Force on Higher Education and Society 2000.

21. Carnoy et al. 2014, p. 362.

22. For more discussion, see part 3. Keynes described economics as "a science of thinking in terms of models joined to the art of choosing models which are relevant to the contemporary world." Human capital theory is ideologically relevant but not empirically grounded. Keynes (1936) 1973a, p. 296; Carabelli and Cedrini 2014, p. 31. As economist Tony Lawson (2012) remarks: "The fundamental problem of modern economics is that methods are repeatedly applied in conditions for which they are not appropriate" (p. 1).

23. Geiger 2014.

24. Schofer and Meyer 2005, pp. 900, 916.

25. Data analyses by the author. See Marginson 2016.

26. Scott 2015, pp. 47–48.

27. Kharas and Gertz 2010, pp. 5–6.

28. Mahbubani 2013, pp. 11–12.

10. THE SPREAD OF SCIENCE

1. Castells 2000, pp. 70–71.

2. Internet Live Stats 2015. In early 2015 worldwide Internet use was estimated at 3,089 million, 40 percent of the world's population. Penetration in the United States exceeded 87 percent. An Internet user is defined as someone who has Internet access at home.

3. Clark 1998a, p. 6.

4. Vest 2007, p. 4.

5. Borghans and Cörvers 2010.

6. See NSF 2014, Appendix Tables, pp. 588–594.

7. Bush 1945.

8. NSF 2014.

9. The output of nations with small numbers of papers is mostly carried by doctoral and postdoctoral scholars who study internationally, often publishing jointly with American or European advisers.

10. Research by the author in Moscow research establishments, 2013.

11. NSF 2014. For example, in 2012 the rate of coauthorship between the United States and Canada was 14 percent higher than expected, given the overall intensity of coauthorship by the United States with all countries, and by Canada with all countries. The figures for the other countries were Mexico, 8 percent; Chile, 5 percent; Israel, 29 percent; China, 10 percent; South Korea, 25 percent; and Taiwan, 22 percent.

11. THE GLOBAL MULTIVERSITY

1. It is Kerr's final point in the Preface to the 2001 edition of the lectures—Kerr 2001b, p. x.

2. Cole 2009, p. 465.

3. For the change in China, see Huang 2015.

4. Salmi 2009; Huang 2015.

5. Cremonini et al. 2014, p. 351.

6. An exception is the ranking developed by Scimago, based on the Elsevier Scopus journal collection. The main Scimago Lab (2015) listing combines universities and nonuniversity research institutes.

7. Marginson 2006; 2008; 2011a; 2011b.

8. Marginson 2014b.

9. Cheng 2011.

10. *Times Higher Education* 2015.

11. QS Top Universities 2015.

12. Hazelkorn 2011; Locke 2011; Sauder and Espeland 2009.

13. Hazelkorn 2011.

14. Salmi 2009; Altbach and Salmi 2011; Hazelkorn 2011.

15. Carnoy et al. 2014, p. 368.

16. Salmi 2009, p. 3.

17. Ibid., pp. 6–7.

18. Ibid., p. 7.

19. Ibid., pp. 36–37.

20. Ibid., pp. 9–10, 52–60.

21. Ibid., pp. 60–64.

22. Ibid., pp. 12–13.

23. Ibid., p. 73.

24. Matthew 25:29: "For unto every one that hath shall be given, and he shall have abundance." Robert Merton (1968) first used the term "Matthew effect" in relation to the accumulation of reputation by leading research scientists.

25. See also the discussion of research on American institutional stratification by Davies and Zarifa (2012) in part 3.

26. Formerly the Research Assessment Exercise.

27. For example, for Finland, France, and Germany, see Cremonini et al. 2014, pp. 348–354; for the various programs in East Asia, see Yang and Welch 2012; Huang 2015; Yonezawa and Shimmi 2015; Kim 2010, pp. 355–356; and Byun, Jon, and Kim 2013. For a summary of WCU programs in all countries up to 2009, see Salmi 2009, pp. 85–91. For the most recent summary, see Salmi 2015.

28. Salmi 2011, p. 326.

29. For example, in China: Rui Yang 2014; Rhoads and Szelenyi 2011, p. 55.

30. Wang, Wang, and Liu 2011, pp. 53–56.

31. Ibid., p. 56.

32. Rhee 2011, p. 117.

33. For further discussion of internationalization in East Asia, see Bhandari and Lefebure 2015; in China, Huang 2015; and in Japan, Yonezawa and Shimmi 2015.

34. Altbach 2011, p. 22.

35. Mahbubani 2013, p. 83.

36. Borghans and Cörvers 2010, p. 260. In 1948–1957 in the Netherlands, 72 percent of all doctoral theses were in Dutch, but in 1998–2007 that proportion had dropped to 14 percent. In Denmark, the proportion in the national language shifted from 56 to 15 percent; in Norway, theses in Norwegian were 50 percent of all PhDs in 1948–1957 but there were none in Norwegian fifty years later. In contrast there was almost no change in France, with more than 99.5 percent of theses in French in both periods. In Germany the proportion of theses in German fell, but only slightly, from almost 100 percent in 1948–1957 to 95 percent in 1998–2007. Ibid., pp. 261–262.

37. Carnoy 1974.

38. Cremonini et al. 2014.

39. Universitas21 2015.

12. SYSTEMS AND STRATIFICATION

1. Bourdieu 1988.

2. Hirsch 1976; Marginson 1997.

3. OECD 2014a, pp. 84–100.

4. Valimaa 2011.

5. Frank and Cook 1996; Marginson 1997; Marginson 2006; Duncan 2015.

6. Clark 1960.

7. Carnoy et al. 2014, pp. 373–374.

8. Marginson and Marshman 2013.

9. Trow 1963/1964, quoted in Shattock 2012, pp. 118–119. The 1963 Robbins Report was unsuccessful in its attempt to establish a growth-oriented unitary sector of universities. Instead, the United Kingdom decided to create polytechnics to facilitate growth at a lower unit cost in public funding, as in California (Shattock 2012, p. 120). Robbins's unitary view was implemented after 1992, at a time when participation was far higher than in 1963 but universities were expanding their income from nongovernment sources, which helped pay for the costs of research.

10. Ibid., p. 124.

11. This statement was correct up to 2015. The Netherlands *hogescholen* have been granted a limited capacity to conduct applied research projects. A further extension of their research role is possible.

12. Postiglione 2011.

13. Huang 2015.

14. Carnoy et al. 2014, p. 369.

15. Postiglione 2014.

16. Carnoy et al. 2014, p. 368, argues this in relation to the BRICS countries.

17. Reisberg 2014.

18. Marginson 2013.

13 AMERICAN UNIVERSITIES IN THE GLOBAL SPACE

1. Castells 2000; Marginson 2010b; Marginson 2011a.

2. Rui Yang 2014.

3. *ICEF Monitor* 2015.

4. CSIC 2015.

5. Borghans and Cörvers 2010, p. 240.

6. OECD 2014a, p. 344.

7. IIE 2015.

8. NSF 2014, Appendix Tables, p. 385.

9. Bound and Turner 2010, p. 111.

10. Ibid., p. 231.

11. Global public goods are "goods that have a significant element of non-rivalry and/or non-excludability and are made broadly available across populations on a global scale. They affect more than one group of countries" (Kaul, Grunberg, and Stern 1999, pp. 2–3).

12. Shanghai Jiao Tong University, Center for World-Class Universities 2015.

13. Ibid.

14. Leiden University 2015; Scimago Lab 2015.

15. Leiden University 2015.

16. NSF 2014.

17. See the collected chapters in Bhandari and Lefebure 2015.

18. Mahbubani 2013, pp. 11.

14. ENTER THE DRAGON

1. Holcombe 2011, p. 3.

2. Gernet 1996, pp. 28–29.

3. Holcombe 2011, p. 33.

4. Ibid., p. 38.

5. Mahbubani 2013, p. 41, notes that this was emphasized by Mao Zedong.

6. Ibid., pp. 1–2. China published more books than the rest of the world together until about 1500.

7. OECD 2012, p. 43.

8. Ibid.; World Bank 2015.

9. Li 2010, pp. 273–275.

10. Ministry of Education, China 2015.

11. World Bank 2015.

12. Bray 2007.

13. Levin 2011.

14. OECD 2014a, p. 245.

15. Ministry of Education, China 2015.

16. Carnoy et al. 2014, p. 373.

17. Note, however, there is controversy over the meaning of the Shanghai PISA results. Tom Loveless (2013) at the Brookings Institute has argued that average PISA scores in Shanghai are boosted by the exclusion of many migrant workers' children from Shanghai high schools under the *hukou* system of household registration.

18. Ibid., p. 14.

19. Jerrim 2014, p. 4.

20. Ibid., pp. 15–16.

21. Ibid., p. 11 and p. 25.

22. Ibid., p. 16.

23. See the national system case studies of China, Taiwan, South Korea and Japan in Freeman, Marginson, and Tytler 2015.

24. OECD 2014b.

25. Calonge 2015.

26. Jacques 2012.

27. World Bank 2015.

28. Ibid.; CIA 2015. The Taiwan estimate is based on the 1990 to 2010 period.

29. OECD 2012, p. 39.

30. OECD 2015.

31. Cole 2009, p. 3.

32. Tran et al. 2014.

33. Marginson 2010a.

15. HIGHER EDUCATION IN CHINA AND THE UNITED STATES

1. Mahbubani 2013, p. 166.

2. Huang 2015.

3. Zha 2015.

4. Habermas 1989.

5. Hayhoe 2011.

6. Zha 2011. Chinese Minister Yuan Guiren was calling on this ethic of positive responsibility when he said in early 2015 that professors must "not complain, vent personal grievances or convey negative emotions to their students" (Zha 2015). Thus the regime mobilizes faculty as an instrument of rule.

7. Mahbubani 2013, pp. 154–157.

8. Zha 2015.

9. Rhoads and Szelenyi 2011, p. 8.

10. Ibid., p. 100.

11. Clotfelter 2010, pp. 16–17; Kim and Zhu 2010. For historical discussion of U.S.-China higher educational exchange since the late 1970s, see the various chapters in Li 2015.

12. NSF 2014.

13. IIE 2015.

14. *ICEF Monitor* 2015.

15. At the time of writing, the NYU program was just becoming established in China and faced critics at home. It is to be hoped that it can survive the difficult early years.

16. Said 1993, p. 20.

17. Dewey (1927)1980, p. 38.

18. Wimmer and Schiller 2002.

19. Sen 1992.

20. Singer 2002, p. 12.

21. Dewey (1927)1980, pp. 45–46.

16. HIGHER EDUCATION AFTER CLARK KERR

1. Kerr 2001b, p. 227.

2. Deresiewicz 2014, p. 62.

3. Washburn 2005, p. 2.

4. Bok 2003; Kirp 2004.

5. Kerr 2003.

6. OECD 2104a, pp. 150–170.

7. Hansen 2011, p. 43.

8. Rhoades, 2008.

9. For a few examples of many, Arum and Roksa 2014; Deresiewicz 2014; Katsikas 2015; Warner 2015; Berrett 2015.

10. Vest 2007, p. 11.

11. Helms 2015, p. 5.

17. THE IMPOSSIBILITY OF PUBLIC GOOD

1. Lukes 1973; Amadae 2003, p. 122.

2. Amadae 2003, p. 84, pp. 103–104.

3. Ibid., p. 106.

4. Ibid., p. 124.

5. Dewey (1927) 1980.

6. Amadae 2003, p. 84.

7. Arrow (1951) 1963, p. 29.

8. Amadae 2003, p. 114.

9. Ibid., p. 131.

10. Friedman 1953.

11. In characteristic fashion, James Buchanan (1975) was to spell out the full implications of this notion of absolute individualism without J.S. Mills's constraint, or any other constraint deriving from sociability: "In a strictly personalized sense, any person's ideal situation is one that allows him full freedom of action and inhibits the behavior of others so as to force adherence to his own desires. That is to say, each person seeks mastery over a world of slaves" (p. 92).

12. Ibid., p. 111.

13. Buchanan 1997, p. 85.

14. Buchanan and Tullock 1962, pp. 3, 265.

15. Ibid., p. 18.
16. Ibid., p. 95, pp. 305–306, 314–315.
17. Ibid., pp. 12, 35, 132, 284, 315.
18. Smith (1759) 2004. The point is made also by Amadae 2003, p. 205.
19. Buchanan 1975, p. 161.
20. Ibid., p. 201.
21. Buchanan 1979, p. 271
22. Piketty 2014, p. 493.
23. Buchanan 1975, p. 147.
24. Ibid., p. 42.
25. Ibid., p. 84.
26. For example, Buchanan and Wagner 1977, p. 65.
27. Friedman and Friedman 1980, p. x.
28. Friedman 1962.
29. Buchanan and Devletoglou 1970.

18. THE IMPOSSIBILITY OF TAXATION

1. Rosenfeld 2012.
2. Kerr 2003, pp. 288–311.
3. The counterculture "summer of love" began in the Haight-Ashbury district of San Francisco in 1967.
4. Kerr 2003, p. 16.
5. Berrett 2015.
6. Pelfrey 2004, pp. 53–54.
7. Ibid., pp. 56–57.
8. Ibid., pp. 69–70; Callan 2012, p. 70.
9. Bentele 2013, pp. 31–33.
10. Piketty 2014, p. 509; Stiglitz 2013, p. xxxi. For more discussion of trends in inequality, see chapter 19.
11. Kerr 2001a, p. 189.
12. Callan 2012, pp. 67, 69.
13. Douglass 2011a, p. 28.
14. Douglass 2013, pp. 5–6.
15. Wilton 2014.
16. Smelser 2013, pp. 44–48, p. 85.
17. Douglass 2013, p. 7. These are averages; there are marked variations across the disciplines.
18. Adams 2010, pp. 46–66, especially p. 65.
19. Wilton 2014.
20. Callan 2012, p. 76.
21. Ibid., pp. 74–75.
22. Ibid., p. 76.
23. *Sacramento Bee* 2013.
24. Klugman 2013, pp. 11–12.

25. Pelfrey 2012, p. 70.

26. Rothblatt 2007, p. 269.

27. Pelfrey 2012, p. 158.

28. Kerr (1963) 2001b, p. 218.

29. Rothblatt 2007, p. 268.

30. Callan 2012, p. 80.

31. Hansen 2011, pp. 42–43.

32. Douglass 2011a, p. 22.

33. Ibid., p. 27.

34. Callan 2012, p. 80

35. Ibid., pp. 72–73.

36. Ibid., p. 73.

37. Douglass 2011a, p. 21.

38. Callan 2012, p. 71.

39. Ibid., p. 79.

19. ECONOMIC AND SOCIAL INEQUALITY

1. Hennessy 2014, p. 47.

2. Piketty 2014; Stiglitz 2013; Dorling 2014; OECD 2014c.

3. For example, Piketty 2014, pp. 315–316; Saez 2013; Atkinson, Piketty, and Saez 2011; Smeeding 2005; OECD 2014c.

4. Piketty 2014, pp. 319, 256.

5. Ibid., p. 265.

6. Saez 2013, p. 3.

7. Ibid., pp. 7–9.

8. OECD 2014c, p. 1.

9. Ibid., p. 2, p. 5.

10. Piketty 2014, p. 249.

11. Sommeiller and Price 2015. The authors show that measured inequality and relative and absolute incomes of the top 1 percent are greater in their calculations than those of Piketty and Saez,.

12. Pastor and Braun 2015.

13. Economic Policy Institute and Center on Budget and Policy Priorities 2012.

14. Short 2014, pp. 9–10.

15. Luhby 2015; Burds-Sharp and Lewis 2015.

16. Ibid., p. 316.

17. Stiglitz 2013, p. 26.

18. Milanovic for IMF 2011, p. 8; Piketty 2014, pp. 304, 321; Stiglitz 2014, p. 243.

19. Autor, Katz, and Kearney 2008, for example, p. 318; Mouw and Kalleberg 2010; Wolff and Zacharias 2013, pp. 88–90.

20. Piketty 2014, pp. 264–265.

21. Ibid, pp. 300–301.

22. Bentele 2013, pp. 37–39.

23. Piketty 2014, p. 303.

24. Stiglitz 2013.

25. Bentele 2013, p. 33.

26. Hanley 2011, p. 904. "Under the shareholder value conception of the firm managers orient their decisions toward increasing returns on the assets of the firm to increase their value to shareholders, rather than pursuing profits via growth or market share." This legitimizes "redistributing company profits from workers to managers, executives and stockholders. The theory implies that contribution to the value of company stock (or other measures of profit) should be the basis for compensation, rather than measures of output such as value added to products. This redefinition of valued contributions meriting reward by the firm valorizes managerial and professional roles in the division of labour over production." Note that in the case of supersalaries, the link back to educated attributes ("human capital") is more tenuous than with most income earners. Supersalaries are the outcome not of individual productivity per se, but control not just of the workplace but of private remuneration.

27. Piketty 2014, p. 378.

28. Wisman 2013.

29. Stiglitz 2013, p. xii, p. 17.

30. Ibid., p. 147.

31. Piketty 2014, p. 571.

32. Stiglitz (2013, p. xxiii) states that finance plays a larger role in the growing inequality in the United Kingdom than in the United States. The political economy is more centralized in the United Kingdom, with the finance sector in the City of London playing the dominant role and policy and regulation sustained by the symbiosis between leading private financial institutions, the Bank of England, and the Treasury and the Chancellor's office.

33. For example, Stiglitz 2013; Wisman 2013, p. 921; Mettler 2014, pp. 45–48.

34. For example, Cingano 2014 for OECD; OECD 2014c, p. 9.

35. Cingano 2014; OECD 2014c. The IMF is also concerned about the alleged negative effects of inequality on economic growth: see Milanovic 2011; Berg and Ostry 2011; Ostry et al. 2014. Ostry et al. (2014, p. 23) conclude: "We find that higher inequality is bad for growth for both OECD and non-OECD countries (with the effect higher in OECD than in non-OECD countries)."

36. Oxfam 2014, p. 11.

37. Ibid., p. 13. See also Stiglitz 2013, p. 43, on the same episode.

38. Stiglitz 2013, pp. 148–149.

39. Ibid., p. 159.

40. Ibid., p. 160. Likewise, in the United Kingdom, Dorling (2014, p. 2) cites the results of the annual British Social Attitudes survey in 2012, which found that 82 percent of respondents saw the income gap as too large.

41. Reynolds and Xian, 2014. The authors also find that some respondents believe in both worldviews and others believe in neither (p. 121).

42. For some examples of many, Piketty 2014, pp. 193–194, p. 303, p. 376; Stiglitz 2013 p. xxiii, p. 43, p. 120, p. 308; Dorling 2014, pp. 55, p. 83–90; OECD 2014c, p. 9; Tridico 2012; Wisman 2013, p. 939; Bentele 2013, p. 29, p. 39; Hanley 2011, p. 908.

43. Wisman 2013, p. 925.

44. Stiglitz 2013, p. 120.

45. Stiglitz 2013, p. xxiii and p. 311.
46. Ibid., p. 225.
47. Piketty 2014, pp. 507–508.
48. Stiglitz 2013, p. xxxi.
49. Ibid., p. 496.
50. Piketty 2014, pp. 465–466.
51. Smeeding 2005, pp. 972–973.
52. Wisman 2013, p. 932.
53. Mettler 2014, pp. 87–110.

20. UNEQUAL OPPORTUNITY

1. Corak 2006; Mountford-Zimdars and Sabbagh 2013.
2. Roemer 2004.
3. For example, Thomsen et al. 2013, pp. 457, 471, 474.
4. Soares 2007, p. 167.
5. Piketty 2014, p. 485.
6. See, for example, Deresiewicz 2014; Pinker 2014; Rivera 2011.
7. Unz 2012. The violation of the merit principle in relation to Asian Americans was the subject of a legal challenge to Harvard in 2015 (Schmidt 2015). The long-standing use of nonacademic criteria by the Ivy League enables these universities to discriminate, but the problem may also extend to the public sector (Samson 2013).
8. Hoxby and Avery 2013.
9. Ibid., p. 2.
10. Ibid., pp. 5–6.
11. Ibid., pp. 14–15.
12. Ibid., pp. 38–39, 42.
13. Ibid., p. 1.
14. Ibid., p. 4.
15. Ibid., p. 31.
16. Ibid., pp .17–18.
17. Boliver 2013. See also the findings of Boliver 2011.
18. Boliver 2013, p. 344–345.
19. Hoxby and Avery 2013. See also Borgen 2015, p. 34, and the parallel findings by Chankseliani 2013 on rural disadvantage in Georgia: "equality is understood as equal treatment of all applicants to higher education. In contrast, an equitable system ensures that applicants are treated according to their prior education opportunities, which are often related to family background and geographic location. By analyzing the Georgian case, I argue that a higher education admissions model may guarantee equality but at the same time be inequitable" (p. 426). "Among those with the same measured aptitude, rural applicants are 12 times more likely to apply to one of the least prestigious higher education institutions than are applicants from urban areas" (p. 424).
20. See also Wilkinson and Pickett 2010, p. 113.
21. Boliver 2013, p. 347. This "underadmission" process is a large factor in the United Kingdom. In the case of students with equivalent qualifications, "applying to a Russell

Group university from a private school rather than a state school, or from a White ethnic background rather than a Black Caribbean/African or Pakistani/Bangladeshi one, increases the odds of admission to a Russell Group university by at least as much as having an additional B-grade A-level" (p. 358).

22. Frank and Cook 1996.

23. Hansen 2011, pp. 47–48.

24. Davies and Zarifa 2012, p. 143.

25. Ibid., p. 147.

26. See also Hansen 2011, p. 79.

27. Davies and Zarifa 2012, p. 144.

28. Ibid., p. 145.

29. Ibid., p. 145. The national higher education systems in the United Kingdom and Australia were reformed in the 1985–1995 period along the lines of managed quasi markets. These systems exhibit ongoing tendencies to greater stratification and the relative strengthening of top-tier institutions, although the tendencies are partly contained by policy (Marginson and Marshman 2013).

30. Davies and Zarifa 2012, p. 145.

31. Ibid., p. 146.

32. Ibid., p. 149.

33. Ibid., pp. 149–150.

34. Ibid., pp. 150, 154.

35. Ibid., p. 154.

36. Arum, Gamoran, and Shavit 2007, p. 3.

37. Ibid., p. 4.

38. Lucas 2001, 2009; Triventi 2013, p. 47.

39. Lucas 2001, p. 1652.

40. Lucas 2009, p. 459.

41. Arum, Gamoran, and Shavit 2007, p. 5.

42. Lucas 2009, p. 500.

43. Triventi 2013, p. 48.

44. Borgen 2015, p. 36.

45. Arum, Gamoran, and Shavit 2007, pp. 24–25.

46. Piketty 2014, p. 486.

47. Shavit, Arum, and Gamoran 2007.

48. Cheung and Egerton 2007, p .195.

49. Boliver 2011.

50. Cheung and Egerton 2007, p. 218.

51. Shavit et al. 2007, p. 61.

52. Park 2007, p. 97.

53. Hoxby and Avery 2013; Arum, Gamoran, and Shavit 2007, p. 31.

54. Jonsson and Erikson 2007, p. 137.

55. Ibid., p. 138.

56. Gärtner and Prado 2012.

57. Roksa et al. 2007, p. 189

58. Ibid., p. 165.

59. Ibid., p. 167.
60. Ibid., p. 190.
61. Ibid., p. 169.
62. Rivera 2011, 2012a, 2012b.
63. Rivera 2015.
64. Rivera 2011, p. 72.
65. Ibid., p. 73.
66. Ibid., p. 84.
67. Ibid., p. 75.
68. Ibid., p. 76.
69. Ibid., p. 78.
70. Ibid., p. 78.
71. Ibid., p. 80.
72. Ibid., p. 88.
73. Ibid., p. 72.
74. Ibid., p. 82.
75. Ibid., p. 83.
76. Ibid., p. 82.
77. Ibid., pp. 85–86.
78. Ibid., pp. 87–88.
79. Rivera 2012b, p. 999.
80. Rivera 2012b, pp. 1001–1002.
81. Rivera 2011, p. 88.
82. Rivera 2012a, p. 73.
83. Ibid., p. 85.
84. Tholen et al. 2013, p. 148.
85. Wolniak et al. 2008, p. 125.
86. Ibid., p. 135.
87. Borgen 2015, p. 32.
88. For example, Brand and Xie, 2010.
89. Ibid., p. 293.
90. Ibid., p. 291.
91. Ibid., p. 280.
92. Borgen 2015, p. 34.
93. Ibid., p. 34.

21. HIGHER EDUCATION AND THE ECONOMY

1. Arum and Roksa 2014, pp. 85, 105.
2. Hansen 2011, pp. 80–81.
3. Arum and Roksa 2014, p. 7.
4. Ibid., p. 112.
5. Hansen 2011, p. 43.
6. Lukes 1973.
7. Piketty 2014, pp. 330–331; Dorling 2014, p. 57.

8. OECD 2014a, p. 151.

9. Arum and Roksa 2014, p. 125.

10. Triventi 2013, p. 45.

11. Corak 2012, p. 6.

12. For example, Wolniak et al. 2008, p. 131.

13. Bingley, Corak, and Westergård-Nielsen 2011; Hallsten 2014, p. 20; Borgen 2015.

14. Arum and Roksa 2014, p. 14.

15. Piketty 2014, p. 305.

16. Arum and Roksa 2014, pp. 80–81.

17. Gerber and Cheung 2008, p. 301.

18. Thomas and Zhang 2005, p. 437, p. 440, p. 449, p. 437, p. 440.

19. Dale and Krueger 2011. The authors are more certain that for African American and Hispanic students and students from families with low parental education, returns to selectivity are significant (p. 1).

20. Li et al. 2012, p. 79.

21. Ibid., p. 78.

22. Gerber and Cheung 2008, p. 303.

23. Ibid., p. 313.

24. For example, Arum and Roksa 2014, pp. 80–81, in relation to business studies; Triventi 2013, pp. 55–57; Zhao 2012; Thomsen et al. 2013, p. 471; Hu and Vargas 2015; Hennessy 2014, p. 47.

25. Arum and Roksa 2014, p. 57.

26. Roksa 2005, p. 207.

27. Ibid.

28. Loyalka, Song, and Wei 2012, p. 304; Roksa and Levey 2010.

29. Kelly, O'Connell, and Smyth 2010, p. 655.

30. Roksa and Levey 2010, p. 392.

31. Ibid., p. 389.

32. Ibid., p. 399.

33. Wolniak et al. 2008, p. 131.

34. Roksa and Levey 2010, p. 399.

35. Roksa 2005, p. 226.

36. Triventi 2013, pp. 47–48.

37. Ibid., pp. 54, 45, 53, 55, 57.

38. Goodman 2014.

39. Zhao 2012.

40. Goodman 2014, p. 183. In *Class in Contemporary China*, Goodman remarks that in China, one's social power is the key factor, rather than income or ownership (p. 183). Social power is the way to economic rewards (pp. 29–30); status is one of the contributors to social power; and in China the state fosters the idea that graduation from higher education is the point of entry to the middle class (p. 111). This has lifted higher education's role in social allocation. Party members with college education are four times as likely as those without college to become leading cadre, though there is a circularity here: access to elite higher education is partly a function of parental clout, especially party membership (p. 70, p. 121).

41. Ibid., p. 187.
42. OECD 2014a, p. 109.
43. Wildhagen 2014, p. 19.
44. Arum and Roksa 2011, p. 34. The original source is Schneider and Stevenson 1999, pp. 79–85.
45. Robst 2007, p. 398.
46. Ibid., p. 402.
47. Roksa 2005, p. 225; Roksa and Levey 2010, p. 391.
48. Roksa and Levey 2010, p. 391.
49. Melguizo and Wolniak 2012, p. 383; Robst 2007, pp. 403–404.
50. See, for example, Bingley, Corak, and Westergård-Nielsen 2011; Rivera 2011, 2012a, 2012b; Tholen et al. 2013; Borgen 2015.
51. Thomsen et al. 2013, p. 471.
52. Robst 2007, p. 399.
53. For example, Arum and Roksa 2014, p. 14.
54. Borgen 2015, p. 34.
55. Bingley , Corak, and Westergård-Nielsen 2011, pp. 3, 7, 12.
56. Hussain, McNally, and Telhaj 2009, p. 12, p. 1.
57. Kelly, O'Connell, and Smyth 2010, p. 655.
58. Borgen 2015, p. 40.
59. Ibid., p. 43.
60. Ibid., p. 42.
61. Lemieux 2006, p. 195, p. 196, p. 199.
62. UIS 2015.
63. Piketty 2014, p. 315.
64. Ibid., p. 330.
65. Ibid., p. 308.
66. Hanley 2011, p. 904.

22. HIGHER EDUCATION AND SOCIETY

1. Stiglitz 2013, p.9.
2. Ibid., p. 94.
3. Pell Institute and PennAHEAD 2015, p. 31.
4. Mettler 2014, pp. 4–5, p. 8.
5. Stiglitz 2013, p. 24.
6. OECD 2014c, p. 12.
7. NCES 2015.
8. Mettler 2014, p. 88.
9. Ibid., pp. 168–169.
10. Ibid., p. 108
11. Ibid., pp. 111, 104.
12. Stiglitz 2013, p. 118.
13. Ibid., p. 165.
14. Ibid., p. 3.

15. Ibid., p. 35.

16. Ibid., pp. 36–37.

17. Ibid., pp. 165–166.

18. Corak 2006, p. 18.

19. Ibid., p. 11.

20. Piketty 2014, p. 484.

21. Stiglitz 2013, pp. 22–23.

22. OECD 2014a, p. 93.

23. Park (2007) finds that in relation to universities, the odds ratio for enrollment of students—students whose father completed tertiary education versus students whose father completed only secondary education—moved from about two to about five, moving from oldest cohort to younger cohorts (p. 33). This may indicate a very pronounced skew to nonuniversity HEIs in newly participating families, or it may represent an outcome that contradicts the favourable OECD finding on intergenerational mobility.

24. Chetty et al. 2014.

25. Treiman 2012; Gustafsson, Shi, and Nivorozhkina 2011.

26. Jonsson and Erikson 2007, p. 138.

27. Piketty 2014, p.484.

28. Gurria 2014.

29. Stiglitz 2013, p. 344.

30. Piketty 2014, p. 307.

31. OECD 2010; OECD 2014b; Lee, Lee, and Park 2012; Cingano 2014; Oxfam 2014, for example, p. 18, p. 49.

32. Wilkinson and Pickett 2010, p. 161.

33. Rivera 2015.

34. Deresiewicz 2014, p. 41; Geiger 2015, p. 303.

35. Piketty 2014, p. 424.

36. Arum and Roksa 2014, p. 121; Archibald and Feldman 2011.

37. Parry 2011, p. 135.

38. NCES 2015.

39. Soares 2007, pp. 173–179. Though as Soares (2007) also points out, the proportion of families with at least one child in an elite institution is higher than the attendance rate of all children (p. 181).

40. As above: Borgen 2015; Brand and Xie 2010; Dale and Krueger 2011; Hoxby and Avery 2013.

41. Geiger 2015, p. 305.

42. Arum and Roksa 2014, pp. 11–12. For the original study, see Brint and Cantwell 2010.

43. Arum and Roksa 2014, pp. 21, 37–38, 60–62, 42–44.

44. Ibid., p. 35. For the original study, see Babcock and Marks 2011.

45. Deresiewicz 2014, pp. 14, 69.

46. Pinker 2014.

47. Murphy 2015.

48. Arum and Roksa 2011, 2014, p. 10.

49. Ibid., pp. 8, 12, 14, 54.

50. Armstrong and Hamilton 2013.

51. Marginson 2014b.

52. Vygotsky 1978.

EPILOGUE: AFTER THE DREAM

1. Mettler 2014.

2. Dewey (1927) 1980, pp. 21–22.

3. Bowles 1991, p. 13.

4. Slattery 2015.

5. Stiglitz 2013, p. xxi.

6. Chapman 2006; Chapman and Armstrong 2011; Chapman 2014.

7. Douglass 2011, pp. 35–36.

8. Bill Tierney and Bryan Rodriguez (2014) of the University of Southern California suggest an overall CCC-CSU merger, as part of a process of upgrading the community colleges. They also suggest that all students who graduate within four years from the CSU should be guaranteed a free college education.

REFERENCES

Adams, James. (2010). Is the United States losing its preeminence in higher education? In Charles Clotfelter (ed.), *American Universities in a Global Market* (pp. 33–68). Chicago: University of Chicago Press.

Altbach, Philip. (2011). The past, present and future of the research university. In Philip Altbach and Jamil Salmi (eds.), *The Road to Academic Excellence: The Making of World-Class Research Universities* (pp. 11–32). Washington, DC: World Bank.

Altbach, Philip, and Salmi, Jamil, eds. (2011). *The Road to Academic Excellence: The Making of World-Class Research Universities.* Washington, DC: World Bank.

Amadae, S. M. (2003). *Rationalizing Capitalist Democracy: The Cold-War Origins of Rational Choice Liberalism.* Chicago: University of Chicago Press.

Archibald, Robert, and Feldman, David. (2011). *Why Does College Cost So Much?* New York: Oxford University Press.

Armstrong, Elizabeth, and Hamilton, Laura. (2013). *Paying for the Party: How College Maintains Inequality.* Cambridge, MA: Harvard University Press.

Arrow, Kenneth. ([1951] 1963). *Social Choice and Individual Values.* 2nd ed. New York: Wiley.

Arum, Richard, Gamoran, Adam, and Shavit, Yossi. (2007). More inclusion than diversion: Expansion, differentiation and market structures in higher education. In Yossi Shavit, Richard Arum, and Adam Gamoran (eds.), *Stratification in Higher Education: A Contemporary Study* (pp. 1–35). Stanford, CA: Stanford University Press.

Arum, Richard, and Roksa, Josipa. (2011). *Academically Adrift: Limited Learning on College Campuses.* Chicago: University of Chicago Press.

———. (2014). *Aspiring Adults Adrift: Tentative Transitions of College Graduates.* Chicago: University of Chicago Press.

Atkinson, Anthony, Piketty, Thomas, and Saez, Emmanuel. (2011). Top incomes in the long run of history. *Journal of Economic Literature,* 49 (1), pp. 3–71. www.aeaweb.org/articles?id=10.1257/jel.49.1.3.

Autor, David, Katz, Lawrence, and Kearney, Melissa. (2008). Trends in U.S. wage inequality: Revising the revisionists. *Review of Economics and Statistics,* 90 (2), pp. 300–323.

Babcock, Philip, and Marks, Mindy. (2011). The falling time cost of college: Evidence from half a century of time use data. *Review of Economics and Statistics,* 93, pp. 468–478.

Baker, David. (2011). Forward and backward, horizontal and vertical: Transformation of occupational credentialing in the schooled society. *Research in Social Stratification and Mobility,* 29, pp. 5–29.

Becker, Gary. (1964). *Human Capital: A Theoretical and Empirical Analysis with Special Reference to Education.* Chicago: University of Chicago Press.

Bentele, Keith. (2013). Distinct paths to higher inequality? A qualitative comparative analysis of rising earnings inequality among U.S. states, 1980–2010. *Research in Social Stratification and Mobility,* 34, pp. 30–57.

Berg, Andrew, and Ostry, Jonathan. (2011). *Inequality and Unsustainable Growth: Two Sides of the Same Coin?* IMF Staff Discussion Note, SDN/11/08, April. Washington, DC: International Monetary Fund.

Berrett, Dan. (2015). The day the purpose of university changed. *University World News,* 352, 30 January.

Bhandari, Rajika, and Lefebure, Alessia, eds. (2015). *Asia: The Next Higher Education Superpower?* New York: AIFS/Institute of International Education.

Bingley, Paul, Corak, Miles, and Westergård-Nielsen, Niels. (2011). *The Intergenerational Transmission of Employers in Canada and Denmark.* IZA Discussion Paper No. 5593. Bonn: Institute for the Study of Labor.

Bok, Derek. (2003). *Universities in the Marketplace: The Commercialization of Higher Education.* Princeton, NJ: Princeton University Press.

Boliver, Vikki. (2011). Expansion, differentiation, and the persistence of social class inequalities in British higher education. *Higher Education,* 61, pp. 229–242.

———. (2013). How fair is access to more prestigious UK universities? *British Journal of Sociology,* 64 (2), pp. 344–364.

Borgen, Nicolai. (2015). College quality and the positive selection hypothesis: The "second filter" on family background in high-paid jobs. *Research in Social Stratification and Mobility,* 39, pp. 32–47.

Borghans, Lex, and Cörvers, Frank. (2010). The Americanization of European higher education and research. In Charles Clotfelter (ed.), *American Universities in a Global Market* (pp. 231–267). Chicago: University of Chicago Press.

Bound, John, and Turner, Sarah. (2010). Where do international doctorate students study and how do US universities respond? In Charles Clotfelter (ed.), *American Universities in a Global Market* (pp. 101–127). Chicago: University of Chicago Press.

Bourdieu, Pierre. (1988). *Homo Academicus.* Cambridge, UK: Polity.

Bowen, William, and Tobin, Eugene. (2015). *Locus of Authority: The Evolution of Faculty Roles in the Governance of Higher Education.* Princeton, NJ: Princeton University Press.

Bowles, Samuel. (1991). What markets can—and cannot—do. *Challenge,* July-August, pp. 11–16.

Brand, Jennie, and Xie, Xu. (2010). Who benefits most from college? Evidence for negative selection in heterogeneous economic returns to higher education. *American Sociological Review,* 75, pp. 273–302.

Bray, M. (2007) *The Shadow Education System: Private Tutoring and Its Implications for Planners.* 2nd ed. Paris: UNESCO. http://unesdoc.unesco.org/images/0011/001184/118486e.pdf.

Brint, Steven, and Cantwell, Allison. (2010). Undergraduate time use and academic outcomes: Results from University of California undergraduate experience survey 2006. *Teachers College Record* 112, pp. 2441–2470.

Buchanan, James. (1975). *The Limits of Liberty: Between Anarchy and Leviathan.* Chicago: University of Chicago Press.

———. (1979). *What Should Economists Do?* Indianapolis, IN: Liberty Press.

———. (1997). *Post-socialist Political Economy.* Lyme, CT: Edward Elgar.

Buchanan, James, and Devetoglou, Nicos E. (1970). *Academia in Anarchy.* New York, NY: Basic Books.

Buchanan, James, and Tullock, Gordon. (1962). *The Calculus of Consent.* Ann Arbor: University of Michigan Press.

Buchanan, James, and Wagner, Robert. (1977). *Democracy in Deficit.* New York: Academic Press.

Burds-Sharp, Sarah, and Lewis, Kirsten. (2015). *Geographies of Opportunity. Ranking Well-Being by Congressional District.* Measure of America Series. Brooklyn, NY: Social Science Research Council. http://ssrc-static.s3.amazonaws.com/wp-content/uploads/2015/04/Geographies-of-Opportunity-4.22.2015.pdf.

Bush, Vannevar. (1945*).* Science: *The Endless Frontier.* A Report to the President by the Director of the Office of Scientific Research and Development, July. Washington: United States Government Printing Office. www.nsf.gov/od/lpa/nsf50/vbush1945.htm.

Byun, Kiyong, Jon, Jae-Eun, and Kim, Dongbin. (2013). Quest for building world-class universities in South Korea: Outcomes and consequences. *Higher Education,* 65 (5), pp. 645–659.

Callan, Patrick. (2012). The perils of success: Clark Kerr and the Californian Master Plan for Higher Education. In Sheldon Rothblatt (ed.), *Clark Kerr's World of Higher Education Reaches the 21st Century: Chapters in a Special History* (pp. 61–84). Dordrecht, NL: Springer.

Callender, Claire. (2014). Student numbers and funding: Does Robbins add up? *Higher Education Quarterly,* 68 (2), pp. 164–186.

Calonge, David. (2015). South Korean education ranks high, but it's the kids who pay. *The Conversation,* 30 March.

Carabelli, Anna, and Cedrini, Mario. (2014). Chapter 18 of *The General Theory* further analysed: Economics as a way of thinking. *Cambridge Journal of Economics,* 38, pp. 23–47.

Carnoy, Martin. (1974). *Education as Cultural Imperialism.* New York: David McKay.

Carnoy, Martin, Froumin, Isak, Loyalka, Prashant, and Tilak, Jandhyal. (2014). The concept of public goods, the state and higher education finance: A view from the BRICS. *Higher Education,* 68 (3), pp. 359–378.

Carrington, Damian. (2014). World population to hit 11b in 2100—with 70% chance of continuous rise. *Guardian,* 18 September.

Castells, Manuel. (2000). *The Rise of the Network Society.* 2nd ed. Oxford: Blackwell.

Chankseliani, Maia. (2013). Rural disadvantage in Georgian higher education admissions: A mixed-methods study. *Comparative Education Review,* 57 (3), pp. 424–456.

Chapman, Bruce. (2006). *Government Managing Risk: Income Contingent Loans for Social and Economic Progress*. London: Routledge.

———. (2014). Income contingent loans: Background. In Bruce Chapman, Timothy Higgins, and Joseph Stiglitz (eds.), *Income Contingent Loans: Theory, Practice and Prospects* (pp. 12–28). Basingstoke and New York: Palgrave Macmillan.

Chapman, Bruce, and Armstrong, Shiro, eds. (2011). *Financing Higher Education and Economic Development in East Asia*. Canberra: ANU E-Press.

Cheng, Ying. (2011). *The History and Future of ARWU*. Paper presented to the inaugural meeting of the ARWU International Advisory Board, 30 October, Shanghai.

Chetty, Raj, Hendren, Nathaniel, Kline, Patrick, Saez, Emmanuel, and Turner, Nicholas. (2014). *Is the United States Still a Land of Opportunity? Recent Trends in Intergenerational Mobility*. National Bureau of Economic Research Working Paper No. 19844. www.nber.org/papers/w19844.

Cheung, Sin Yi, and Egerton, Muriel. (2007). Great Britain: Higher education expansion and reform—changing educational inequalities. In Yossi Shavit, Richard Arum, and Adam Gamoran (eds.), *Stratification in Higher Education: A Contemporary Study* (pp. 195–219). Stanford, CA: Stanford University Press.

CIA (Central Intelligence Agency). (2015). *World Factbook*. www.cia.gov/library/publications/the-world-factbook/geos/tw.html.

Cingano, Frederico. (2014). Trends in income inequality and its impact on economic growth. *OECD Social, Employment and Migration Working Papers,* No. 163. Paris: Organisation for Economic Cooperation and Development.

Clark, Burton. (1960). The "cooling-out" function in higher education. *American Journal of Sociology,* 65 (6), pp. 569–576.

———. (1983). *The Higher Education System: Academic Organization in Cross-National Perspective*. Berkeley: University of California Press.

———. (1998a). *Creating Entrepreneurial Universities: Organizational Pathways to Transformation*. Oxford: Pergamon.

———. (1998b). The entrepreneurial university: Demand and response. *Tertiary Education and Management,* 4 (1), pp. 5–16.

Clotfelter, Charles. (2010). Introduction. In Charles Clotfelter (ed.), *American Universities in a Global Market* (pp. 1–29). Chicago: University of Chicago Press.

Cole, Jonathan. (2009). *The Great American University: Its Rise to Preeminence, Its Indispensable National Role, Why It Must Be Protected*. New York: Public Affairs.

Corak, Miles. (2006). *Do Poor Children Become Poor Adults? Lessons from a Cross-Country Comparison of Generational Earnings Mobility*. IZA Discussion Paper No. 1993, March. Bonn: Institute for the Study of Labor (IZA).

———. (2012). Inequality from generation to generation: The United States in comparison. Unpublished manuscript. Graduate School of Public and International Affairs, University of Ottawa, Canada. http://nws-sa.com/rr/Inequality/inequality-from-generation-to-generation-the-united-states-in-comparison-v3.pdf.

Cremonini, Leon, Westerheijden, Don, Benneworth, Paul, and Dauncey, Hugh. (2014). In the shadow of celebrity? World-Class University policies and public value in higher education. *Higher Education Policy,* 27, pp. 341–361.

CSIC (Consejo Superior de Investigaciones Cientificas), Cybermetrics Lab. (2015). *Webometrics Ranking Web of Universities*. www.webometrics.info.

Dale, Stacy, and Krueger, Alan. (2011). *Estimating the Return to College Selectivity over the Career Using Administrative Earnings Data.* NBER Working Paper 17159. Cambridge, MA: National Bureau of Economic Research.

Davies, Scott, and Zarifa, David. (2012). The stratification of universities: Structural inequality in Canada and the United States. *Research in Social Stratification and Mobility,* 30, pp. 143–158.

Deresiewicz, William. (2014). *Excellent Sheep: The Miseducation of the American Elite and the Way to a Meaningful Life.* New York: Free Press.

Dewey, John. ([1927] 1980). *The Public and Its Problems.* New York: H. Holt. Reprinted by Ohio University Press.

Dorling, Danny. (2014). *Inequality and the 1%.* London: Verso.

Douglass, John. (2000). *The California Idea and American Higher Education: 1850 to the 1960 Master Plan.* Stanford, CA: Stanford University Press.

———. (2011a). Can we save the college dream? *Boom: A Journal of California,* 1 (2), pp. 25–42.

———. (2011b). Revisionist reflections on California's Master Plan @ 50. *California Journal of Politics and Policy,* 3 (1). doi:10.2201/1944–4370.1105. www.bepress.com/cjpp/vol3/iss1/1.

———. (2013). *To Grow or Not to Grow? A Post-Great Recession Synopsis of the Political, Financial, and Social Contract Challenges Facing the University of California.* Research and Occasional Paper Series, CSHE.15.13, December. Berkeley: Center for Studies in Higher Education, University of California, Berkeley. www.cshe.berkeley.edu/publications/grow-or-not-grow-post-great-recession-synopsis-political-financial-and-social-contract.

Duncan, E. (2015). Excellence v equity. Special report: Universities. *Economist,* 28 March.

Economic Policy Institute and Center on Budget and Policy Priorities. (2012). Income inequality has grown in California. Infographic. www.cbpp.org/sites/default/files/atoms/files/California.pdf. In Elizabeth McNichol, Douglas Hall, David Cooper, and Vincent Palacios, *Pulling Apart: A State-by State Analysis of Income Trends,* 15 November. Washington, DC: Center on Budget and Policy Priorities. www.cbpp.org/research/poverty-and-inequality/pulling-apart-a-state-by-state-analysis-of-income-trends.

Frank, Robert, and Cook, Philip. (1996). *The Winner-Take-All Society: Why the Few at the Top Get So Much More Than the Rest of Us.* Harmondsworth: Penguin.

Freeman, Brigid, Marginson, Simon, and Tytler, Russell, eds. (2015). *The Age of STEM: Educational Policy and Practice across the World in Science, Technology, Engineering and Mathematics.* New York: Routledge.

Friedman, Milton (1953). The methodology of positive economics. In *Essays in Positive Economics* (pp. 3–43). Chicago: University of Chicago Press.

———. (1962). *Capitalism and Freedom.* Chicago: University of Chicago Press.

Friedman, Milton, and Friedman, Rose (1980). *Free to Choose.* Melbourne: Macmillan.

Gärtner, Svenja, and Prado, Svante. (2012). Inequality, trust and the welfare state: The Scandinavian model in the Swedish mirror. Paper presented at Högre seminariet, Ekonomisk-historiska institutionen, Göteborgs Universitet, 7 November.

Geiger, Roger. (2014). Higher education in high participation systems. Paper presented at the conference of Ontario Confederation of University Faculty Associations, Toronto, 27–28 February.

———. (2015). Does higher education cause inequality? Essay review on Mettler, and Armstrong and Hamilton. *American Journal of Education*, 121 (2), 299–310.

Gerber, Theodore, and Cheung, Sin Yi. (2008). Horizontal stratification in postsecondary education: Forms, explanations, and implications. *Annual Review of Sociology*, 34, pp. 299–318.

Gernet, Jacques (1996). *A History of Chinese Civilization*. 2nd ed. Cambridge, UK: Cambridge University Press.

Gonzalez, Cristina. (2011). *Clark Kerr's University of California: Leadership, Diversity and Planning in Higher Education*. New Brunswick, NJ: Transaction.

Goodman, David. (2014). *Class in Contemporary China*. Cambridge, UK: Polity.

Gray, Hanna Holborn. (2012). *Searching for Utopia: Universities and Their Histories*. Berkeley: University of California Press.

Gurria, Angel. (2014). Tertiary education: The gift that keeps on giving. *University World News*, 340, 24 October.

Gustafsson, Bjorn, Shi, Li, and Nivorozhkina, Ludmila. (2011). Why are household incomes more unequally distributed in China than in Russia? *Cambridge Journal of Economics*, 35, pp. 897–920.

Habermas, Jürgen. (1989). *The Structural Transformation of the Public Sphere*. Cambridge, MA: MIT Press.

Hallsten, Martin. (2014). Inequality across three and four generations in egalitarian Sweden: 1st and 2nd cousin correlations in socio-economic outcomes. *Research in Social Stratification and Mobility*, 35 (1), pp. 19–33.

Hanley, Caroline. (2011). Investigating the organizational sources of high-wage earnings growth and rising inequality. *Social Science Research*, 40, pp. 902–916.

Hansen, Hal. (2011). Rethinking certification theory and the educational development of the United States and Germany. *Research in Social Stratification and Mobility* 29, pp. 31–55.

Hayhoe, Ruth. (2011). Introduction and acknowledgements. In Ruth Hayhoe, Jun Li, Jing Lin, & Qiang Zha, *Portraits of 21st Century Chinese Universities: In the move to mass higher education* (pp. 1–18). Dordrecht, NL: Springer.

Hazelkorn, Ellen. (2011). *Rankings and the Reshaping of Higher Education: The Battle for World-Class Excellence*. Houndmills, UK: Palgrave Macmillan.

Helms, Robin. (2015). Higher education in the United States. Paper prepared for a British Council project on the coordination of large higher education systems, June. Washington, DC: American Council on Education.

Hennessy, Peter. (2014). *Establishment and Meritocracy*. London: Haus Publishing.

Hirsch, Fred. (1976). *Social Limits to Growth*. Cambridge MA: Harvard University Press.

Holcombe, Charles. (2011). *A History of East Asia: From the Origins of Civilization to the Twenty-First Century*. Cambridge, UK: Cambridge University Press.

Hoxby, Caroline, and Avery, Christopher. (2013). The missing "one-offs": The hidden supply of high-achieving, low-income students. *Brookings Papers on Economic Activity*, 46 (1), Spring, pp. 1–65.

Hu, Anning, and Vargas, Nicholas. (2015). Horizontal stratification of higher education in urban China. *Higher Education*, 70 (3), pp. 337–358.

Huang Futao. (2015). Building the world-class research universities: A case study of China. *Higher Education*, 70 (2), pp. 203–215.

Hussain, Iftikhar, McNally, Sandra, and Telhaj, Shqiponja. (2009). *University Quality and Graduate Wages in the UK*. IZA Discussion Paper No. 4043. Bonn: Institute for the Study of Labor (IZA).

Humboldt, Wilhelm von. (1970). *On the Spirit and the Organizational Framework of Intellectual Institutions in Berlin*. Written sometime between autumn 1809 and autumn 1810. See: University reform in Germany, *Minerva*, 8, pp. 242–250.

ICEF Monitor. (2015). Foreign-language study in US declines for the first time in 20 years. 17 February. http://monitor.icef.com/2015/02/foreign-language-study-us-declines-first-time-20-years/.

IIE (Institute for International Education). (2015). Open Doors Data portal. www.iie.org/en/Research-and-Publications/Open-Doors/Data.

Internet Live Stats. (2015). www.internetlivestats.com/internet-users/.

Jacques, Martin. (2012). *When China Rules the World*. 2nd ed. Harmondsworth, UK: Penguin.

Jerrim, John. (2014). Why do East Asian children perform so well in PISA? An investigation of Western-born children of East Asian descent. Unpublished paper. London: Institute of Education.

Jonsson, Jan, and Erikson, Robert. (2007). Sweden: Why educational expansion is not such a great strategy for equality—theory and evidence. In Yossi Shavit, Richard Arum, and Adam Gamoran (eds.), *Stratification in Higher Education: A Contemporary Study* (pp. 113–139). Stanford, CA: Stanford University Press.

Katsikas, Aina. (2015). Same performance, better grades. *Atlantic*, 13 January. www.theatlantic.com/archive/2015/01/same-performance-better-grades/384447/

Kaul, Inge, Grunberg, Isabelle, and Stern, Marc, eds. (1999). *Global Public Goods*. New York: Oxford University Press.

Kelly, Elish, O'Connell, Philip, and Smyth, Emer. (2010). The economic returns to field of study and competencies among higher education graduates in Ireland. *Economics of Education Review*, 29, pp. 650–657.

Kennedy, John. (1961). Address to a Joint Convention of the General Court of the Commonwealth of Massachusetts. State House, Boston, MA, 9 January. www.jfklibrary.org/Asset-Viewer/OYhUZE2Qoo-ogdV7ok9ooA.aspx.

Kerr, Clark. (2001a). *The Gold and the Blue: A Personal Memoir of the University of California, 1949–1967*. Vol. 1: *Academic Triumphs*. Berkeley: University of California Press.

———. ([1963] 2001b). *The Uses of the University*. 5th ed. Cambridge, MA: Harvard University Press.

———. (2003). *The Gold and the Blue: A Personal Memoir of the University of California, 1949–1967*. Vol. 2: *Political Turmoil*. Berkeley: University of California Press.

Keynes, John Maynard. ([1933] 1972). *Essays in Biography*. Reprinted in E. Johnson and D. E. Moggridge (eds.), *The Collected Writings of John Maynard Keynes*, vol. 10. London: Macmillan, for the Royal Economic Society.

———. ([1936] 1973a). *The General Theory and After. Part II: Defense and Development*. Reprinted in E. Johnson and D. E. Moggridge (eds), *The Collected Writings of John Maynard Keynes*, Vol. 14. London: Macmillan, for the Royal Economic Society.

———. ([1936] 1973b). *The General Theory of Employment, Interest and Money*. Reprinted in E. Johnson and D. E. Moggridge (eds), *The Collected Writings of John Maynard Keynes*, vol. 7. London: Macmillan, for the Royal Economic Society.

Kharas, Homi, and Gertz, Geoffrey. (2010). The new global middle class: A cross-over from West to East. In C. Liu (ed.), *China's Emerging Middle Class: Beyond Economic Transformation*. Washington, DC: Brookings Institution Press.

Kim, E. Han, and Zhu, Min. (2010). Universities as firms: The case of U.S. overseas programs. In Charles Clotfelter (ed.), *American Universities in a Global Market* (pp. 163–201). Chicago: University of Chicago Press.

Kim, Sunwoong. (2010). From brain drain to brain competition: Changing opportunities and the career patterns of U.S.-trained Korean academics. In Charles Clotfelter (ed.), *American Universities in a Global Market* (pp. 335–369). Chicago: University of Chicago Press.

Kirp, David. (2004). *Shakespeare, Einstein and the Bottom Line: The Marketing of Higher Education*. Cambridge, MA: Harvard University Press.

Klugman, Joshua. (2013). The advanced placement arms race and the reproduction of educational equality. *Teachers College Record*, 115 (5).

Lawson, Tony. (2012). Mathematical modelling and ideology in the economics academy: Competing explanations of the failings of the modern discipline? *Economic Thought* 1, pp. 3–22.

Lee, Hyun-Hoon, Lee, Minsoo, and Park, Donghyun. (2012). *Growth Policy and Inequality in Developing Asia: Lesson from Korea*. ERIA Discussion Paper 2012–12, July. Jakarta: Economic Research Institute for ASEAN and East Asia. www.eria.org/ERIA-DP-2012–12.pdf.

Leiden University, Centre for Science and Technology Studies. (2015). *The Leiden Ranking 2014*. www.leidenranking.com/ranking/2014.

Lemieux, Thomas. (2006). Postsecondary education and increasing wage inequality. *AEA Papers and Proceedings*. May.

Levin, Henry. (2011). Conversation with the author, 26 September. Teachers College, Columbia University.

Levine, Arthur. (2012). Clark Kerr and the Carnegie Commission and Council. In Sheldon Rothblatt (ed.), *Clark Kerr's World of Higher Education Reaches the 21st Century: Chapters in a Special History* (pp. 43–60). Dordrecht, NL: Springer.

Li, Cheng. (2015). *Bridging Minds across the Pacific: U.S.–China Educational Exchanges 1978–2003*. Lanham, MD: Lexington Books.

Li, Haizheng. (2010). Higher education in China: Complement or competition to U.S. universities? In Charles Clotfelter (ed.), *American Universities in a Global Market* (pp. 269–304). Chicago: University of Chicago Press.

Li, Hongbin, Meng, Lingsheng, Shi, Xinzheng, and Wu, Binzhen. (2012). Does attending elite colleges pay in China? *Journal of Comparative Economics*, 40, pp. 78–88.

Liu, Niancai. (2009). The story of the Academic Ranking of World Universities. *International Higher Education*, 54, pp. 2–3.

Liu, Niancai, and Cheng, Ying. (2005). The Academic Ranking of World Universities. *Higher Education in Europe*, 30 (2), pp. 127–136.

Locke, William. (2011). The institutionalization of rankings: Managing status anxiety in an increasingly marketized environment. In Jung Cheol Shin, Robert Toutkoushian, and Ulrich Teichler (eds.), *University Rankings: Theoretical Basis, Methodology and Impacts on Global Higher Education* (pp. 201–228). Dordrecht, NL: Springer.

Loveless, Tom. (2013). PISA's China problem. *Brown Center Chalkboard* (blog), 9 October. www.brookings.edu/blogs/brown-center-chalkboard/posts/2013/10/09-pisa-china-problem-loveless.

Loyalka, Prashant, Song, Yingquan, and Wei, Jianguo. (2012). The effects of attending selective college tiers in China. *Social Science Research* 41, pp. 287–305.

Lucas, Samuel. (2001). Effectively maintained inequality: Education transitions, track mobility, and social background effects. *American Journal of Sociology,* 106 (6), pp. 1642–1690.

———. (2009). Stratification theory, socioeconomic background, and educational attainment: A formal analysis. *Rationality and Society,* 21, pp. 459–511.

Luhby, Tami. (2015). California: The Nation's Most Unequal State. *CNN Money International,* 6 May. http://money.cnn.com/2015/05/05/news/economy/california-unequal/.

Lukes, Steven. (1973). *Individualism.* Oxford: Basil Blackwell.

Mahbubani, Kishore. (2013). *The Great Convergence: Asia, the West, and the Logic of One World.* New York: Public Affairs.

Marginson, Simon. (1997). *Markets in Education.* Sydney: Allen and Unwin.

———. (2006). Dynamics of national and global competition in higher education. *Higher Education,* 52, pp. 1–39.

———. (2007). The public/private division in higher education: A global revision. *Higher Education,* 53, pp. 307–333.

———. (2008). Global field and global imagining: Bourdieu and worldwide higher education. *British Journal of Sociology of Education,* 29 (3), pp. 303–315.

———. (2010a). Nation. In Peter Murphy, Michael Peters, and Simon Marginson, *Imagination: Three Models of Imagination in the Age of the Knowledge Economy* (pp. 225–325). New York: Peter Lang.

———. (2010b). Space, mobility and synchrony in the knowledge economy. In Simon Marginson, Peter Murphy, and Michael Peters, *Global Creation: Space, Mobility and Synchrony in the Age of the Knowledge Economy* (pp. 117–149). New York: Peter Lang.

———. (2011a). Imagining the global. In Roger King, Simon Marginson, and Rajani Naidoo (eds.), *Handbook of Higher Education and Globalization* (pp. 10–39). Cheltenham, UK: Edward Elgar.

———. (2011b). Strategising and ordering the global. In Roger King, Simon Marginson, and Rajani Naidoo (eds.), *Handbook of Higher Education and Globalization* (pp. 394–414). Cheltenham, UK: Edward Elgar.

———. (2013). The impossibility of capitalist markets in higher education. *Journal of Education Policy,* 28 (3), pp. 353–370.

———. (2014a). Student self-formation in international education. *Journal of Studies in International Education,* 18 (1), pp. 6–22.

———. (2014b). University rankings and social science. *European Journal of Education,* 49 (1), pp. 45–59.

———. (2016). High participation systems of higher education. *Journal of Higher Education,* 87 (2), pp. 243–267.

Marginson, Simon, and Considine, Mark. (2000). *The Enterprise University: Power, Governance and Reinvention in Australia.* Cambridge, UK: Cambridge University Press.

Marginson, Simon, and Marshman, Ian. (2013). System and structure. In Gwilym Croucher, Simon Marginson, Andrew Norton, and Julie Wells (eds.), *The Dawkins Revolution 25 Years On,* pp. 56–74. Melbourne: Melbourne University Publishing.

Melguizo, Tatiana, and Wolniak, Gregory. (2012). The earnings benefits of majoring in STEM fields among high achieving minority students. *Research in Higher Education,* 53, pp. 383–40.

Merton, Robert (1968). The Matthew effect in science. *Science,* 159, pp. 56–63.

Mettler, Suzanne. (2014). *Degrees of Inequality: How the Politics of Higher Education Sabotaged the American Dream.* New York: Basic Books.

Milanovic, Branko. (2011). More or less. *Finance and Development,* September, pp. 6–11.

Ministry of Education, China. (2015). China. Paper prepared for British Council project on Large Higher Education Systems. British Council: London.

Mountford-Zimdars, Anna, and Sabbagh, Daniel. (2013). Fair access to higher education: A comparative perspective. *Comparative Education Review,* 57 (3), pp. 359–368.

Mouw, Ted, and Kalleberg, Arne. (2010). Occupations and the structure of wage inequality in the United States, 1980s to 2000s. *American Sociological Review,* 75 (3), pp. 402–431.

Murphy, Peter. (2015). *Universities and Innovation Economies: The Creative Wasteland of Post-Industrial Society.* Farnham, UK: Ashgate.

NCES (National Center for Educational Statistics). (2015). Table 303.10: Total fall enrollment in degree-granting postsecondary institutions, by attendance status, sex of student, and control of institution. *Digest of Education Statistics.* http://nces.ed.gov/programs/digest/d13/tables/dt13_303.10.asp.

NSF (National Science Foundation). (2014). *Science and Engineering Indicators 2014.* www.nsf.gov/statistics/seind14/.

Newman, John Henry. ([1852–1858] 1996). *The Idea of a University.* New Haven, CT: Yale University Press.

OECD (Organisation for Economic Cooperation and Development). (2012). *Industrial Policy and Territorial Development: Lessons from Korea.* Paris: OECD.

———. (2014a). *Education at a Glance 2014.* Paris: OECD.

———. (2014b). *PISA 2012 Results in Focus: What 15-Year-Olds Know and What They Can Do with What They Know.* Paris: OECD.

———. (2014c). *United States: Tackling High Inequalities, Creating Opportunities for All.* Paris: OECD.

———. (2015). *Main Science and Technology Indicators.* http://stats.oecd.org/Index.aspx?DataSetCode = GERD_FUNDS.

Ostry, Jonathon, Berg, Andrew, and Tsangarides, Charalambos. (2014). *Redistribution, Inequality, and Growth.* IMF Staff Discussion Note 14/02. Washington, DC: IMF.

Oxfam. (2014). *Working for the Few: Political Capture and Economic Inequality.* Oxford: Oxfam GB.

Park, Hyunjoon. (2007). Korea: Educational expansion and inequality of opportunity for higher education. In Yossi Shavit, Richard Arum, and Adam Gamoran (eds.), *Stratification in Higher Education: A Contemporary Study* (pp. 87–112). Stanford, CA: Stanford University Press.

Parry, Gareth. (2011). Mobility and hierarchy in the age of near-universal access. *Critical Studies in Education,* 52 (2), pp. 135–149.

Pastor, Manuel, and Braun, Dan. (2015). The California chasm: A look at income inequality in the golden state. Huffpost Politics, *Huffington Post,* 12 February. www.huffingtonpost. com/2015/02/12/california-income-inequality_n_6673042.html.

Pelfrey, Patricia. (2004). *A Brief History of the University of California.* 2nd ed. Berkeley: University of California Press.

———. (2012). *Entrepreneurial President: Richard Atkinson and the University of California, 1995–2003.* Berkeley: University of California Press.

Pell Institute and PennAHEAD. (2015). *Indicators of Higher Education Equity in the United States: 45-Year Trend Report.* 2015 rev. ed. Washington, DC, and Philadelphia: Pell Institute and PennAHEAD, Graduate School of Education, University of Pennsylvania. www.pellinstitute.org/downloads/publications-Indicators_of_Higher_Education_ Equity_in_the_US_45_Year_Trend_Report.pdf.

Piketty, Thomas. (2014). *Capital in the Twenty-First Century.* Trans. Arthur Goldhammer. Cambridge, MA: Belknap Press of Harvard University Press.

Pinker, Steven. (2014). The trouble with Harvard. *New Republic,* 4 September. www.newrepublic.com/article/119321/harvard-ivy-league-should-judge-students-standardizedtests.

Postiglione, Gerard. (2011). The rise of research universities: The Hong Kong University of Science and Technology. In Philip Altbach and Jamil Salmi (eds.), *The Road to Academic Excellence: The Making of World-Class Research Universities* (pp. 63–100). Washington, DC: World Bank.

———. (2014). Reforming the Gaokao. *University World News,* 325, 20 June.

QS Top Universities. (2015). *QS World University Rankings.* www.topuniversities.com/ university-rankings.

Reagan, Ronald. (1989.) Farewell address to the nation. Broadcast from the White House, Washington, DC, January 11. https://reaganlibrary.archives.gov/archives/ speeches/1989/011189i.htm.

Reisberg, Liz. (2014). The alarming expansion of the for-profits. *World View* (blog). *Inside Higher Ed,* 27 October. www.insidehighered.com/blogs/world-view/alarmingexpansion-profits.

Reynolds, Jeremy, and Xian, He. (2014). Perceptions of meritocracy in the land of opportunity. *Research in Social Stratification and Mobility,* 36, pp. 121–137.

Rhee, Buyung Shik. (2011). A world-class research university on the periphery: The Pohang University of Science and Technology, the Republic of Korea. In Philip Altbach and Jamil Salmi (eds.), *The Road to Academic Excellence: The Making of World-Class Research Universities* (pp. 101–127). Washington, DC: World Bank.

Rhoads, Robert, and Szelenyi, Katalin. (2011). *Global Citizenship and the University: Advancing Social Life and Relations in an Interdependent World.* Stanford, CA: Stanford University Press.

Rhoades, Gary. (2008). The centrality of contingent faculty to academe's future. *Academe,* 94 (6), pp. 12–15.

Rivera, Lauren. (2011). Ivies, extracurriculars, and exclusion: Elite employers' use of educational credentials. *Research in Social Stratification and Mobility,* 29, pp. 71–90.

———. (2012a). Diversity within reach: Recruitment versus hiring in elite firms. *Annals of the American Academy of Political and Social Science,* 639, pp. 71–90.

———. (2012b). Hiring as cultural matching: The case of elite professional service firms. *American Sociological Review,* 77 (6), pp. 999–1022.

———. (2015). *Pedigree: How Elite Students Get Elite Jobs.* Princeton, NJ: Princeton University Press.

Robst, John. (2007). Education and job match: The relatedness of college major and work. *Economics of Education Review,* 26, pp. 397–407.

Roemer, John. (2004). Equal opportunity and intergenerational mobility: Going beyond intergenerational income transition matrices. In Miles Corak (ed.), *Generational Income Mobility in North America and Europe.* Cambridge, UK: Cambridge University Press.

Roksa, Josipa. (2005). Double disadvantage or blessing in disguise? Understanding the relationship between college major and employment sector. *Sociology of Education,* 78 (3), pp. 207–232.

Roksa, Josipa, Grodsky, Eric, Arum, Richard, and Gamoran, Adam. (2007). United States: Changes in higher education and social stratification. In Yossi Shavit, Richard Arum, and Adam Gamoran (eds.), *Stratification in Higher Education: A Contemporary Study* (pp. 165–191). Stanford, CA: Stanford University Press.

Roksa, Josipa, and Levey, Tania. (2010). What can you do with that degree? College major and occupational status of college graduates over time. *Social Forces* 89 (2), pp. 389–416.

Rosenfeld, Seth. (2012). *Subversives: The FBI's War on Student Radicals and Reagan's Rise to Power.* New York: Farrar, Straus and Giroux.

Rothblatt, Sheldon. (2007). *Education's Abiding Moral Dilemma: Merit and Worth in the Cross-Atlantic Democracies, 1800–2006.* Oxford: Symposium Books.

———. (2012a). Clark Kerr: Two voices. In Sheldon Rothblatt (ed.), *Clark Kerr's World of Higher Education Reaches the 21st Century: Chapters in a Special History* (pp. 1–42). Dordrecht, NL: Springer.

———. (2012b). Preface. In Sheldon Rothblatt (ed.), *Clark Kerr's World of Higher Education Reaches the 21st Century: Chapters in a Special History* (pp. xiii-xv). Dordrecht, NL: Springer.

Sacramento Bee. (2013). California's high school graduation rate rises sharply. *Capitol Alert* (blog), 9 April. http://blogs.sacbee.com/capitolalertlatest/2013/04/californias-high-school-graduation-rate-rises-sharply.html.

Saez, Emmanuel. (2013). Striking it richer: The evolution of top incomes in the United States. Unpublished manuscript, September 3. Berkeley: University of California, Berkeley, Department of Economics, Econometrics Laboratory. http://eml.berkeley.edu//~saez/saez-UStopincomes-2012.pdf.

Said, Edward. (1993). *Culture and Imperialism.* New York: Vintage.

Salmi, Jamil. (2009). *The Challenge of Establishing World-Class Universities.* Washington: World Bank. http://siteresources.worldbank.org/EDUCATION/Resources/278200-1099079877269/547664-1099079956815/547670-1237305262556/WCU.pdf.

———. (2011). The road to academic excellence: Lessons of experience. In Philip Altbach and Jamil Salmi (eds.), *The Road to Academic Excellence: The Making of World-Class Research Universities* (pp. 323–347). Washington, DC: World Bank.

———. (2015). Excellence strategies and world-class universities. In Ellen Hazelkorn (ed.), *Global Rankings and the Geopolitics of Higher Education: Understanding the Influence and Impact of Rankings on Higher Education, Policy, and Society.* New York: Routledge.

Samson, Frank. (2013). Altering public university admission standards to preserve white group position in the United States: Results from a laboratory experiment. *Comparative Education Review,* 57 (3), pp. 369–396.

Sauder, Michael, and Espeland, Wendy. (2009). The discipline of rankings: Tight coupling and organizational change. *American Sociological Review,* 74 (1), pp. 63–82.

Schmidt, Peter. (2015). Groups allege systematic anti-Asian bias against Harvard. *Chronicle of Higher Education,* 363, 2 May.

Schneider, Barbara, and Stevenson, David. (1999). *The Ambitious Generation: America's Teenagers Motivated but Directionless.* New Haven, CT: Yale University Press.

Schofer, Evan, and Meyer, John. (2005). The worldwide expansion of higher education in the twentieth century. *American Sociological Review,* 70, December, pp. 898–920.

Scimago Lab. (2015). *Scimago Institutions' Rankings.* www.scimagoir.com/.

Scott, Peter. (2015). New languages and landscapes for higher education. UCL Institute of Education, University College London. Paper for seminar at University of Warwick, 26–27 March.

Sen, Amartya. (1992). *Objectivity and Position.* Lindley Lecture, The University of Kansas. Lawrence: University of Kansas.

———. (2000). *Development as Freedom.* New York: Basic Books.

Shanghai Jiao Tong University, Center for World-Class Universities. (2015). *Academic Ranking of World Universities* (ARWU). www.shanghairanking.com/World-University-Rankings-2014/USA.html.

Shattock, Michael. (2012). Parallel worlds: The Californian Master Plan and the development of British higher education. In Sheldon Rothblatt (ed.), *Clark Kerr's World of Higher Education Reaches the 21st Century: Chapters in a Special History* (pp. 107–127). Dordrecht, NL: Springer.

Shavit, Yossi, Arum, Richard, and Gamoran, Adam, eds. (2007). *Stratification in Higher Education: A Contemporary Study.* Stanford, CA: Stanford University Press.

Shavit, Yossi, Ayalon, Hanna, Chachashvili-Bolotin, Svetlana, and Menahem, Gila. (2007). Israel: Diversification, expansion and inequality in higher education. In Yossi Shavit, Richard Arum, and Adam Gamoran (eds.), *Stratification in Higher Education: A Contemporary Study* (pp. 39–62). Stanford, CA: Stanford University Press.

Short, Kathleen. (2014). The Supplemental Poverty Measure: 2013. *Current Population Reports.* P60–251. Washington, DC: United States Census Bureau. www.census.gov/content/dam/Census/library/publications/2014/demo/p60-251.pdf.

Singer, Peter (2002). *One World: The Ethics of Globalization.* New Haven, CT: Yale University Press.

Slattery, L. (2015). Equality movement gains support in unlikely places. *Sydney Morning Herald,* 26 April. www.smh.com.au/comment/equality-movement-gains-support-in-unlikely-places-20150426-1mtbma.html.

Slaughter, Sheila, and Leslie, Larry. (1997). *Academic Capitalism: Politics, Policies, and the Entrepreneurial University.* Baltimore: Johns Hopkins University Press.

Slaughter, Sheila, and Rhoades, Gary. (2004). *Academic Capitalism and the New Economy: Markets, States, and Higher Education*. Baltimore: Johns Hopkins University Press.

Smeeding, Timothy. (2005). Public policy, economic inequality, and poverty: The United States in comparative perspective. *Social Science Quarterly*, 86 Supplement (s1), pp. 955–983.

Smelser, Neil. (2001). Foreword. In Clark Kerr, *The Gold and the Blue: A Personal Memoir of the University of California*. Vol. 1: *Academic Triumphs* (pp. xix–xxvii). Berkeley: University of California Press.

———. (2003). Foreword. In Clark Kerr, *The Gold and the Blue: A Personal Memoir of the University of California*. Vol. 2: *Political Turmoil* (pp. xv–xxv). Berkeley: University of California Press.

———. (2013). *Dynamics of the Contemporary University: Growth, Accretion, and Conflict*. Berkeley: University of California Press.

Smith, Adam. ([1759] 2004). *The Theory of Moral Sentiments*. New York: Barnes and Noble.

Soares, Joseph. (2007). *The Power of Privilege: Yale and America's Elite Colleges*. Stanford, CA: Stanford University Press.

Sommeiller, Estelle, and Price, Mark. (2015). *The Increasingly Unequal States of America. Income Inequality by State, 1917 to 2012*. Washington, DC: Economic Policy Institute. www.epi.org/publication/income-inequality-by-state-1917-to-2012/.

Stiglitz, Joseph. (2013). *The Price of Inequality*. London: Penguin.

Task Force on Higher Education and Society. (2000). *Higher Education in Developing Countries: Peril and Promise*. Washington, DC: World Bank.

Teichler, Ulrich. (2009). *Higher Education and the World of Work: Conceptual Frameworks, Comparative Perspectives, Empirical Findings*. Rotterdam, NL: Sense.

Tholen, Gerbrand, Brown, Phillip, Power, Sally, and Allouch, Annabelle. (2013). The role of networks and connections in educational elites' labour market entrance. *Research in Social Stratification and Mobility*, 34, pp. 142–154.

Thomas, Scott, and Zhang, Liang. (2005). Post-baccalaureate wage growth within 4 years of graduation: The effects of college quality and college major. *Research in Higher Education*, 46 (4), pp. 437–459.

Thomsen, Jens, Munk, Martin, Eiberg-Madsen, Misja, and Hansen, Gro. (2013). The educational strategies of Danish students from professional and working class backgrounds. *Comparative Education Review*, 57 (3), pp. 457–480.

Tierney, William, and Rodriguez, Bryan. (2014). *The Future of Higher Education in California: Problems and Solutions for Getting In and Getting Through*. Los Angeles: Pullias Center for Higher Education, Rossier School of Education, University of Southern California.

Times Higher Education. (2015). Times Higher Education *World University Rankings*. www.timeshighereducation.co.uk/world-university-rankings/

Tran, Ly, Marginson, Simon, Do, Hoang, Do, Quyen, Le, Truc, Nguyen, Nhai, Vu, Thao, Pham, Thach, and Nguyen, Huong. (2014). *Higher Education in Vietnam*. New York: Palgrave.

Treiman, Donald. (2012). The "difference between heaven and earth": Urban–rural disparities in well-being in China. *Research in Social Stratification and Mobility*, 30, pp. 33–47.

Tridico, Pasquale. (2012). Financial crisis and global imbalances: its labour market origins and the aftermath. *Cambridge Journal of Economics,* 36, pp. 17–42.

Triventi, Moris. (2013). The role of higher education stratification in the reproduction of social inequality in the labor market. *Research in Social Stratification and Mobility,* 32, pp. 45–63.

Trow, Martin. (1963/1964). Robbins: A question of size and shape. *Universities Quarterly,* 18, pp. 117–132.

———. (1970). Reflections on the transition from mass to universal higher education. *Daedalus,* 99 (1), pp. 1–42.

———. (1973). *Problems in the Transition from Elite to Mass Higher Education.* Berkeley, CA: Carnegie Commission on Higher Education.

———. (2000). *From Mass Higher Education to Universal Access: The American Advantage.* Research and Occasional Paper CSHE 1.00. Berkeley: Center for Studies in Higher Education, University of California Berkeley.

UIS (UNESCO Institute for Statistics). (2015). Education. *UIS.Stat.* United Nations Educational, Social and Cultural Organization. http://data.uis.unesco.org/.

UNDESA (United Nations Department of Educational and Social Affairs). (2012). *World Urbanization Prospects: The 2011 Revision.* New York: United Nations.

UNDP (United Nations Development Programme). (2013). *Humanity Divided.* Washington: UNDP.

Universitas21. (2015). *U21 Ranking of National Higher Education Systems.* 2014 ed. www.universitas21.com/article/projects/details/152/u21-ranking-of-national-higher-education-systems.

Unz, Ron. (2012). The myth of American meritocracy. *American Conservative,* December, pp. 14–51.

Valimaa, Jussi. (2011). The corporatisation of national universities in Finland. In Brian Pusser, Ken Kempner, Simon Marginson, and Imanol Ordorika (eds.), *Universities and the Public Sphere: Knowledge Creation and State Building in the Era of Globalization* (pp. 101–119). New York: Routledge.

Vest, Charles. (2007). *The American Research University from World War II to World Wide Web: Governments, Private Sector, and the Emerging Meta-University.* Berkeley: University of California Press.

Vygotsky, Lev. (1978). *Mind in Society: The Development of Higher Psychological Processes.* Cambridge, MA: Harvard University Press.

Wang, Qi, Wang, Q. H., and Liu, Niancai. (2011). Building world-class universities in China: Shanghai Jiao Tong University. In Philip Altbach and Jamil Salmi (eds.), *The Road to Academic Excellence: The Making of World-Class Research Universities* (pp. 33–62). Washington, DC: World Bank.

Warner, Marina. (2015). Universities should not become corporate affiliates. *University World News,* 362, 10 April.

Washburn, Jennifer. (2005). *University Inc.: The Corporate Corruption of Higher Education.* New York: Basic Books.

Werfhorst, Herman van de. (2002). Fields of study, acquired skills, and the wage benefit from a matching job. *Acta Sociologica,* 45, pp. 286–303.

Wildhagen, Tina. (2014). Unequal returns to academic credentials as a hidden dimension of race and class inequality in American college enrollments. *Research in Social Stratification and Mobility*, 38, pp. 18–31.

Wilkinson, Richard, and Pickett, Kate. (2010). *The Spirit Level: Why Equality Is Better for Everyone*. London: Penguin.

Wilton, John. (2014). PowerPoint presentation supplied by Vice-Chancellor, Administration and Finance, University of California Berkeley, October.

Wimmer, Andrea, and Schiller, Nina. (2002). Methodological nationalism and beyond: Nation-state building, migration and the social sciences. *Global Networks*, 4 (2), pp. 301–334.

Wisman, Jon. (2013). Wage stagnation, rising inequality, and the financial crisis of 2008. *Cambridge Journal of Economics*, 37, pp. 921–945.

Wolff, Edward, and Zacharias, Ajit. (2013). Class structure and economic inequality. *Cambridge Journal of Economics*, 37, pp. 1381–1406.

Wolniak, Gregory, Seifert, Tricia, Reed, Eric, and Pascarella, Ernest. (2008). College majors and social mobility. *Research in Social Stratification and Mobility*, 26, pp. 123–139.

World Bank. (2015). *Data*. http://data.worldbank.org.

Yang, Po. (2014). *Chinese Higher Education Expansion*. Paper presented at the Summer School on Higher Education Research, National Research University–Higher School of Economics, Institute of Education, Pushkin, St. Petersburg, 13 June.

Yang, Rui. (2014). China's strategy for internationalization of higher education: An overview. *Frontiers of Education in China*, 9 (2), pp. 151–162.

Yang, Rui, and Welch, Anthony. (2012). A world-class university in China? The case of Tsinghua. *Higher Education*, 63 (5), pp. 645–666.

Yonezawa, Akiyoshi, and Shimmi, Yukiko. (2015). Transformation of university governance through internationalization: Challenges for top universities and government policies in Japan. *Higher Education*, 70 (2), January. http://link.springer.com/article/10.1007/s10734-015-9863-0.

Zha, Qiang. (2011). Is there an emerging Chinese model of the university? In Ruth Hayhoe, Jun Li, Jing Lin, and Qiang Zha, *Portraits of 21st-Century Chinese Universities: In the Move to Mass Higher Education* (pp. 451–471). Dordrecht, NL: Springer.

———. (2015). Reading Xi's modern twist on Plato's *The Republic*. *World View* (blog), 9 March. *Inside Higher Ed*. www.insidehighered.com/blogs/world-view/reading-xi's-modern-twist-plato's-"-republic".

Zhao, Wei. (2012). Economic inequality, status perceptions, and subjective well-being in China's transitional economy. *Research in Social Stratification and Mobility* 30, pp. 433–450.

INDEX